Advances in
Library Resource Sharing

Advances in Library Resource Sharing

VOLUME 1	1990

Edited by Jennifer Cargill and Diane J. Graves

Meckler

Westport · London

Advances in
Library Resource Sharing

ISSN 1052-262X   ISBN 0-88736-490-X

Editors-in-Chief

Jennifer Cargill
Rice University

Diane J. Graves
*University of Illinois
at Chicago*

Associate Editor
Jim Ivers

Managing Editor
Doreen Beauregard

Senior Vice President
Anthony Abbott

Publisher
Alan M. Meckler

Advances in Library Resource Sharing (ISSN 1052-262X) is published annually by Meckler Publishing, the publishing division of Meckler Corporation. Copyright © 1990 Meckler Publishing. All rights reserved.

Subscriptions: $55.00 per year. Please add $5.00 for foreign subscriptions. Orders from North and South America should be sent to Meckler Publishing, 11 Ferry Lane West, Westport, CT 06880; from elsewhere to Meckler Ltd., Grosvenor Gardens House, Grosvenor Gardens, London SW1W 0BS, UK.

Editorial submissions may be made to Diane J. Graves, 4043 Wolf Road, Western Springs, IL 60558.

Printed on acid free paper. Printed and bound in the United States of America.

Contents

IV. The Future of Resource Sharing

V. Suggested Readings: An Annotated Bibliography

Introduction

Like bibliographic instruction, resource sharing is a library concept which is always in practice to some extent, but varies in popularity from time to time depending on the economic health of library budgets versus the cost of acquiring materials. Over the past 15 years, libraries have experienced dramatic rises in materials costs, owing to fluctuations in dollar value on the world market, inflation, the burgeoning list of scientific publications (particularly serials), and related factors. Resource sharing has become easier in that new technologies facilitate the sharing of information about who owns what, and the items themselves are more easily transmitted from one place to another than was true even 5 years ago. However, resource sharing is also a topic of some debate since libraries are under pressure from local constituencies to acquire everything.

The editors became interested in the topic of resource sharing after noticing that it was a concept which received a fair amount of attention from the profession at conferences, in the literature of librarianship, and even in casual conversations among colleagues. As academic librarians, we heard a number of our colleagues discuss the concept of "access versus collections;" however, we saw little of that concept in practice. Collection development officers at research libraries, for instance, tend to share a concern that they provide the most complete collection possible—to their own constituencies. Librarians at smaller institutions complain that they are unable to buy everything their patrons requested, and that access to nearby research collections often is seriously restricted.

We know that attempts to develop shared collection development strategies within geographic areas also poses challenges. Core collections tend to duplicate one another, while some specialized collections are hoarded with the zeal of the priests in Umberto Eco's *The Name of the Rose*. Librarians at private institutions frequently feel resentful that they should be obligated to share access to their collections with patrons not affiliated with their universities. And public institutions often resent having to provide service to all comers simply because their libraries are mostly tax-supported, especially when the tax revenues are insufficient to provide adequate resources and services to their primary patrons. Resource sharing becomes a topic of evaluation and debate within consortium membership.

To muddy the waters further, conversations with colleagues revealed that the lack of standards in networks, telecommunications, searching and database structures of integrated online systems, and vendor packages is rendering more difficult some efforts to share access to information. Copyright law imposes additonal restrictions on resource sharing arrangements. Certainly the time-honored promotion and tenure system, as well as the accreditation agencies for various disciplines, further hamper librarians' efforts to stretch budgets without restricting patron access to needed bibliographic tools. Membership in research associations often depends on a formula that includes volume counts.

After considering the implications of the kinds of comments we were hearing and reading, we decided that an annual volume on resource sharing issues would be timely and perhaps of value to our colleagues. We agreed that the best coverage for a first volume would include an overview of the history of resource sharing, a look at current resource sharing practices, their successes and failures, a consideration of legal issues, and finally some "blue-sky" projections on the future of resource sharing and librarianship itself.

The articles we solicited from colleagues revealed to us that clearly, traditional means of resource sharing are no longer sufficient, and that new methods and perspectives are under development as we write. Within this volume are more than one article suggesting that the library as we know it now is on the wane, and that visionary information professionals will become informed about standards for transmitting information. They will train themselves and their staffs to think of sharing access to information rather than the actual bibliographic units that may not really answer the needs of the researcher.

Other articles discuss the present tense, and cite both encouraging and disheartening case studies of resource sharing efforts currently in practice. While some of these are real success stories, the personal experiences of a researcher trying to use various resource sharing systems is less encouraging, and probably fairly representative of the experiences of many academics whose needs are not answered by the collections of their host institutions.

Perhaps the most alarming trend revealed by a volume of collected essays such as this one is the fact that while librarians have been monumentally successful at cooperating on cataloging standards, networking, the implementation of the MARC format and other efforts, resource sharing collectives have almost always experienced a degree of failure. For a variety of reasons, efforts to expand access to information through cooperative ventures have met with insurmountable odds. Hopefully, *Advances in Library Resource Sharing* will serve as a catalyst for discussion about this trend, and will encourage all of us to consider ways to circumvent our self-imposed barriers before the new technologies enable information users to circumvent the library!

The Editors

Library Cooperation: A Historical Perspective and a Vision for the Future

Richard M. Dougherty
Professor, School of Information and Library Studies
University of Michigan
and Carol Hughes, Visiting Lecturer, School of Information and
Library Studies, University of Michigan

In the presidential address given to the American Library Association in 1905, Ernest Cushing Richardson deplored the inadequacy of the nation's major libraries and stated that the "remedy" for this situation would be found: "First, in cooperation in purchase and distribution...Second, [in] cheapening the postal rates [and]...Third, [in the] considerable extension of the cooperative book list."[1] Herbert Kellar, head of the Library of Congress' Experimental Division of Library Cooperation, echoed this strategy in 1941, and succinctly called it a concern for "acquisition, control and mobility" of materials.[2]

For 85 years the library community has been struggling with how best to promote the acquisition, control and mobility of materials among libraries. The library profession has mounted and operated cooperative projects on all three fronts which few other professions or organizations could have accomplished. This tri-partite framework for resource sharing has been developed in an attempt to enable people at every level of society to find the information they are seeking.

But a shift is occurring in the environment of library cooperation. Technology has caught up with Richardson's plan. The library community has been given tools to apply his remedy in ways that far outstrip anything he could have envisioned. However, in the process of giving librarians what they've always said they wanted in order to serve the needs of patrons, technology is challenging the traditional roles and relationships of the information transaction. Resource sharing in the 21st century will require a rearticulation of our cooperative goals based on a fresh vision of what is required in order to meet the new and more demanding expectations of library users.

This chapter is not intended to be a comprehensive account of the history of library cooperation. It is intended to serve as a general overview of issues and trends in library cooperation, particularly within the research library community. Hopefully this overview will inspire a fresh perspective about future courses which libraries might take in working together to address the information needs of our particular communities.

Historical Context

The library community has addressed the need for widening users' access to information in a variety of ways. Programs have ranged from the development of interlibrary loan networks and coordinated acquisitions agreements to cooperative collection development systems. Resource sharing has not always been focused on materials, as cooperative reference programs and joint storage facilities demonstrate. Some programs have been little more than informal agreements among neighboring colleagues; other programs have been regional or national in scope with strictly defined protocols.

One of the oldest traditions in library cooperation has been the sharing of bibliographic information. In 1885, the Smithsonian published the earliest national union list, consisting of scientific and technical journals. Two of the most significant efforts for national bibliographic resource sharing were sponsored by the Library of Congress (LC) when its card distribution service and the National Union Catalog were both begun in 1901. All the early activity in this area was not confined to the East coast—in 1909, California developed a union card catalog of public library holdings.[3]

Much of this bibliographic information had location information attached to it. The development of the first interlibrary loan code by the American Library Association (ALA) in 1917 began a long term effort within the profession to formalize procedures for access when ownership was not possible.

Union list development was a predominant activity of the 1920s. The publication of the *Union List of Serials in Libraries of the United States and Canada* in 1927 was one of the most notable achievements of that decade. But programs for the support of shared cataloging and the development of formal interinstitutional cooperative arrangements received a significant boost in the 1930s. Federal programs aimed at stimulating a recovery from the Depression also stimulated library cooperation.[4]

The Library of Congress and universities such as Harvard, Chicago and Illinois had been publishing cataloging for several years. But with the establishment of the Library of Congress' Cooperative Cataloging Division in 1932, this sharing of information was soon expanded to almost 400 libraries in the United States and Canada.[5]

Several interinstitutional cooperative arrangements of varying degrees of formality were also born in the 1930s. Duke University and the University of North Carolina began their long and productive relationship. The Claremont Colleges banded together in 1931 to "establish a joint order and catalog department to serve the three libraries."[6] The Association of Research Libraries (ARL) was founded in 1932. Bibliographic centers were formed to maintain regional union lists and support interlibrary loan activities. One of the earliest of these organizations was the Bibliographical Center for Research in Denver, founded in 1934 with a $10,000 grant from the Carnegie Corporation. It was followed in 1940 by the Pacific Northwest Bibliographic Center, Seattle, which was also started with a Carnegie grant.[7]

World War II's disruption of the acquisition of foreign materials gave an impetus to one of the most notable and long-lived programs for the enhancement of our nation's intellectual resources, the Farmington Plan. The Farmington Plan proposed that "libraries having research collections join in a cooperative undertaking to bring to this country and make available through one of the cooperating libraries at least one copy of every book and pamphlet published anywhere in the world...that might reasonably be expected to have interest to a research worker in America. It [was] further proposed that each item so acquired shall be catalogued promptly and listed in the Union Catalogue at the Library of Congress."[8]

Keyes Metcalf, Librarian at Harvard University and one of the original drafters of the Plan, stated that "librarians are...on the horns of a dilemma. They are overwhelmed with the costs arising from the little-used material they have acquired and are acquiring, and yet the research scholar of the United States does not have at his command a large proportion of the material that is needed if he is to pursue his studies in out-of-the-way lines. The Farmington Plan was proposed to correct this situation without increasing library expenditures and with the hope that ultimately it will reduce them."[9]

In 1942, Archibald MacLeish, then Librarian of Congress, convened a committee in Farmington, Connecticut, composed of himself, Metcalf, and Julian Boyd, librarian at Princeton. The work of this committee evolved into the Plan sponsored by the Association of Research Libraries and funded partially by a grant from the Carnegie Corporation. On January 1, 1948, the Farmington Plan went into operation, receiving materials from Sweden, Switzerland and France.

The world of western European scholarship was divided among participating libraries on the basis of the LC subject classification system, although local strengths were acknowledged in the assignment of areas of responsibility. In 1952 a complementary program for publications from The East and South Asia, Latin America, Africa, Eastern Europe and the Near East was begun, with collecting responsibilities divided along geographic lines.

But there were difficulties in accommodating institutional changes in program emphasis and a general lack of clarity about the extent of any single library's commitment. Concerns about duplication of effort arose as LC began the National Program for Acquisitions and Cataloging in the mid-1960s, about the time that it began to acquire foreign publications with unspent funds from Public Law 480 accounts. The Farmington Plan was formally ended in 1972, as was the Latin American Cooperative Acquisitions Program.[10]

One of the lessons of the Farmington Plan was that cooperation needs an organizational structure to support it. One of the most important cooperative organizations for academic libraries was the Midwest Interlibrary Center in Chicago, founded in 1949. Originally intended as a cooperative storage center for ten midwestern university libraries, this organization changed its name in 1965 to the Center for Research Libraries (CRL), expanded its membership base, and broadened its mission in regards to the acquisitions of lesser used materials.

The development of cooperative organizations took on an entirely new significance for libraries as the computer began to change the face of library operations. The first major cooperative effort in automation within academic libraries, the Columbia/Harvard/Yale Medical Library project, operated from 1962 to 1966. This project used an online system for both card production and access to bibliographic information. Several factors contributed to the closure of the project, including competing institutional priorities, technological problems and storage costs.[11]

In the mid-1960s, the Library of Congress took the lead by developing the MARC format for machine readable cataloging and offering both the format and the data from its own cataloging operation to any organization willing to experiment. This development set the ground rules for the future. In this fashion, "the approach was adopted that programs should be built from the ground up and based on immediate needs rather than plans constructed around the concept of an ideal system."[12] The future of networking in the United States was set on a course of distributed systems and diverse protocols. Technology became the dominant factor in the design of cooperative systems for the "acquisition, control and mobility" of materials.

Out of all the libraries and groups of libraries that took advantage of the opportunity to develop systems with the MARC tapes, three emerged in the 1970s as the major sources of online bibliographic network services. The Ohio College Library Center (OCLC, later renamed the Online Computer Library Center), the Washington Library Network (WLN), and the Research Libraries Group (RLG), each developed systems which were quite different from each other, but which served the needs of their library members quite well.

Maciuszko points out that the late 1960s and the 1970s marks the shift of leadership in cooperative library developments from the public library sector to academic libraries.[13] Campuses were already engaged in the capital investment needed to develop and maintain large online databases, aided by the infusion of interest and money made by the federal government into academic research communities during this period. The increased use of technology as a tool of cooperation began to require a level of standardization in practice unprecedented in library history. Balancing the tension between local autonomy and cooperative standards became one of the major challenges of cooperative activity.

Much of the literature of the 1970s refers to OCLC as the de facto national network. There could have been several reasons for this statement, all of which still affect network operations today. OCLC serves the largest number and variety of libraries with the largest database. Additionally,

OCLC serves as the primary national database for machine-readable serials records in its role as the CONSER host (formerly the CONversion of SERials Project, and now the Cooperative ONline SERials Program). Creation of a huge database was the strategy OCLC chose for supporting resource sharing.

The other two utilities chose different strategies for development. WLN did not seek members outside the northwest part of the country, choosing instead to market its software that others might duplicate what it had done. RLG, from the beginning, consciously limited its membership. The intent in the formation of the group was to deal programmatically with issues facing research libraries, such as cooperative collection development, preservation and interlibrary lending. A bibliographic database was the means by which these programs could be launched.[14] Thus the world of networked library cooperation maintained three very different but equally viable alternative utilities during this decade.

Perhaps the search for a de facto national network merely reflected the general mood of the times which also exhibited itself in the call for a national mechanism to cope with the new budgetary austerity which research libraries were facing in the 70s. "The effects of the rising [acquisitions] costs and the heavy use of the interlibrary loans systems caused librarians to seek assistance at the national level. Although not a new concept, the National Periodicals Center (NPC) began to gain prominence within the library field."[15]

In the early 1970s, a group of studies were conducted for the Association of Research Libraries on interlibrary lending of materials in academic libraries. These studies focused on the characteristics of interlibrary loans made by academic libraries, on the use of centralized and regionalized interlibrary loan centers, on the potential for using time-sharing networks for improving communication and management of interlibrary loans, and on methods for financing interlibrary loans.[16-19] In 1974, another ARL report recommended that there be established a National Periodical Resources Center since almost one-half of all academic interlibrary loans had been reported in the earlier studies to be from the periodical literature.[20] The National Commission on Libraries and Information Science (NCLIS) was also studying this issue, and it set up a Task Force on a National Periodicals System which reported in 1977 that the Library of Congress should develop a National Periodicals Center (NPC) as part of a three-tiered program for improving national access to periodical literature.[21]

This plan did not come to fruition. The library community did not coalesce in its support of the concept and "as a result, then, of interpersonal, inter-institutional, and inter-industry frictions, of an inadequate knowledge base, and perhaps of characteristic bureaucratic reactions, librarians tended to generate paper instead of actions around the NPC concept."[22]

Contributing to the lack of coalescence behind the NPC were concerns about how copyright issues would be handled, whether most publishers would collaborate, and whether technology would soon make dependence upon a centralized collection anachronistic. These issues were raised to NCLIS in an Arthur D. Little, Inc., report on alternative systems of access to serial publications.[23] In 1979, LC "which had planned to direct the NPC project for its first two years, decided to bow out, claiming it could not locate the requisite amount of funding and space...[The NPC] seems to have been tabled indefinitely."[24]

The library community has often exhibited ambivalence toward the concept of national or centralized services. As Shank has stated: "There is a natural tendency in American society to favor the local environment."[25] Although a great deal of time and energy were spent in contributing to the growth of large online databases in the 1970s, there remained a resistance toward a perceived loss of local autonomy and a sense that the governance of these organizations should operate according to the wishes of the membership rather than out of a centrally developed corporate plan.

As OCLC grew, it developed formal relationships with other regional library cooperative organizations which could serve as service centers, brokering OCLC to individual libraries in their geographic areas. Some of these regional cooperative organizations, such as the Michigan Library Consortium, were newly formed for this purpose. Other organizations which became service centers, like NELINET, had existed longer than OCLC and they already had a pattern of services to which they added OCLC brokering.

As networks grew into mature organizations, the level of complexity for any given library increased exponentially in the 1970s: in the relationships among libraries and between each library and its bibliographic utility of choice, in the decision to make a financial commitment to the costs of online cataloging and dues for various tiers of cooperative programs, and in the unease some libraries felt about being called upon to be part of a national network with the concomitant responsibilities for participation in the programs and governance of all the various cooperative organizations to which the library might belong.

The research libraries that belonged to RLG sometimes found themselves within a state which was developing state-wide, multitype-library, OCLC-based resource sharing programs or in a smaller regional area where the local cooperative was developing network based services. Directors in such states felt pressure to participate in the state program rather than in the research library-based programs of RLG. Some officials were fond of referring to RLG as "elitist." The dichotomy between research libraries which chose to remain in OCLC and those which chose to join RLG was an important factor in the pattern of resource sharing throughout the decade of the seventies. Its influence was felt into the 1980s as the need for bridging this technological gap gave an impetus to the development of the Linked Systems Project (LSP). When completed, the LSP will permit organizations such as LC, OCLC, and RLG to exchange bibliographic records electronically—a long-awaited milestone in the history of resource sharing.

In the early seventies, McAnally and Downs had included political pressures to develop effective resource sharing programs and to computerize library operations in their seminal assessment of the changing role of research library directors. They quoted Charles Buckman as stating that a director could probably restore the university's confidence in the library and its director by accepting and implementing "some significant national programs that really come [sic] to grips with fundamental problems of providing information and knowledge for people working in the universities."[26] Library cooperation was becoming a more important factor in determining an individual director's success on the local campus.

Maciuszko writes that "[OCLC] forced librarianship to abandon the traditional viewpoint of an independent library and to embrace the new idea of a library as part of a network sharing common experiences, resources and responsibilities for the betterment of all concerned."[27] Certainly, the emphasis on standardization which participation in automated library cooperation demanded was changing the way even the smallest library operated. It may have seemed that this transformation within the profession had been accomplished when Maciuszko wrote this, but local interests had not yet been universally relegated to second place in the hearts of librarians. The forces at work in this process of metamorphosis still generated quite a bit of friction as the ramifications of the use of resource sharing technology became apparent in the 1980s.

In December 1982, OCLC displayed a notice of copyright on its database. As Rowland Brown, President of OCLC, stated in a letter to Robert Clark, President of the Chief Officers of State Library Agencies (COSLA): "Our copyright action should not be perceived as representing any change in OCLC policy or any lessening of our support for resource sharing. The OCLC membership has always assumed that OCLC's management would find the means of reconciling the need to maximize resource sharing and public access while maintaining the integrity, viability and cost effectiveness of the system in the membership's collective interests. We see copyright as simply one of many factors...assisting us in carrying out this balanced policy."[28]

Individual libraries and networks did not view OCLC's move to register a copyright of its database in the same light. Concerns quickly arose about restrictions which could be enforced on a local library's use of its OCLC records. One response of many collected by the AMIGOS Bibliographic Council, Inc., stated that "OCLC's unilateral action to copyright the database is in my view most inappropriate. It certainly runs counter to the implicit understanding between OCLC and the participating libraries and implies radical changes in the nature of our relationship."[29] SOLINET released a resolution of its Board of Directors stating, "Any unilateral copyright claim on the database constitutes a radical and ominous departure from the heretofore cooperative efforts of OCLC, the networks, and the member libraries."[30]

In a subsequent letter to the entire OCLC membership, Brown reaffirmed OCLC's benign intent in applying for a registration of copyright of the database as he wrote, "Almost all of the present and contemplated uses of general member libraries' OCLC-derived records remain unrestricted under the criteria adopted by our Board...In those cases where there is a question, the OCLC Board will apply the guidelines as broadly as practicable in order to facilitate resource sharing, with the understanding that OCLC has the concomitant duty to apply them so as not to diminish the future strength of the *Online Union Catalog* or to jeopardize the economic viability of OCLC."[31]

Regardless of one's assessment of the necessity for OCLC's copyright registration, it could be said that this debate initiated a significant increase in the library community's awareness of the economic value of its cooperative efforts—an economic value which was much more than the sum of the value of its individual records. It also underscored the ambivalence of librarians toward governance of sophisticated cooperative organizations by corporate plan, rather than by membership wishes.

The precise interrelationship between libraries and networks did not became clearer over the next few years. Susan Martin, one of the pioneer analysts of networks, stated, in *Library Networks, 1986-87—Libraries in Partnership*, "both OCLC and RLG are operating under the assumption that they are in control of their own destiny and in control of the way distributed processing is designed...That assumption is likely to be false, however, since libraries will purchase local systems that appeal to them and only then worry about the way the local system will interface with the utility."[32] In the same report, Martin also pointed out that, "It often seems as if librarians take networks and bibliographic utilities for granted, while they emphasize local problems and issues. However, the current structure of library networks has molded the political and social environment of the library world itself."[33]

Technology was providing the dream of librarians for over 100 years—a virtual national database—while it simultaneously offered ever increasing options for autonomy in local systems and independence from national programs. Who was molding whom, and to what degree, were two of the most challenging questions of the 1980s.

Most libraries were involved in the molding process, however. The sixth edition of The Report on Library Cooperation reported that from 1980-86 single type library cooperatives increased in number by 12%, multitype library cooperatives increased 164%, and that 30 multi-state networks were in operation.[34] Networks and cooperatives were now a fact of life for most of the library community.

On the national level, two major cooperative programs were laying the groundwork for the next generation of cooperation. The Linked Systems Project gave the major utilities and the Library of Congress the opportunity to "search for a way to enable cost-effective system-to-system communication that would facilitate sharing of the large resources of records building up at the three bibliographic utilities."[35] Building on the Library of Congress' experience with sharing authority records with the RLG computer system in the Name Authority Cooperative (NACO), and with an eye on international work on standards for computer protocols, LC, RLG, OCLC, and WLN discussed through the late 1970s and early 1980s how records might be shared among them. These discussions did not lead to a quick agreement. McCallum notes that, "this basic hesitancy to link the utilities" was due to the competition inherent among the utilities and to the concern over third-party use of records and copyright issues.[36]

By 1985, however, all three utilities were working with LC to develop procedures which could handle the transfer of any type of record for use in cataloging or interlibrary loan transactions. The potential applications of LSP extend beyond transfer of records among utilities to the transfer of records between utilities and individual libraries, and among libraries—a fact which was not lost on the library community as another trend began to manifest itself: the proliferation of the "local system."

The term "local system" generally refers to a set of automated tools available for library operations. As the technological sophistication of locally maintained integrated online systems increased and as the price of such systems decreased, many libraries made the investment. With these integrated local systems, libraries acquired the ability to update and enter data directly into the local catalog without waiting for tapeloads from a utility. The possibility of transferring records from locally mounted MARC tapes or from local CD-ROM MARC databases made it possible to became increasingly self-sufficient, bypassing the need to pay the telecommunications and use charges of the bibliographic utilities. Financially this was attractive, yet it endangered two decades of work toward building large databases for resource sharing— and in-depth resource sharing was exactly what the members of RLG were organizing to accomplish.

In 1979, RLG developed its first mechanism for in-depth resource sharing: the RLG Conspectus. This tool, based on the LC classification system, is a method of describing, in terms which allow for comparison with other institutions, the level of comprehensiveness at which an institution is collecting materials in any given subject area. In 1981, the Association of Research Libraries (ARL) adapted this tool for use by its membership in the North American Collections Inventory Project (NCIP) and it was successful in supporting the widespread application of the Conspectus within the research library community.

But even though this and other academic cooperative collection development programs experienced a surge of activity during the 1980s, most programs remained vaguely defined and were used primarily as vehicles for communication or for general coordination of serials subscriptions.[37] Farrell and Reed-Scott, in their article on the NCIP, state that "while a strong cooperative spirit clearly exists, that spirit has not been molded into a complete construct capable of supporting on a national scale the complex and difficult decision of resource allocation and coordination."[38]

The reasons for this lack of a construct are varied, but Hewitt and Shipman suggest that it primarily involves inadequate program design and operational strategies rather than resistance from faculty or library staff. From the data gathered in their survey of ARL libraries, they have assessed a need for empirical studies on "strategies and techniques for dividing collecting responsibility, decision models and selection procedures in the context of cooperative collection development agreements, communication among bibliographers, and organizational structure at the implementation level."[39]

Work continues on the cooperative collection development front.

Perhaps the experience now being gained in cooperative preservation programs will provide some answers on how to construct effective broadly-based collection development programs. Farrell and Reed-Scott suggest that the RLG Conspectus has great potential as a framework for future advances if its complexity of application can be reduced and its documentation completed.[40] Certainly this arena of resource sharing will be increasingly important to any effort to maintain a sufficient national collection of information resources.

The past 85 years have seen remarkable accomplishments in library cooperation. The logistics of acquisition, control and mobility of materials have improved dramatically since the beginning of the century. This is largely due to the substantial achievements of the library community in the standardization of protocols and record formats. Yet the fact remains that resource sharing has remained a secondary strategy in the repertoire of librarians.

Unfulfilled Promise

Regardless of progress to date, the perception remains that library cooperation has not fulfilled its promise for increasing access to information for users. Moran quotes Reynolds as stating that it can be demonstrated "that library cooperation has not solved the important problems of the library, but only responded to their symptoms."[41]   Moran then continues with his own observation that he did "not mean to suggest that no real value has resulted from the cooperative programs that exist, but that the results are insignificant when related to expectations, the models that have existed for same time, and the orientation of librarians toward cooperation."[42]

Discerning the reasons for this lack of performance will be essential if resource sharing is to reach its potential as a primary strategy for meeting the information needs of the future. In examining the underlying structure of resource sharing as it has developed over the past century, three themes emerge which might profitably be re-examined in light of current predictions about the challenges which the library community will face in the future. These three themes, which are part of the foundation of most resource sharing structures operating today, are:

1. the primacy of locally based services and collections over resource sharing systems;
2. the role of the librarian as the interpreter and mediator of users' information transactions outside of the local collection; and
3. the focus on delivering bibliographic units rather than on delivering information.

Primacy of Local Collections and Services

There are many reasons why locally based services and collections have been first and last in the hearts of librarians. Local users want local availability on a convenient shelf. Limited financial resources have been spent "at home." Librarians take professional pride in being able to fulfill users' requests directly.

One other explanation claims that resource sharing suffers in the quest for the prestige which comes with bigger collections. "Consumer-oriented studies can determine when direct access to materials is required—the core collection—and when the access needed is to one specific item best provided on demand [from another library]...The political problems of such a changed approach cannot be minimized. For so many years the size of a library's own collection has been its claim to fame and a shift to emphasizing its services would be seen as revolutionary. In fact, the revolution has already happened, outside libraries, and the requirement is to reconnect the library to the new information systems."43

At times, the primacy of local collections and services over resource sharing systems has became an actual hurdle for users. In his speech, "The Importance of People Networking," Atkinson concluded that librarians should "deal with the realities of library use by our patrons and by ourselves and our colleagues rather than with the myths that surround them knowing that the relatively artificial processes that we have evolved often serve as a barrier to effective library service both on the local library level and certainly for interlibrary network library services."44

His example was of a professor who had to go to the local public library to initiate an interlibrary loan request rather than requesting it from the University of Illinois' interlibrary loan department. It seems that since Illinois owned the item, but all copies were in circulation, the rules prohibited an ILL request, requiring instead that the professor wait for a copy to be recalled. Judging that he didn't have the time to wait for a recall, the professor took extra steps to circumvent the library's rules to get what he needed. It might be interesting to reflect on how many users have sufficient knowledge of how libraries operate to be able to manipulate the system to achieve that level of utility.

White states that "it is clear that the academic library materials budget is aimed at ownership and not at access...[This] amounts to a double penalization for the user." The first penalty for the user comes from not having available what the user needs, whether because it was not bought or because it is otherwise unavailable for that user. The second penalization comes from making the patron wait unreasonable amounts of time to receive the material requested and perhaps even charging him/her for the borrowing of this material.45 A third penalization could be added that, upon finally having obtained the requested material, an abbreviated loan period usually demands that the material be returned soon after receipt.

The philosophy underlying this emphasis of local collections over resource sharing needs to be examined. If it is agreed that nearly 80% of the document needs of a library can be satisfied by 20% of the collection, why are users who request materials which librarians did not have the foresight to acquire relegated to a slow and personally costly secondary system, while library budgets and professional expertise remain focused on acquiring the 80% of a collection which will rarely be used?

Librarian as Mediator

Systems have been built for librarian to librarian communication, not for end-user access. The implicit assumption has been that building sophisticated systems to help librarians with the "acquisition, control and mobility of materials" would satisfy the needs of the users. However, a few writers have called into question the quality of the library profession's knowledge of and assumptions about what users really want and need.

Ballard makes particularly challenging statements about how librarians have disregarded users' preferences in the design of resource sharing systems. He states that the majority of users primarily want convenience, and that "a patron's use of a...library...is virtually limited to selection from the books on the shelf at the time of the visit." With what justification, he asks, do libraries create elaborate and expensive tiered-systems for resource sharing when it is only a small proportion of users who require this?[46]

Although Ballard was addressing resource sharing in public libraries, the research library community has also acknowledged this paradox. Rothstein noted that interlibrary loans account for only about 1% of the total lending activity in a research library.[47] Chapin suggested that "before we develop grandiose networking schemes, at great expense, perhaps we should have a better idea as to what needs are not being met by traditional programs."[48]

Ignorance of users' needs compounds the problems of disregarding known preferences. Lynch, in a 1976 article on the effect of networks and other cooperative enterprises on the function of reference, stated that, "despite great effort, the profession still is lacking in basic knowledge of users, their information needs and the uses to which information is put." As critical as this is to local reference services, it becomes essential to "the process of reference in a systems framework."[49]

Focus on Bibliographic Units

Nitecki echoed Lynch's concern about the profession's lack of knowledge about user information needs. She took it a step further to discuss the inadequacy of resource sharing systems which are based on delivering bibliographic units rather than information. Acknowledging that automation has made great strides in assisting in the location and request for materials, she noted, "we are still faced with insufficient techniques for accurately identifying actual user needs and delivering the specific information required. Often an identified citation is a hoped-for solution. After waiting for its delivery and examining it, the user may find it to be inadequate and so must begin the search anew."[50]

Even sophisticated users can be disappointed when attempting to obtain information from a system designed to handle documents rather than information. Kilgour reported that he had "obtained on interlibrary loan three currently published books whose titles gave strong indication that the books would contain what he wanted. Two of them contained nothing, and the third only a single sentence that was useful. Nevertheless, the title accurately described the books; they were not frauds."[51]

One analysis suggests that all the internal operations of a library must be re-evaluated in the context of the need to form external networks of information services. Shaw has suggested that a library's "approach [to information services] derives from an outmoded conception of the kinds of tasks that ought to go on in libraries—tasks that were never really systematically designed, but which simply evolved, and are based on a purpose that has to do with collecting and lending books. Consequently the total system is often misconceived as a data management system—bigger, faster, more flexible, more universally accessible—but still targeted only to message manipulation rather than informing."[52]

Changing User Expectations

The library profession is at a critical juncture. Gaining an increased understanding of users' needs will be the key to librarians' future role in the knowledge transfer process. Improved design of information-oriented resource sharing systems which are used as effectively as local services and collections will also be essential.

Our profession is facing a future in which it must clearly demonstrate its utility to its constituencies or risk being relegated to an ever-decreasing role in the new information society. If it has become axiomatic that no individual library can hope to serve the information needs of all of its users, the profession must now decide what can be done to strengthen the systems of library cooperation which already exist and what new systems will be needed to accomplish our goal of information delivery. However, merely extrapolating from past experience will probably not be adequate to give us the answers we're seeking. "We are in danger of trying to solve tomorrow's problems with yesterday's tools—those tools being computerization, MARC, AACR2, yesterday's networking."[53]

Multiple Options

The user of tomorrow will have many options for the delivery of information services. Direct information services to users will depend in part upon a growing availability of electronic sources designed for access by those who are not information professionals. The development of such services is in full swing in both the profit and the non-profit sector. RLG and OCLC are actively developing direct user services. Bibliographic information vendors, such as DIALOG, and telecommunications vendors, such as the SOURCE, are joining publishers in the provision of full-text delivery systems. Direct services are most likely to be developed first in the more highly commercial subject areas, but gradually such services will be developed to serve the needs of users in other disciplines.

The question of whether libraries and librarians can retain their "customers" in an increasingly competitive environment is still being debated. Over ten years ago, Braunstein wrote that the choice between using a library or using a commercial source was an economic choice, depending upon how the user valued his/her time and how efficient use of the library was for acquiring the desired information. He concluded that any effort which increased the speed and convenience of library use, and which reduced the time which the user must spend to put the data into a personally usable format would enhance the "competitive stance" of libraries.[54] Efficient resource sharing systems will be essential if individual libraries wish to maintain their niche in the information delivery market.

Speed and Convenience

Many authors have projected what the user of the future will require from information services. One point on which most agree is that users will go to the quickest and most convenient source for what they need. Increasingly, turnaround times of two weeks or more for document delivery will "not only be unattractive to library users, but may in some instances render the service intended by interlibrary loans useless." [55]

The history of interlibrary loan has been one of developing rules for how libraries as institutions would relate to each other. Rules, policies, and procedures have always been necessary for any type of coherent system. However, the basis of many procedures has been that of protecting a lending institution from "overuse" rather than that of service for the library user. Requests for response by telefacsimile are the exception rather than the rule. Often the arrival of fax requests are treated as disruptions in an orderly workflow. Interlibrary loan systems which require users to appear in person at a central point to place requests and to retrieve materials will have to compete with systems which are accessible from a user's workstation and which provide direct document delivery.

Interlibrary loan departments will need to be staffed, organized and evaluated according to a new definition of response quality. Loan periods which hamper users at remote sites may have to be discarded. A reappraisal of resource sharing policies will be necessary lest we "use rules as an excuse for not providing service rather than as a means for facilitating service."[56]

Individualized Service

Both commercial and library-based user services will need to accommodate an increase in users' demand for individualized tailoring of information and information access systems. This tailoring of information access has two dimensions. One dimension is that of accommodating the personal logic of the user in the information request. Molholt calls this the trend toward "individuation" of information services. "We have traditionally forced individuals into conforming roles. They had to search using standardized formats…they had to accept our world view as presented in the related term structure we created for the systems. In the near future, users will be able to use their own thought patterns, their own associations and views of the world, to retrieve information."[57]

The other dimension of tailored information services is that of focusing on the user's specific information need rather than on the retrieval of bibliographic units. Drake states that, "library users in ever greater numbers want information and data to be customized to their particular problem. They are not content with a stack of paper, volumes of abstracts, a printout of citations from an online service, or a box of census tapes…[Librarians] have been like the salespeople who believe that their customers buy books because they want books. The reality is that most people buy books and information services because they want to know, to learn, or to solve a problem."[58]

Current resource sharing systems were not designed to be "user friendly" for library staff, not to mention library users. Interlibrary loan offices frequently operate at a physical and intellectual distance from information services. They are designed to handle the delivery of items, leaving any assessment of the value of the item entirely to the patron. As libraries begin to customize local information services, the resource sharing operations of the library will also have to be re-evaluated.

Users have always wanted information that was timely, convenient, and customized. Technology is now growing in its capacity to meet these demands. How well libraries and resource sharing systems incorporate these characteristics into their services will be critical to their success in the future. Systems which create obstacles between the use of local resources and remote resources, which are so complex that they require the mediation of an information professional, which are slow, and which are based on traditional bibliographic units rather than the delivery of information will be inadequate to meet the majority of users' needs. If librarians can't create successful information delivery systems, the role of libraries in the information society of the future will shrink dramatically.

Challenges for the Future of Resource Sharing

If understanding users' needs is the key to the future, librarians must became much more knowledgeable about what each individual user requires in terms of content, timeliness, and customization. To accomplish this, it is apparent that interviewing skills will become paramount in library services. What has been termed the "reference interview" will be required of librarians operating in resource sharing programs as well as those at the reference desk. If we assume that the resource sharing request is an information-based request rather than a bibliographic unit-based request, the need for professional assistance is clear and the distinction blurs between reference and interlibrary loan functions.

Many have acknowledged that the profession has an unfortunate lack of skill in this technique, however, even at the reference desk. In a recent study Durrance found that "only one quarter of the librarians were thought to be excellent interviewers...and only 27% found out what the questioner really needed."[59]

A major challenge faces librarianship in re-focusing our professional skills on the user rather than on documents. It will be increasingly necessary for a librarian to develop a closer relationship with his/her "client," much like that which other professionals develop. This professional relationship may well include a greater performance accountability for information service staff and a relinquishment of the traditional cloak of anonymity which has distinguished librarianship from other professions. A greater sensitivity to the privacy with which a user expects his/her question to be handled will also be necessary as the possibility of using cooperative information services increases. The future will require librarians to operate as knowledge professionals rather than collection professionals.

Technology is now, and it will remain, both a force for progress and an obstacle to progress. Impressive advances in bibliographic resource sharing have been made because the power of technology was harnessed by the use of standards like MARC. The lack of standardization which remains in the world of telecommunications, applications software, electronic mail protocols, etc., will need to be addressed before the information society can become a reality. Technological advances will probably continue to outstrip the ability of people to link the old and the new. The development of standards and bridging software will be a continuing challenge.

The shift from print-based materials to electronic materials will present us with more than just the technological task of creating systems for seamless electronic resource sharing. Each discipline will vary in the speed with which its information base is built electronically because of the nature of research in that discipline. Disciplines in which data is more time-sensitive will shift more quickly to electronic sources. Resource sharing systems will have to accommodate access to both formats for a long time to come.

The shift to non-print collections is an important variable in resource sharing both logistically and politically. Logistically, we may have to acknowledge that print-based resource sharing has limits to the speed with which it can accomplish its task. The hierarchy which is in place handled over 3,527,700 loaned items and 1,095,500 borrowed items in 1987-88 in ARL libraries. ACRL statistics for the same period report that smaller university libraries loaned over 803,300 items and borrowed over 517,700. The current system is already handling millions of items annually. Without an entirely new paradigm, it may not be possible to achieve further significant advancements in the performance of resource sharing systems.

Some refinements may still be possible in the current interlibrary loan model. Interlibrary loan staffs could begin to develop guidelines for a triage system for handling requests. Establishment of priorities among requests could be made according to the degree of urgency or the size of a fee paid. White suggests that an increased use of ingenuity, personal contacts and commercial sources coupled with increased economic incentives for lenders would increase response quality.[60] Interlibrary loan rules and procedures which delay and inhibit information use could be changed. But unless the content of documents is digitized, a dramatic increase in speed of delivery is unlikely, and speed is becoming increasingly more important to users.

Refinements in the electronic bibliographic record used as the base for interlibrary loan are also being explored. The addition of tables of contents, abstracts, book reviews, and indexes to the work described are all possibilities for enhancing access to the information contained within the bibliographic unit.

Politically, the shift to non-print collections has serious ramifications. For example, academic reward systems must be overhauled. Currently this reward system is based on publication of research and scholarship in specialized paperform publications. Publication in electronic format should ease pressure on libraries to have large local collections of little-used, highly specialized periodicals merely to satisfy the publish-or-perish syndrome. The population of journals which could be considered for resource-sharing would be expanded.

Moreover, universities and their faculties will have to stop using "bigger libraries are better" as a recruiting technique for graduate students and faculty. The university community will need to acknowledge the role which access to remote resources plays in its knowledge base. "In addition, many electronic resources, such as remote sensing data or large text files, will require cooperative support. The resulting interdependence will not easily co-exist with institutional pride."[61] But such an acknowledgment of interdependence is necessary on the part of the entire university community if librarians are to be politically empowered to use resource sharing as a primary service strategy.

The barriers to enhancing resource sharing are significant, but they cannot be allowed to block the profession's continued progress in this area. Librarians must be actively engaged in helping to design information systems which provide information, not documents. The profession can continue to work toward and lobby for the development of industry standards to facilitate sharing. Librarians can also play a leadership role in helping scholars re-evaluate their relationship with publishers who care more for profits than effective scholarly communication.

Perhaps the most important issue which librarianship must confront in order to maintain a central role in the future development of information services is that of shared collection development and document delivery. Campus administrators are slowly growing in their collective consciousness about the need for institutional interdependence in information resources. Librarians must take a leadership role now in designing effective systems to prove their ability to exploit the resources which have been given to their care.

Significant investments have been made in building research collections and in building networking systems. If librarians and the networks they have built cannot pay back that investment soon, they are likely to lose their claim to a role as full partners in the national knowledge transfer system.

The ability of librarians to participate fully in the development of the national knowledge network is already threatened by the trend toward the maintenance of local systems at the expense of supporting national resource sharing systems. Such a suboptimization of intellectual resources is fundamentally at odds with the best interests of a national information system. The profession's claim to a national vision is compromised by library policies which treat scholars from outside the library's primary constituency as second class citizens in terms of access and services rendered. These practices belie the rhetoric so often heard that cooperation is essential because no library can be self-sufficient. "If self-sufficiency is not an attainable goal, then mutual sufficiency becomes a compelling need. And this raises the problem from the narrow parochial view of the individual library to the status of a national problem to which all librarians must address themselves."[62]

Conclusion

The history of library cooperation and resource sharing is one of which the profession can be very proud. But the future will demand a new paradigm. The spirit of this age is high-technology combined with individualized and personalized response. "It is multi-optioned...The age is entrepreneurial, decentralized and self-reliant."[63]

Library resource sharing systems will have to conform to the spirit of the age if they are to be useful to the majority of information seekers. These systems will have to be seamless to the user, making the use of remote sources as easy as local sources. They will not require the constant mediation of a librarian for procedural or logistical purposes. They will be information based rather than document based and will include access to many full-text electronic sources. They will accommodate the individual user's unique needs.

What then will be the role of the librarian? "Librarians will serve as network managers, facilitating the usage of collections in many libraries. Expanded and enhanced access to information will occur, without requiring redundant collections, as more libraries became part of larger, networked collections."[64] Librarians will be pathfinders for people venturing outside the boundaries of their accustomed information universe.

The "new librarianship" in colleges and universities cannot stop at the boundaries of the campus. It must encompass an interinstitutional, even global, vision of what information resources exist focused on a personal understanding of an individual's information needs. The challenges are daunting, but the rewards for success will be tremendous.

Notes

1. Richardson, Ernest Cushing. "The Adequacy of American Libraries as Regards Their Books. Extract from the Presidential Address, ALA Conference, Portland, OR, July 1905" in General Library Cooperation and American Research Books; Collected Papers by Ernest Cushing Richardson. Yardley, PA: F.S. Cook & Son, 1930, p. 3-4.
2. Kellar, Herbert. Memorandum on Library Cooperation. (Washington, D.C.: Library of Congress, 1941).
3. Kraus, Joe W. "Prologue to Library Cooperation." *Library Trends* 24(2): 173 (October 1975).
4. Weber, David C. "A Century of Cooperative Programs Among Academic Libraries." *College & Research Libraries* 37(3): 205-21 (May 1976).
5. Ibid.
6. Ibid.
7. Weber, David C. and Lynden, Frederick C. "Survey of Interlibrary Cooperation" in *Proceedings of the Conference on Interlibrary Communications and Information Networks,* Airlie House, 1970, edited by Joseph Becker. (Chicago: American Library Association, 1971) p. 69-81.
8. Metcalf, Keyes. "The Farmington Plan," *Harvard Library Bulletin* 2(3): 296 (Autumn 1948).
9. Ibid., 300.
10. Edelman, Hendrik. "The Death of the Farmington Plan." *Library Journal* 98 (8): 1251-1253 (April 15, 1973).
11. Weber and Lynden, Op. cit.
12. Stevens, Norman. "Library Networks and Resource Sharing in the United States: an Historical and Philosophical Overview." *Journal of the American Society for Information Science* 31(6): 406 (November 1980).
13. Maciuszko, Kathleen. *OCLC: A Decade of Development, 1967-1977.* (Littleton, CO: Libraries Unlimited, Inc., 1984).
14. Bryant, Douglas W. "Strengthening the Strong: the Cooperative Future of Research Libraries." *Harvard Library Bulletin* 24(1): 5-16 (January 1976).
15. Webreck, Susan J. "National Periodicals Center" in *Encyclopedia of Library and Information Science,* vol. 40, suppl. 5. (New York: Marcel Dekker, 1986). p. 322.
16. Palmour, Vernon E., et al. *A Study of the Characteristics, Costs and Magnitude of Interlibrary Loans in Academic Libraries.* (Westport, CT: Greenwood Publishing Co., 1972).
17. Stevens, Rolland E. *A Feasibility Study of Centralized and Regionalized Interlibrary Loan Centers.* (Washington, D.C.: Association of Research Libraries, 1973).
18. Hayes, Robert M. *Final Report for a Study of a System for Inter-library Communication (SILC).* (Los Angeles: Becker & Hayes, 1974).
19. Palmour, Vernon E., Olson, Edwin E., and Roderer, Nancy K. *Methods of Financing Interlibrary Loan Services* (Rockville, MD: Westat, 1974).
20. Palmour, Vernon E., Bellassai, Marcia C., and Gray, Lucy M. *Access to Periodical Resources: a National Plan.* (Rockville, MD,: Westat, 1974).
21. National Commission on Libraries and Information Science. Task Force on a National Periodicals System. Effective Access to the Periodical Literature: a National Program. (Washington, D.C.: National Commission on Libraries and

Information Science, 1977).

22. Biggs, Mary. "The Proposed National Periodicals Center, 1973-1980: Study, Dissension, and Retreat." *Resource Sharing and Information Networks* 1(3/4): 2 (Spring/Summer 1984).

23. Little, Arthur D., Inc. *A Comparative Evaluation of Alternative Systems for the Provision of Effective Access to Periodical Literature; a Report to the National Commission on Libraries and Information Science.* (Washington, D.C.: National Commission on Libraries and Information Science, 1979).

24. Webreck, Op. cit. p. 324.

25. Shank, Russell. "The Socio-economic Environment for Regional Library Network Development." *Resource Sharing & Library Networks* 1(4): 21 (Summer 1982).

26. McAnally, Robert N., and Downs, Robert B. "The Changing Role of Directors of University Libraries." Reprinted in *College and Research Libraries* 50 (3): 317 (May 1989).

27. Maciuszko, Op. cit. p. 214.

28. Rowland Brown to Robert L. Clark, 5 August 1983.

29. "AMIGOS Members Respond to OCLC Issues." 20 October 1983. (A collection of statements from individual library members.)

30. "Resolution of the SOLINET Board of Directors regarding the Proposed OCLC/Network Contract." 14 September 1983.

31. Rowland Brown to OCLC membership, 31 October 1983.

32. Martin, Susan K. *Library Networks, 1986-87—Libraries in Partnership.* (White Plains, N.Y.: Knowledge Industry, 1986) p. 167.

33. Ibid. p. 170.

34. Wareham, Nancy. *The Report on Library Cooperation, 1986.* 6th ed. (Chicago: Association of State and Cooperative Library Agencies, 1986).

35. McCallum, Sally. "The Linked Systems Project: Implications for Library Automation and Networking." in *Advances in Library Automation and Networking, vol. 1.* (Greenwich, CT: Jai Press, 1987) p. 2.

36. Ibid. p. 3-4.

37. Hewitt, Joe A. and Shipman, John S. "Cooperative Collection Development Among Research Libraries in the Age of Networking: Report of a Survey of ARL Libraries" in *Advances in Library Automation and Networking, vol. 1.* (Greenwich, CT: Jai Press, 1987) p. 189-232.

38. Farrell, David and Reed-Scott, Jutta. "The North American Collections Inventory Project: Implications for the Future of Coordinated Management of Research Collections." *Library Resources and Technical Services* 33(1): 15-28 (January 1989).

39. Hewitt and Shipman, Op. cit. p. 223.

40. Farrell and Reed-Scott, Op. cit. p. 27.

41. Moran, Robert F. "Library Cooperation and Change." *College and Research Libraries* 39(4): 268 (July 1978).

42. Ibid., 269.

43. Martin, Nolene P. "Interlibrary Loan and Resource Sharing: New Approaches." *Journal of Library Administration* 3(3/4): 107 (Fall/Winter 1982).

44. Atkinson, Hugh. "The Importance of People Networking: July 7, 1985." *Resource Sharing and Information Networks* 4(1): 89 (Fall 1987).

45. White, Herbert S. "Ownership is Not Always Availability—Borrowing May Not Satisfy Access Needs" in *Access to Scholarly Information: Issues & Strate*

gies, edited by Sul Lee. (Ann Arbor, MI: Pierian Press, 1985) p. 2-3.

46. Ballard, Thomas. *The Failure of Resource Sharing in Public Libraries and Alternative Strategies for Service.* (Chicago: American Library Association, 1986) p. 273.

47. Rothstein, Samuel. "The Extended Library and the Dedicated Library: a Skeptical Outsider Looks at Union Catalogues and Bibliographic Networks." *Cataloging & Classification Quarterly* 2(1/2): 103-20 (1982).

48. Chapin, Richard E. "Limits of Local Self-Sufficiency" in Becker, Op. cit., 58.

49. Lynch, Beverly. "Networks and Other Cooperative Enterprises: Their Effect on the Function of Reference." *Research Quarterly* 15(3): 202 (Spring 1976).

50. Nitecki, Danuta. "Document Delivery and the Rise of the Automated Midwife," *Resource Sharing and Information Networks* 1(3/4): 95 (Spring/Summer 1984).

51. Kilgour, Frederick. "EIDOS and the Transformation of Libraries. "*Library Journal* 112(16): 47 (October 1, 1987).

52. Shaw, Ward. "Toward Broader Networks." *Resource Sharing & Library Networks* 1(1): 3-4 (Fall 1981).

53. Gapen, D. Kaye. "Strategies for Networking in the Next Ten Years." *Journal of Library Administration* 8(3/4): 122 (Fall 1987).

54. Braunstein, Yale M. "Costs and Benefits of Library Information: the User Point of View." *Library Trends* 28(1): 79-87 (Summer 1979).

55. Budd, John. "Interlibrary Loan Service; a Study of Turnaround Time." *RQ* 26 (1): 79 (Fall 1986).

56. Drake, Miriam A. "Management of Information." *College and Research Libraries* 50(5): 527 (September 1989).

57. Molholt, Pat. "Libraries and the New Technologies: Courting the Cheshire Cat." *Library Journal* 113(19): 39 (November 15, 1988).

58. Drake, Miriam A. "From Print to Nonprint Materials: Library Information Delivery Systems." *EDUCOM Bulletin* 23(1): 29 (1988).

59. Durrance, Joan C. "Reference Success: Does the 55 Percent Rule Tell the Whole Story?" *Library Journal* 114(7): 36 (April 15, 1989).

60. White, Op. cit.

61. Lewis, David W. "Inventing the Electronic University." *College and Research Libraries* 49(4): 302 (July 1988).

62. Kronick, David A. "Goodbye to Farewells—Resource Sharing and Cost Sharing." *Journal of Academic Librarianship* 8(3): 134 (July 1982).

63. Matheson, Nina. "The Academic Library Nexus." *College and Research Libraries* 45(2): 211-12 (May 1984).

64. Murr, Lawrence E. and Williams, James B. "The Roles of the Future Library." *Library Hi Tech* 5(3): 11 (Fall 1987).

Interlibrary Loan: Past, Present, Future

Thomas L. Kilpatrick
Head of Interlibrary Loan
Morris Library
Southern Illinois University at Carbondale

The concept of library resource sharing is rooted in the nineteenth century interlibrary loan movement, but has expanded in recent years to encompass a diversity of library activities for which responsibility can be shared. Because of commonality of purpose and repetition of effort from library to library, cooperative programs have evolved to provide improved and more economical services to individual libraries and the library community as a whole. Interlibrary loan, union lists, shared cataloging projects, last copy storage facilities, cooperative collection development programs, and other endeavors involving cooperation are commonly considered resource sharing. However, the original and most often cited example remains interlibrary loan.

Interlibrary loan is defined in the National Interlibrary Loan Code, 1980, as "...a transaction in which library material, or a copy of the material, is made available by one library to another upon request."[1] In a broader sense, interlibrary loan is a logical extension of reference service as unmet needs at a local library are satisfied by a neighboring library on a reciprocal basis.

History

Interlibrary loan is a relatively recent concept in the history of libraries. The single, underlying purpose for the development of early libraries was the preservation of knowledge. Most libraries were privately owned and endowed, established to meet specific needs, and restricted in use to the owner and select clientele, including certain friends, clergy, scholars, and students. Libraries pursued their objectives through acquisition. Providing for the intellectual needs of users was a secondary priority, at best. Circulation of materials to either local or remote users did nothing to further the libraries' goals, and was generally not done.

Early scholars were at the mercy of librarians and library owners who guarded their collections well and maintained close control over access. Information about libraries and collections was sketchy and spread by word of mouth. To gain access to materials in a library, scholars had to travel to the library, and were expected to use the resources on site. Handwritten copies of documents were sometimes provided, but the lending of books or manuscripts was rare. Loans, when they did occur, were the result of long and arduous negotiations between the scholar and the library holding the desired documents.

The concept of interlibrary loan was first proposed early in the seventeenth century when Nicolas Claude Fabri de Peiresc (1580-1637) recommended that mechanisms for a reasonably free exchange of materials be established among certain European libraries. Peiresc, a French humanist who had developed contacts in libraries throughout Europe and served as intermediary for many scholars in negotiating loans, made the proposal in 1634 while attempting to negotiate a loan from the Royal Library in Paris to the Barberini Library in Rome. After more than a year, a handwritten copy of the requested document was provided, but Peiresc's broader proposal was never adopted. Individually negotiated loans remained the norm for the next two hundred fifty years.[2]

The gentleman's agreement employed by early European libraries when lending documents to distant scholars was adopted in the United States and prevailed well into the nineteenth century. By the mid-1800s, libraries in the United States had begun what Pings calls the "socialization process."[3] This involved a redefinition of goals, with greater emphasis placed on the needs of users. As libraries assumed the responsibility for provision as well as preservation of knowledge, librarians began to feel an obligation to obtain and provide unowned materials on demand.

Loan negotiations became inconvenient and cumbersome, and a few libraries began lending books for the use of remote scholars at the written request of their local libraries. In what may have been the first survey of libraries ever conducted in the United States, C. C. Jewett, in 1849, enquired of more then 900 libraries: "Is there any regulation by which books may be lent by courtesy to persons at a distance? If so, what is it?" At that time, fourteen libraries responded positively to the question, but most placed restrictions of various kinds on the use of materials loaned to other libraries. However, the groundwork for standardized interlibrary lending was being laid.[4]

A quarter century later, in the premier issue of *Library Journal*, a letter by Samuel S. Green expressed the frustration of many librarians with the lack of an interlibrary loan system in the United States, and proposed an agreement among reference libraries to lend books to each other for short periods of time upon request.[5] Other librarians concurred,[6] and during the next forty years gradual but steady progress was made in developing interlibrary loan service and standardizing procedures. By the turn of the century, the National Library of Medicine, the Boston Public Library, the University of California Library, and many others were routinely sharing items from their collections with scholars working in other locations, setting precedent for future interlibrary lending, and developing workable interlibrary loan procedures in the process.[7]

The first steps toward standardizing mechanisms for sharing of library resources were taken in 1912 when C. H. Gould, Chair of the American

Library Association Committee on Coordination, asked three members of the committee to draft rules for the conduct of interlibrary loans and present their thoughts in a symposium at the ALA Conference in Ottawa. Herbert Putnam of the Library of Congress, William Coolidge Lane of Harvard, and J. L. Gillis of the California State Library presented widely divergent opinions,[8] which may have been the reason that three years were allowed to lapse before further action was taken.

In 1915, Henry Eduard Legler, Chair of the ALA Publishing Board, requested that work on the interlibrary loan regulations be continued, with the intention of publishing them when they were completed. In June, 1916, the first draft of "Regulations for the Conduct of Inter-Library Loans" was presented to the Committee on Coordination for comment.[9] Six months later, during ALA Midwinter, a final draft was presented to the ALA Council and approved with only minor changes. It was a liberal code for the times, providing for borrowing privileges to both the researcher and the average reader at no cost to the borrowing library other than postage and insurance.[10] While the 1916 code precipitated ideological discussion and backlash which became evident in subsequent codes, it remained in force until a revision was completed and adopted in 1940.[11] Later versions were adopted in 1952, 1968, and 1980.[12]

Other documents have been developed over the years to expand, explain, and facilitate the interlibrary loan process. Among them are a standard interlibrary loan form in the 1950s,[13] a model interlibrary loan code for regional, state, local, and other special groups of libraries in 1968,[14] and an interlibrary loan procedures manual, written by Sarah Katharine Thomson (1970) and revised by Virginia Boucher (1984).[15]

Issues

Since its inception, interlibrary loan has been a controversial practice. For more than one hundred years, the basic concept has been debated along with such issues as lending of journals, copyright restrictions, charging of lending fees, need for a national lending library, resource sharing networks, and automation. Progress has been made in resolving many of these issues. Others remain unresolved and provide a sure topic for discussion wherever librarians congregate. Meanwhile, librarians have made judgments based on their degree of acceptance, or rejection of the interlibrary loan concept, and have incorporated those judgments into policies for their libraries that may approximate, but do not always follow, the National Interlibrary Loan Code or common practice.

While Samuel S. Green, Melville Dewey, Bunford Samuel, and others wrote in favor of organizing and liberalizing interlibrary loan, an equal number of librarians assumed conservative or negative viewpoints. Herbert Putnam acknowledged the need for interlibrary loan in order to provide the unusual book for the unusual reader, and William Coolidge Lane supported the philosophy of interlibrary loan services for scholars, but neither was willing to support the concept in a broad sense.[16] Others refrained from speaking out against interlibrary loan, but chose not to acknowledge the need or participate in the process.

Approval of the "Code of Practice for Inter-Library Loans" in 1916 did little to encourage participation of individual libraries, but did precipitate additional debate concerning the issues. Advocates of interlibrary loan considered approval of the code to be a victory. In reality, the code had little impact, for it had no legal status. Those libraries that accepted and supported the interlibrary loan concept did so out of a service orientation and were already participating in the process, while those that opposed it continued business as usual, denying service or providing it selectively to those who could prove need.

In 1926, Malcolm Young of Princeton spoke out for extending interlibrary loan privileges to graduate students in addition to university faculty who qualified for the service automatically by virtue of their status as scholars.[17] Most librarians took a cautious view of the proposal in spite of the liberal interlibrary loan code. Anne Stokely Pratt of Yale had voiced the hesitation of many when she spoke before the College and Reference Section of ALA in 1922. In her presentation she noted a 30% increase in interlibrary loan activity between 1912 and 1922, called attention to the escalating costs involved in responding to requests from other libraries, and entertained the idea of charging lending fees for requests filled.[18] While taking opposing points of view, both Young and Pratt voiced valid concerns of the library community, prompting Margaret Hutchens of the University of Illinois to summarize the dilemma in her statement: "The question is how to reconcile the laudable wishes of borrowing libraries to satisfy the demands of their readers and the reluctance of the lending libraries to accede to all the demands..."[19]

Malcolm Young's proposal did not become a reality until several years later. In fact, progress was so slow and so little change was noted as a result of the "Code of Practice for Interlibrary Loan" that Harold Russell of the University of Minnesota was prompted to write, some twenty years after it was adopted, that: "The so-called 'interlibrary loan code' of 1917 set up certain standards of practice which have been honored more in the breach than in the observance. It is to be suspected that a majority of library people do not even know of its existence."[20] In fact, librarians knew of the code, but chose not to acknowledge it.

The 1940 revision of the National Interlibrary Loan Code was the result of years of discussion, study, and negotiation. In 1937, in response to years of negative criticism of interlibrary loan practices, ALA's Board on Resources of American Libraries appointed Donald Coney of the University of Texas to "...draw up a code for interlibrary loan practice to be submitted to the board before its next meeting."[21] This did not occur, but encouraged action in other arenas. The following year, the Association of College and Reference Libraries took up the issue. Harold Russell was appointed Chair of a committee to revise the code, and at the suggestion of ACRL prepared an article-by-article analysis of the 1916 document. He summarized his analysis by recommending reaffirmation of the earlier code, with additions and changes to bring it up to date.[22] The task of revision was finally completed, and the new code was approved and published in 1940.

The 1940 National Interlibrary Loan Code was far less liberal than its predecessor. It was written from an academic library perspective; limited interlibrary loan privileges to researchers; provided justification for lending fees; acknowledged copyright restrictions; and gave the lending library far greater discretion in determining lending policies than the earlier document.[23]

Reversal of the liberal code was a major victory for library conservatives who maintained dominance over interlibrary loan ideology for the next forty years. Revisions of the code in 1952 and 1968 made only minor changes while reaffirming the 1940 document. Only with the 1980 revision did the National Interlibrary Loan Code approach the liberality of the original 1916 version. Controversy still continues. Increasing numbers, costs, and perceived abuses of the interlibrary loan system are the major arguments against a liberal code. An ideology of sharing, service, and reciprocity remain the basis for positive arguments.

Little has been written about the lending of journal literature on interlibrary loan, although it has been a companion issue with the lending of books in the interlibrary loan debate. Early considerations did not differentiate journal literature from monographs, perhaps because it was not immediately perceived as an issue. However, few librarians have been willing to lend journals, particularly recent issues and high use titles. Unlike monographic requests that involve the use of an entire book, journal requests usually involve only one article or a small portion of a volume. In such instances, librarians have been willing to supply copy in lieu of a loan. Scholars have been willing to use copy even though early copy methods were often time-consuming, quality was often less than satisfactory, and costs were sometimes prohibitive.

Early copy was provided in handwritten or typewritten form. As the number of journal requests increased, librarians began seeking alternative ways of supplying the requested information, but none gained acceptance in American libraries until well into the twentieth century. As early as 1839, a Belgian medical student named Albrecht Breyer invented a method of copying pages from books and manuscripts that did not require the use of a camera.[24] Two years later, Fox Talbot, an English scientist, introduced a method of photography that made use of sensitized paper rather than metal plates.[25] Both processes were used sparingly in libraries, usually for copy and preservation of manuscripts, rare books, and other special materials rather than for processing of interlibrary loan requests. In 1900, Abbe Rene Graffin of the Institute Catholique in Paris developed the photostat process. This fast and inexpensive method of producing copy was quickly adopted by the major libraries in Europe for many processes including interlibrary loan, but it remained unnoticed in the United States for another ten years.[26]

The Crerar Library of Chicago was the first American library to report the use of photoduplication processes, but was probably not the first library to own a copy machine. In 1912, J. C. M. Hanson reported to the College and Reference Section of ALA on the Crerar experience.[27] At the same conference, William Coolidge Lane recommended application of the method to interlibrary loan: "It is...suggested that the possession of a cameragraph for making rotary bromide prints, or other similar device by which facsimile copies can be made inexpensively, would often enable a library to send a satisfactory copy of portions of a rare book or manuscript in place of lending the original."[28] Many large academic and research libraries purchased photocopy facilities between 1910 and 1920, but it wasn't until the early 1960s that electrostatic photocopy equipment was made available, and photocopy as it is known today became standard in libraries of all sizes and types throughout the United States.[29]

Microfilm was the other alternative to lending prior to introduction of the Xerox machine in 1960. Microfilm was never totally adequate from the perspective of either the providing library or the user. Few libraries invested in microfilm equipment, and those that did found film production expensive and time-consuming.[30] From the patron's point of view, microfilm was cumbersome to use, the wait for an article to be filmed was too long, and the cost was often prohibitive, all of which led to apathy toward the medium on the part of general users and many scholars.[31]

Photocopy and journal access have become issues as the numbers of requests for journal literature have increased. Neither the 1916 nor the 1940 National Interlibrary Loan Code made reference to journal literature. However, the 1952 code includes "current issues of periodicals" among the categories of materials that libraries should not request. Formalization of that restriction, coupled with ever increasing demands for journal literature, may have hastened the development of photocopy equipment and the acceptance of photocopy as an alternative to lending of journals on interlibrary loan.

As requests for journal literature increased and were increasingly filled through photoduplication rather than loan of the original work, the question of copyright infringement began to arise. The Copyright Law of the United States, enacted in 1909 and codified in 1947, was the copyright legislation in force when the cameragraph was introduced into the United States and when the Xerox machine was introduced some forty years later. Briefly, the Copyright Law granted to the holder of copyright the privilege of printing, reprinting, publishing, copying, or vending any work registered in his name by the Copyright Office. Works subject to copyright registration included books, periodicals, lectures, dramatic compositions, musical compositions, maps, works of art, reproductions of works of art, scientific drawings or models, photographs, prints, and motion pictures. The length of copyright was twenty-eight years with the option of renewal for an additional twenty-eight years. Infringement of copyright left the infringer liable for injunction, damages, and reimbursement of profits to the proprietor of the copyright. No provision was made for copy or distribution of study copies by a library.[32]

To correct a perceived flaw in the copyright law, the doctrine of fair use was developed through case law over a period of years to provide for reasonable use of published material by scholars, researchers, and writers. Defined in its simplest terms by Abe A. Goldman, the fair use doctrine "...permits the reproduction, for legitimate purposes, of material taken from a copyrighted work to a limited extent that will not cut into the copyright owner's potential market for the sale of copies."[33] Fair use has never been precisely defined, and thus has been invoked to justify a variety of circumstances, from the quoting of a portion of a published work by a writer to the production of multiple copies of a portion of a book or journal for educational purposes to the copying of an article by a library employee in response to an interlibrary loan request. While the doctrine has proved to be a saving grace for libraries, it has been the bane of many authors and for-profit publishers who regard it as a quasi-legal tool for avoiding the payment of royalty fees.

The doctrine of fair use in relation to interlibrary loan photocopying was tested in the courts in the late 1960s and early 1970s. In 1968, the Williams and Wilkins Company, a for-profit publisher of journals in the field of medicine, filed suit against the United States in the U. S. Court of Claims for infringement of copyright by the National Institutes of Health and the National Library of Medicine. Since the 1950s, the two libraries had routinely provided photocopy in response to interlibrary loan requests in lieu of lending journals on interlibrary loan.

In the suit, Williams and Wilkins alleged that the defendants, "the National Institutes of Health (NIH) and the National Library of Medicine (NLM) have infringed plaintiff's copyrights in medical journals by making unauthorized photocopies of articles from...*Medicine, Journal of Immunology, Gastroenterology,* and *Pharmacological Reviews,*" all published by Williams and Wilkins. The original allegations claimed unauthorized copying of eight articles from five volumes of the four journals and requested compensation for the infringement. However, the case was broadened substantially before it was settled, and became an issue between authors and publishers seeking just compensation for their work and librarians seeking freedom to copy within limits.

In 1982, James F. Davis, Commissioner of the Court of Claims, issued a report on Williams and Wilkins v. The United States, in which he ruled that the unauthorized photocopying of articles from copyrighted journals constituted copyright infringement that could not be defended under the doctrine of fair use.[34] In November, 1973, the Court overturned the report in a split, four to three decision.[35] Williams and Wilkins appealed the decision to the U. S. Supreme Court, who split four to four, with one abstention, thus letting stand the previous decision in favor of libraries and their photocopying practices.[36]

In many respects, the Williams and Wilkins case was a hollow victory for libraries, for as the case was being reviewed by the Federal Courts, the United States Congress was in the process of revising the copyright law. Little more than a year after the Williams and Wilkins decision, P.L. 94-553, The Copyright Revision Act of 1976, was passed by Congress and signed by the President, to become effective January 1, 1978. The new law addressed many of the copyright issues encountered by librarians involved in interlibrary loan, including the doctrine of fair use and the provision of photocopy in lieu of interlibrary loan. In the process, it negated the impact of the Williams and Wilkins case, but codified the intent of that decision into federal law.[37]

The doctrine of fair use was a radical addition to copyright law resulting from the Williams and Wilkins case and its impact on Congress. As in previous copyright law, The Copyright Revision Act of 1976 provides for the exclusive rights of reproduction of copyrighted works to lie with the copyright owner. However, it also provides for reasonable use of copyrighted material for the purposes of criticism, comment, news reporting, teaching, scholarship, and research under the fair use provision of the new law. Although the definition of fair use is left deliberately vague, the law provides four factors to be used in determining fair use. These are:
1. the purpose and character of the use;
2. the nature of the copyrighted work;
3. the amount and substantiality of the portion used; and
4. the effect of the use on the potential market for the work.

The new law also allows the provision of photocopy in lieu of interlibrary loan. Section 108 (d) provides for the copying of a single article or a small portion of a copyrighted work for purposes of interlibrary loan, provided:
1. the copy becomes the property of the user;
2. the library has no indication that the copy will be used for other than private study, scholarship, or research;
3. the library displays a warning of copyright at the place where copying is done and on each copy; and
4. requests are not in such aggregate quantities as to substitute for purchase of or subscription to the work. Responsibility for compliance with the copyright law lies with the library requesting the work rather than the library filling the request.[38]

To further clarify the fair use provision of the new copyright law, the National Commission on New Technological Uses of Copyrighted Works (CONTU) wrote guidelines which dealt with photocopying of copyrighted materials for interlibrary loan and certain other purposes. The CONTU Guidelines do not define such terms as "fair use" or "aggregate quantities" as used in the law, but specify limits beyond which a library may be at risk of prosecution for copyright infringement. Briefly summarized, the guidelines concern only materials published within the last five years. They stipulate that no more than one article per journal issue or five articles per journal title may be requested by a single library during a single calendar year. Exceptions are granted if the requesting library owns the volume in question or has a current subscription to the journal. CONTU did not deal with requests for materials older than five years.[39]

Although the new copyright law is an improvement over the 1909 version, it does not address the fine points of the copyright issue. Congress has left to the courts the responsibility for determining limits of copy protection and fair use. To date, little has been done, probably because of the high cost of litigation. A few copyright cases have been filed, but nothing of the impact of Williams and Wilkins. None have addressed interlibrary loan photocopy practices. Most have been withdrawn or settled out of court. Meanwhile, copyright remains an unsettled issue. Authors and publishers seek stricter interpretation and enforcement of the copyright law, while librarians deal with increasing numbers of requests, maintain detailed records to ensure copyright compliance, and lobby to maintain the status quo in the provision of photocopy for interlibrary loan purposes.

As a result of the Williams and Wilkins Case, the Copyright Revision Act of 1976, and continuing pressures by publishers and librarians, copyright compliance has become a prominent issue in interlibrary loan. Many journal publishers have begun publishing royalty information for the articles appearing in their publications. The Copyright Clearance Center, established in the 1970s, expedites royalty payments. Many document supply services now include royalty fees in the total cost of an article. In summary, progress has been made on a procedural level in reconciling interlibrary loan and copyright, but many basic issues remain unresolved.

The nature and function of interlibrary loan has changed more since 1960 than any time in the history of libraries, primarily because of the combined effect of library networks and automated systems. Reciprocal interlibrary loan agreements between neighboring or like libraries began to appear in the nineteenth century. These agreements eventually evolved into alliances of several institutions agreeing to share book and journal resources on request. Most were formed among academic and research libraries attempting to meet the needs of scholars. The impetus for large-scale library networking grew out of the needs of public and special libraries for greater access to materials not held locally rather than out of the academic library community.

Library networks bound by geographical lines have become commonplace in the years since 1960. Most were developed within state boundaries with interlibrary loan as their primary function, but have expanded into other areas of networking and resource sharing as library technology has developed. Most have the state library as a driving force and have been supported through Library Services and Construction Act (LSCA) funds. Examples of library networks of this sort include the Illinois Library and Information Network (ILLINET), the New York State Interlibrary Loan Network (NYSILL), and the Minnesota Interlibrary Telecommunications Exchange (MINITEX).

ILLINET is representative of the early interlibrary loan networks that have expanded and evolved to accommodate new technologies and meet the changing needs of member libraries. ILLINET was created by the Illinois Legislature in 1965. The law, known as the Library System Act of 1965, made provision for eighteen library systems distributed geographically throughout the state for the purpose of providing interlibrary loan and supplemental services to public libraries. The Act designated four permanent research and reference centers to serve as backup for the systems, and provided for the selection of other special resource centers as needed.[40] ILLINET was designed as a hierarchical network with four components or levels:

1. local libraries;
2. library systems;
3. research and reference centers; and
4. special resource centers.

In 1973, ILLINET expanded from a public library network to a multitype network with the opening of membership to academic libraries in January; then special libraries later in the same year. Membership was opened to school libraries in 1975.[41] In the summer of 1989, ILLINET had 2316 members.

The national health information network is the most sophisticated and best known example of a network designed around a specific subject discipline. The Medical Library Assistance Act of 1965 authorized the National Library of Medicine to fund medical library development in seven areas, including a national system of regional medical libraries to enhance resource sharing and information dissemination. Eleven regions were established, covering the United States, each with a designated central library to perform administrative support for the program and to provide backup services for the network's member libraries.

The Regional Medical Library Program was conceived as a four-tiered hierarchical network, with basic unit libraries at the lowest level, medical school libraries and a designated regional medical library at the intermediate level, and the National Library of Medicine at the top. Information dissemination activities included:

1. the conduct of literature searches by computer;
2. generation of computer current awareness listings;
3. the provision of copies of documents;
4. the provision of reference services;
5. the conduct of training and orientation programs for medical library staff;
6. support for specialized information centers.

The medical library network has evolved since 1965, reducing the number of regions from eleven to seven, and incorporating new technologies into its operation.

Originally utilizing mail and TWX as the major modes of transmitting requests, the medical library network has taken advantage of advances in telecommunication technologies over the years. The introduction of DOCLINE, an automated interlibrary loan request routing system developed by the National Library of Medicine and implemented in 1985, has increased the availability and accessibility of journal information on interlibrary loan. The use of telefacsimile equipment for transmitting the requested document has drastically reduced response time.[42]

Networking implies the use of automated processes, and most interlibrary loan networks have integrated one or more forms of automation into their processing, communication, and record-keeping routines. When the library networking movement began in the 1960s, teletype (TWX) was on the cutting edge of telecommunication technology and was quickly adopted as a standard transmission method for requests in most interlibrary loan networks because of its speed of transmission and ease of use. TWX remained the technology of choice through the 1970s, giving way to other processes only after the introduction of interlibrary loan subsystems by the major online cataloging services, i.e., OCLC, RLIN, and WLN. Developments in microcomputer technology and enhancements in telecommunications in the 1980s added still other options. Once communications software was developed and telecommunications modems became commonplace, electronic mail systems such as the American Library Association's ALANET were established with loan templates to expedite the interlibrary loan process. Electronic bulletin board software expanded interlibrary loan capabilities, particularly for networks of small libraries in which few or none of the members had access to large online systems. And dial access to online catalogs and circulation systems became a reality.

Telefacsimile is the most recent technology to be adapted to interlibrary loan networking. Simply defined as "...a photocopy machine that can transmit text and pictures over the telephone,"[43] the technology has existed for several years. Model III facsimile equipment, the current standard, has only recently been developed to a point that the quality of transmission, transmission time, and telecommunication cost for sending a document are within acceptable limits for library use. Many networks now include a telefacsimile component for both the transmission of requests and the fast delivery of journal articles and other short items that would otherwise be photocopied and sent through the mail.

The development of networks and the integration of automated procedures into their routines have had major impact on libraries. The effect has been phenomenal growth in the number of interlibrary loan transactions and expanded availability of information for the library patron, combined with reductions in processing time, response time, and cost per transaction for the library.

Processing an Interlibrary Loan Request

Interlibrary loan procedures have undergone vast change because of networking and automation, but rules and guidelines remain basically the same. The National Interlibrary Loan Code, first approved in 1916 and revised periodically, remains an interlibrary loan standard in spite of its rocky history and lack of legal status. The code sets forth the tenets of interlibrary loan, designates responsibilities of the borrowing and the lending library, and prescribes

borrowing and lending procedures. It has served as a model for state and regional codes and as a basis for reciprocal agreements and consortia. The
ALA approved interlibrary loan request form, which dates from the 1950s,
has been reviewed and refined periodically, but still calls for the basic data
elements identified as essential in the 1950s. Originally devised for use in
mail transactions, the form was adapted to a free text format usable with
TWX in the 1960s. It suggested a format for various automated interlibrary
loan systems and subsystems in the 1980s, and is being recommended as a
standard format for telefacsimile transactions in the 1990s. Virginia Boucher's *Interlibrary Loan Practices Handbook* (1984) and its predecessor Sarah
Katharine Thomson's *Interlibrary Loan Practices Handbook* have documented and interpreted the interlibrary loan process as it has evolved.

Library materials in any format may be requested on interlibrary
loan. Requests for books, single periodical articles, newspapers on microfilm,
doctoral dissertations, masters theses, and government publications are considered routine, and should be answered in a reasonable length of time by a
lending library. Requests for films, phonograph records, machine readable
data files, software, audio and video cassettes, compact discs, and other non-
print items are often noncirculating in the lending library, and filling such a
request may prove to be a challenge for the borrower. However, requests for
such materials may be filled if the staff of the borrowing library are persistent
and innovative.

The very nature of interlibrary loan implies a less than perfect success rate. Requests are frequently for items that are out of print, esoteric in
nature, old and/or rare, out of scope of the library's collection policy, or currently popular items for which the local demand exceeds the supply. Reference books, journals, genealogy and local history, unique items, and materials that may constitute a shipping problem are identified as potential
problems in the National Interlibrary Loan Code. Alternatives to borrowing
the original may be required to fill such requests. Patrons placing interlibrary
loan requests should be made aware of potential difficulties and should be
contacted periodically concerning the status of any requests that have not
been received within a reasonable period of time.

Interlibrary loan requests should be verified prior to sending. Verification is a two part function involving the checking of bibliographic information for accuracy and the identification of possible lending libraries through
the use of union catalogs, holdings lists, online bibliographic databases, and
other standard bibliographic tools. Verification and location of monographic
titles may often be accomplished in one step. Journal articles may require verification of the bibliographic data through the use of indexes and location of
holding libraries through the use of union catalogs. A third step is necessary
for journal articles and other items to be photocopied. Monitoring for copyright compliance is the responsibility of the borrowing library. A file of previous photocopy requests must be maintained by the borrowing library, as set
forth by the Copyright Revision Act of 1976, and each request must be
checked prior to sending in order to determine compliance with the law or the

CONTU Guidelines.

When verification and location have been completed, the request may be transmitted to a prospective lending library through a variety of methods. These include mail, automated systems such as OCLC, RLIN, WLN, and DOCLINE, the automated circulation system of the lending library, telefacsimile, electronic mail, telephone, or any other mode of transmission agreed upon by both the borrowing and the lending libraries. When an interlibrary loan is entered into a network or automated system, guidelines, protocols, and formats designed for that system prevail.

It is the responsibility of the lending library to respond to an interlibrary loan request in a timely manner. A variety of responses are possible:

1. The item may be loaned;
2. A photocopy may be provided if the requesting library has indicated copyright compliance and a willingness to pay any charges incurred;
3. An interim response may be sent setting forth conditions under which the item might be provided; and
4. A negative response may be sent, often accompanied by a brief explanation for the denial.

The borrowing library should have established procedures for contacting the patron when the requested item arrives, for control of the item while it is on loan, for renewal if necessary, and for return of the item in the manner specified by the lending library. Since the safety of an item is the responsibility of the borrowing library until it is returned to its owner and all charges are cleared, shipping records, insurance forms, and other documents concerning the transaction should be maintained until notification of return is received, or until a reasonable length of time has passed. Invoices for loan or photocopy should be processed promptly honoring any special procedures specified by the providing library.

The Future of Interlibrary Loan

Interlibrary loan has experienced phenomenal growth since the 1950s, and there is no indication that the trend will be reversed in the foreseeable future. The world's expanding knowledge base, improved bibliographic access, and faster information retrieval coupled with decreased financial support have reduced the ability of libraries to purchase materials necessary to meet the needs of their patrons and have increased reliance on interlibrary loan as an alternative. Automation and improved interlibrary loan procedures have reduced the waiting time for delivery of information. Development of consortia and networks dedicated to resource sharing have expedited request and delivery of materials. Liberalization of the National Interlibrary Loan Code and development of liberal state and regional codes have increased acceptance of interlibrary loan as a standard function of most libraries. The combined effect of all these influences has been vast increases in the volume of interlibrary loan traffic from library to library.

Interlibrary loan is a labor-intensive service in which increases in borrowing and lending activity lead to a need for additional staff, space, equipment, supplies, communications support, and postage, all of which require funding. As with most services in which there is no tangible product, support of interlibrary loan often falls short of need, while requests for additional funding go unheeded. Many libraries have developed policies to discourage interlibrary loan. The number of libraries that refuse to participate in the interlibrary loan process, limit cooperation to members of their state or regional network, or charge lending fees for use of their materials is gradually increasing.

Development in interlibrary loan continues, particularly in the area of automation. Proprietary online cataloging networks such as OCLC, RLIN, and WLN have developed interlibrary loan subsystems and continue to improve and enhance their systems to make the communication of interlibrary loan requests faster and easier.

Telefacsimile transmission, which is a relatively old technology in terms of automation, has gradually evolved to the point of practical applicability in interlibrary loan. Using telefax as a transmission method an interlibrary loan request may be sent and a response received within minutes. Meanwhile, equipment is being developed with internal memory that will substantially reduce the processing time for a request by allowing copy, storage, and transmission of documents in one convenient operation. Fax boards for microcomputers are available that permit transmission of documents from telefax machine to microcomputer or vice versa. The next logical step is the incorporation of telefacsimile into an automated interlibrary loan subsystem to expedite the transmission of requests and responses through the subsystem. What does it mean for the future? Probably one compact, convenient, and easy-to-use terminal through which requests can be entered and transmitted, and full-text responses transmitted and received as quickly as the supplying library can search and input the requested document.

Development of online public access catalogs (OPAC) in libraries has also had a positive effect on interlibrary loan. As libraries convert from card catalogs to OPACs, dial-up access to their catalogs becomes technically possible. A patron with a microcomputer, a modem, and a communications software package should be able to dial into the library's database, search the catalog for needed items, and perhaps even charge them for delivery to home or office. With such technology in place, the logical next step is to offer dial access to other libraries and patrons of other libraries.

The Illinois Library and Information Network (ILLINET) has been a leader in interlibrary loan and resource sharing using these automated procedures. The Interconnect Project began in 1976 when the Illinois State Library, the Suburban Library System, and the North Suburban Library System implemented dial access to each others' CLSI circulation systems. Over the years, other libraries with CLSI systems have joined the Interconnect Project. In the 1980s, a similar network developed among libraries with UTLAS systems. Today's technology is such that participation need not be limited to CLSI or

UTLAS libraries, and many libraries are crossing system lines and dialing into databases at will to check other libraries' holdings and place requests for needed materials.

Illinois' Library Computer System (LCS) and the companion ILLI-NET Online (IO) illustrate the same possibilities on a much grander scale. LCS is an online public access circulation system that was developed for the University of Illinois at Champaign/Urbana, then brokered to other academic libraries throughout the state. In 1989, thirty academic libraries were using LCS for circulation. In addition, terminals with search and charge options have been placed in the eighteen ILLINET systems headquarters, in the Illinois State Library, and in other strategic libraries in the state to provide those libraries with convenient online access to the collections of LCS libraries. Interlibrary loan and resource sharing via LCS have become common practice in Illinois with more than 2,000,000 interlibrary loan transactions initiated between 1980 and 1988.[44]

In 1988, ILLINET Online (IO) was implemented. IO is a statewide online public access catalog providing cataloging and holdings information for the 375 ILLINET/OCLC member libraries in the state. Although circulation and remote charging capabilities are still available only in the databases of the thirty LCS libraries, IO has become a valuable verification/location tool for interlibrary loan librarians throughout the state. The most recent system innovations are dial-up IO searching capabilities and LCS charging capabilities for any library or individual with a valid identification number. These options should drastically alter the look of interlibrary loan in Illinois. Meanwhile, the Illinois experience illustrates the potential for interlibrary loan and resource sharing made possible through automation and suggests developments that may eventually become a reality on a national and international scope.

Finally, certain information utilities and journal publishers have begun providing full-text search and retrieval of journal articles through online methods. These developments hold implications for interlibrary loan, but the implications are still unclear, since libraries and end users have equal access to these online information providers.

In little more than fifty years, interlibrary loan has evolved from a troublesome, auxiliary service provided to certain clientele in some libraries to a standard service available to all. As the need for information grows, as libraries' purchasing power declines, and as automation makes access to information easier, demand for information will increase. Interlibrary loan will increase in direct proportion to that demand for information. Libraries, as service organizations, must respond to the needs of their clientele in order to maintain viability. Since the provision of unowned material on demand has become an important aspect of library service, interlibrary loan and resource sharing can only increase. Libraries will change and interlibrary loan will evolve, but as long as there are libraries, as long as there are patrons needing materials, and as long as there are service oriented librarians, interlibrary loan will flourish as a vital component of the information search and distribution process.

Notes

1. "National Interlibrary Loan Code, 1980," *Reference Quarterly* 20 (Fall 1980): 29 -31.
2. Francis W. Gravit. "A Proposed Interlibrary Loan System in the Seventeenth Century." *Library Quarterly* 16 (October 1946): 331-34.
3. Vern M. Pings. *Interlibrary Loans: A Review of Library Literature, 1876-1965*. (Detroit: Wayne State University School of Medicine Library, 1966).
4. Smithsonian Institution Board of Regents. Fourth Annual Report...to the Senate and House of Representatives...1849. (Washington: Printers to the Senate, 1850).
5. Samuel S. Green. "The Lending of Books to One Another by Libraries." *Library Journal* 1 (September 1876): 15-16.
6. Melville Dewey. "Interlibrary Loans." *Library Notes* 3 (1888): 405-07; Bunford Samuel. "Mutual Book Lending Between Libraries." *Library Journal* 17. (September 1892): 373.
7. "Inter-Library Loans," *Library Journal* 23 (February 1898): 61; "Inter-Library Loans," *Library Journal* 23 (March 1898): 104.
8. Charles H. Gould; Herbert Putnam; William Coolidge Lane; and J. L. Gillis. "Committee on Co-ordination." *American Library Association Bulletin* 6 (July 1912): 96-101.
9. Charles H. Gould. "Report of the Committee on Co-ordination." *American Library Association Bulletin* 10 (July 1916): 349 51.
10. "Code of Practice for Inter-Library Loans." *American Library Association Bulletin* 11 (January 1917): 27-29.
11. "Proposed Interlibrary Loan Code." *American Library Association Bulletin* 34 (March 1940): 199 200, 216.
12. "Revised Code," *Library Journal* 65 (October 1, 1940): 802 03; "General Interlibrary Loan Code 1952." *College and Research Libraries* 13 (October 1952): 350-58; "National Interlibrary Loan Code, 1968." *College and Research Libraries News* 29 (September 1968): 271-72; "National Interlibrary Loan Code, 1980." *RQ* 20 (Fall 1980): 29-31.
13. "Standardization of Interlibrary Loan Forms," *Medical Library Association Bulletin* 43 (October 1955): 554.
14. "Model Interlibrary Loan Code for Regional, State, Local or Other Special Groups of Libraries," *Special Libraries* 59 (September 1968): 528-30.
15. Sarah Katharine Thomson. *Interlibrary Loan Procedure Manual*. (Chicago: American Library Association, 1970); Virginia Boucher. *Interlibrary Loan Practices Handbook*. (Chicago: American Library Association, 1984).
16. Charles H. Gould; Herbert Putnam; William Coolidge Lane; and J. L. Gillis. "Committee on Co-ordination." *American Library Association Bulletin* 6 (July 1912): 96-101.
17. "College and Reference Section," *American Library Association Bulletin* 20 (October 1926): 501-02.
18. "College and Research Libraries Section." *Library Journal* 47 (August 1922): 661.
19. Margaret Hutchens. "Summary and Discussion of Papers on Interlibrary Loans," *American Library Association Bulletin* 20 (October 1926): 503-05.
20. Harold G. Russell. "Some Unsolved Problems in Reference Service." *American Library Association Bulletin* 32 (October 1938): 847-49.

21. "Action Taken at Meeting on Resources of American Libraries." *American Library Association Bulletin* 31 (April 1937): 228.
22. Harold G. Russell. "The Interlibrary Loan Code." *American Library Association Bulletin* 33 (May 1939): 321-25, 354.
23. "Proposed Interlibrary Loan Code." *American Library Association Bulletin* 34 (March 1940): 199-200, 216.
24. Arnold Sadow. "Copying Library Materials by Photographic Methods Other Than Microphotography." (Masters thesis, Pratt Institute, 1955).
25. Hubbard W. Ballou. "Photography and the Library." *Library Trends* 5 (October 1956): 265-93.
26. William Z. Nasri. "Reprography." *Encyclopedia of Library and Information Science.* (New York: Marcel Dekker, 1978, v. 25), pp. 230-39.
27. J. C. M. Hanson. "College and Reference Section." *Library Journal* 37 (August 1912): 445 -46.
28. William Coolidge Lane. "A Statement of General Policy in Regard to Inter-Library Loans." *American Library Association Bulletin* 6 (912): 97-99.
29. Don Wharton. "Xerox—The Invention That Hit the Jackpot." *Reader's Digest* 86 (March 1965): 121-24.
30. Herman H. Fussler. "Microphotography and the Future of Interlibrary Loans." *Journal of Documentary Reproduction* 2 (March 1939): 3-10.
31. Ralph R. Shaw. "Should Scientists Use Microfilm?" *Library Quarterly* 14 (July 1944): 229 -33.
32. U. S. Code, Title 17. (1976).
33. Abe A. Goldman, "Philosophical Bases of Copyright." *Encyclopedia of Library and Information Science.* (New York: Marcel Dekker, 1971, v. 6), pp. 63-75.
34. Ralph R. Shaw. "A Review of the Commissioner's Report: Williams & Wilkins v. the U. S." *American Libraries* 3 (October 1972): 987-99.
35. Benjamin W. Rudd. "Court Overturns Copyright Infringement Report." *Library of Congress Information Bulletin* 32 (December 14, 1973): 440-41.
36. "Copyright Update." *American Libraries* 6 (June 1975): 344.
37. U. S. Code, Title 17, (1982).
38. Copyright Revision Act of 1976: P.L. 94-553, as signed by the President, October 19, 1976: Law, Explanation, Committee Reports. (Chicago: Commerce Clearing House, 1976).
39. *Librarian's Guide to the New Copyright Law.* (Chicago: American Library Association, 1977).
40. "The Multitype Library Network." *Illinois Libraries* 57 (June 1975): 364-444.
41. Linda Lucas; Teresa M. Fox; and Daniel G. Zack. *An Evaluation of the Illinois Interlibrary Loan Network.* (Urbana: University of Illinois, Graduate School of Library Science, 1977).
42. Alison Bunting. "The Nation's Health Information Network: History of the Regional Medical Library Program." *Medical Library Association Bulletin* 75 (July 1987 Supplement): 1-62.
43. "Test Reports on 19 Facsimile Machines," *Library Technology Reports* 24 (September/October 1988): 616-716.
44. Bernard G. Sloan. "Resource Sharing at the Statewide Level: ILLINET On-line," *Illinois Libraries* 71 (March/April 1989): 185-88.

The Center for Research Libraries: One Model for Cooperative Resource Sharing

James R. Mouw
Acquisitions Librarian, University of Chicago

In his remarks at a program on the Center for Research Libraries (CRL) held just prior to the American Library Association Annual conference in New Orleans in 1988, Joseph Boisse, member of the Center for Research Libraries board and University Librarian at the University of California, Santa Barbara summed up his view of the Center when he said:

> The Center for Research Libraries represents, in my view, one of the most successful examples of shared collection development and shared use of resources in the library world. In fact, the Center, which is about to celebrate its fortieth anniversary, is the oldest continuing research library cooperative. Like any other organization, it has, over the years, had its ups and downs, its good years and its bad. It remains, nonetheless, an outstanding example of what a group of research libraries can achieve in trying to meet a common goal: bringing people and information together.[1]

Mr. Boisse points to the unique purpose of the Center for Research Libraries. It is arguably the primary example of a member-run institution devoted solely to resource sharing; it has held that role for more than forty years. No publication concerning cooperative resource sharing would be complete without a discussion of the Center for Research Libraries. The purpose of this paper is to present an overview of the history of the Center for Research Libraries, and to highlight some of the services offered. The center for Research Libraries is perhaps one of the most discussed and written about American library institutions. Scores of articles and news reports have been published over the years. I conclude my article with a bibliography of some of the more important publications that the reader may consult for more in-depth information.

The Center for Research Libraries serves many functions including that of a depository for seldom used monographic materials. In this chapter my discussion will be largely limited to the Center's role in the sharing of serial resources.[2]

History

The Center for Research Libraries began its existence in 1949 when it was formed by several midwestern research universities as the Midwest Inter-

Library Corporation. Since that time it has undergone one name change and has made many adjustments to its various policies and services.

In a 1983 article in the *Journal of Academic Librarianship*, Donald Simpson identified three distinct phases in the development of the Center for Research Libraries.[2] The first of these he labels as Evolution and Metamorphosis. He characterizes the Center's focus during this period "as a collection" with few purchases and the bulk of the collection coming from deposits.[3] In his article in the *Journal of Library History*, Louis Kaplan reports that the original driving force came not from librarians, but from the presidents of the institutions who envisioned the center as a cooperative storage facility.[4]

The librarians, however, responded with a proposal that gave "no less prominence to acquisitions than to storage."[5] The founding document of 1948 listed four recommended areas of cooperation. They were:

1. The coordination of collecting policies for the region as a whole, to avoid unnecessary duplication.
2. Improvement and simplification of technical and bibliographical processes to avoid duplication of effort and provide better service.
3. Provision of accessible and economical housing of little-used material for the good of the region as a whole.
4. Acquisition for the region of materials needed for a forward looking research program, but not now available.[6]

Thirteen institutions had become members by the end of the first fiscal year and by the end of its last year as the Midwest Inter-Library Corporation there were 21 members: six private institutions, fourteen public, and the John Crerar Library.

Mr. Kaplan summarizes seven advantages of membership in the corporation. They were:

1. The existence of a central library, built with outside funds, reduced the need for space in the member libraries. By virtue of weeding duplicates from the Center, the region as a whole benefitted.
2. The value of the materials jointly purchased exceeded the assessments paid by each institution.
3. Physical access, and bibliographic access to a lesser extent, were facilitated. The "package" programs, such as dissertations, college catalogs, and textbooks, simplified the search for such materials. Bibliographic access was promoted by supplying catalog cards for the miscellaneous serials and separates and for the newspapers. The failure to provide cards for the other collections was a matter of concern to some of the librarians.
4. Cataloging costs were reduced; the majority believing that there was no need to catalog items within well-defined programs; those, for example, seeking a foreign dissertation were expected to inquire at the Center.
5. Normally, materials requested on loan were delivered more promptly from the Center than loans made elsewhere, and the loans could be kept for a longer period. Furthermore, the expectation was advanced that

member libraries would be more considerate of each other's requests.

6. Because few readers entered the book stack of the central library, certain materials which otherwise suffer damage in an open book stack were better protected, this being especially true of unbound material.

7. The central library as a "neutral" territory in which materials could be deposited without arousing excessive feelings of rivalry.[7]

This first phase ended in 1965 with the decision to open membership to institutions beyond the midwest region. The Center assumed its present name at this time.

Mr. Simpson identifies Phase Two as the period from 1965 up to 1975. This period is characterized by a rapid growth in membership and by the addition of another membership category, that of Associate Member. At the same time, the number of active programs was expanded to include six categories: direct acquisitions, demand acquisitions, purchase proposals, deposits (with caution), loan from the collection, and special microform projects.[8]

Phase Three began in 1975 with the establishment of the Journals Access Service (JAS). The program "brought together CRL's various current journals collection components with a quasi-contractual relationship with the recently-established British Library Lending Divisions's journal photocopy service to overseas customers...and moved CRL into active involvement with journals in a way different than the acquisitions of serials as part of deposited or purchased collection programs. For some members. particularly those with little or no local identification with CRL collections, CRL services became somewhat synonymous with journal supply."[9]

This program has been seen by some to have caused a weakening of the central purpose of the Center for Research Libraries. The emphasis placed on the JAS was perceived to have come at the expense of other services. The JAS was abandoned in 1986.

Present Situation

The world of librarianship in 1989 is very different from that when the Center for Research Libraries was established forty years ago. The Center has continually adjusted its focus to maintain its viability as an institution. Major changes include periodic adjustments to its membership categories and criteria, and the implementation or discontinuance of various services such as the Journal Access Service that was introduced and then later abandoned. In addition to its Board of Directors, the Center has formed two advisory panels: the Collection Development Officers Advisory Panel and the Interlibrary Loan Officers Advisory Panel. The two panels, comprised of librarians from the member institutions, help guide the policies of the Center. Linda A. Naru, Planning and Development Officer at the Center, emphasized the role of these groups when she said, "The experiences and practical advice from public service and collection development staff at member libraries that have successfully transformed the concept of cooperative collections development into service to the patron can help librarians formulate local policy and procedures to improve use of the Center."[10]

In recent years, the Center has been involved in a process of assessment and planning. One of the results of this process has been a new statement of the Center's Mission and Objectives. The text of this statement was printed in the Center's newsletter, *Focus,* in 1988. The text is as follows:

> The Center for Research Librariies [sic] is a not-for-profit corporation established and operated by scholarly and research institutions to strengthen and library and information resources and to enhance the accessibility of those resources.

The Center for Research Libraries functions as a cooperative, membership-based research library dedicated to acquiring, storing, preserving, providing bibliographic access to, and lending/delivering from a collection that complements and supplements the collections of the major research libraries of North America, thereby assisting individual member libraries in meeting the needs of their local users.

The organizational objectives articulated are as follows:

- Systematically strengthen and preserve the Center's collections for future scholarship.
- Improve access to the Center's collections. Extend membership participation, involvement and commitment to Center programs and activities.
- Increase the awareness in the library and scholarly communities of the Center's contributions to efforts to ensure the availability of the scholarly research materials.
- Develop a secure and growing financial base for the Center's programs and operations.
- Increase the Center's participation in and contribution to national efforts within the scope of the Center's programs for cooperative collection development, preservation, and bibliographic and physical access.
- Manage the Center's internal operations more effectively and efficiently.[11]

This new statement of mission illustrates the Center's continued efforts to remain an effective means of cooperative resource sharing in the coming years.

Collection Development Policy

The preceding section on the history of the Center for Research Libraries listed some of the overall goals of the Center. While these goals are diverse they combine to form one overall goal: that the Center will maintain collections of materials not readily available elsewhere and will provide access to those collections. The Collection Development program of the center reflects that goal. While the collections are indeed diverse, they all exist in accordance with the overriding goal of access to materials not widely held elsewhere.

The best brief description of these collections that the author has seen can be found in a paper presented by Sheila Dowd at the New Orleans conference and later published in *Library Acquisitions: Practice and Theory*. She categorized the collections into two broad areas. They are:

1. a "general collection, miscellaneous in its content...formed principally of older research materials deposited by members, and of expensive materials (especially microform and reprint editions) selected by the membership through purchase proposal balloting."
2. and "special collections...consist[ing] of types of material which are widely agreed to be of scholarly importance, but for which one national collection may be sufficient."[12]

As examples of the most important of the special collections, she lists: the foreign doctoral dissertation collection, the Foreign Newspaper Microfilm Project, archival materials in microform or facsimile, foreign scientific and technical publications, and the area studies collections concentrating especially on Africa, East Asia, South Asia and Southeast Asia.[13]

These collections combine to form the backbone of the rationale for the existence of the Center for Research Libraries. Implicit in that statement is the assumption that these materials are unique or at least not readily available elsewhere. The only scientific testing of the collections' uniqueness that the author has seen was conducted by Sarah Thomas and published in a 1985 article in *College and Research Libraries*.[14]

Ms. Thomas studied a sample of the OCLC records for the Center's serials collection. In her methodology she states that "CRL holds an estimated 50,000 current and retrospective serial titles. Approximately 13,500 are currently received. By spring 1984, 15,389 serials had been cataloged in machine-readable form. This study concentrated primarily on those titles available in machine-readable form and coded as currently received by CRL. Just under half, or 48.46 percent of these 15,389 serial titles, are estimated to fall in this category."[15]

It is important to note that the study was limited to serial titles and to items represented in machine-readable format. The results may have been somewhat different if the total holdings were represented. She studies materials in five languages: Urdu, Japanese, Russian, English, and German. Her results showed that "According to this sample [of 1,069 titles], 20.66 percent of titles held by CRL in these five languages were unique to CRL."[16] This means that almost 80 percent of the titles were NOT unique to the Center for Research Libraries. However, the scope of the study did not extend to investigate how many of these non-unique titles were actually available for loan from the other holding libraries or to the completeness of the holdings. In their 1988 article, "Evaluating Membership in a Resource-Sharing Program: The Center for Research Libraries," John Rutledge and Luke Swindler note that "Since [Sarah Thomas's] article appeared, CRL has cancelled approximately 1,100 subscriptions to titles widely held by members. The level of uniqueness has probably increased."[17]   To the author's knowledge, this hypothesis has not been tested.

In his article, "Toward a Viable Program for CRL—Back to Basics," Joseph A. Rosenthal sums up the present situation when he says: "Although the Center's collections are large and extensive, it is only in a very, very few areas that they are sufficiently comprehensive to be relied upon by North American research libraries to the point where libraries can discontinue collections development in specific fields of publication."[18]

Access to the Collections

The Center for Research Libraries has always recognized that adequate bibliographic access to its collections is vital to the Center's success. It has provided this access in a variety of ways with various levels of bibliographic sophistication. These means of access can be divided easily into two types: cataloged and uncataloged materials.

Many of the collections of the Center are cataloged, and users can obtain holdings information from any of a variety of sources. Records have been added to national bibliographies for many years, including the *National Union Catalog* and *New Serials Titles* as well the *National Register of Microform Masters* and the *United States Newspaper Program National Union List*. In addition to these printed sources, CRL holdings are now added to the OCLC and RLIN databases. The majority of the Center's serials and newspapers are now online.

There are also large portions of the Center's collection that are not cataloged. In her article "Bibliographic Access to the Center for Research Libraries' Collections," Virginia Boucher categorizes these materials into four broad areas: titles that are "in scope," titles appearing in published bibliographies, titles appearing in published guides, and those materials covered in the Center's guides to collections.[19]   She goes on to explain that while these materials are not cataloged by the Center, access is still possible. Titles that are clearly in scope although not specifically listed in various lists or guides can be requested without confirming holdings. In other cases, printed bibliographies or guides exist for collections held by the Center and these guides are often widely held in research libraries. Confirmation of the citation in the printed guide and subsequent confirmation of the Center's holding of the collection will result in the desired material. In some cases, the Center itself has provided guides that aid access to specific portions of the collections. These generally list materials available within broad categories such as:

- Center for Research Libraries. *British and Irish materials*, 1987; or,
- Ignashev, Sergie P. *Soviet serials currently received at the Center for Research Libraries: a checklist* 2nd ed. 1985.[20]

The librarian must be somewhat diligent to make maximal use of the collections of the Center for Research Libraries. As shown above, access of one type or another is available for many of the materials, but not all in any one place, and not all of the materials are fully or even partially cataloged. Most effective use of the collections of the Center for Research Libraries requires that well trained staff be able and willing to make use of a variety of access tools.

One advantage of the Center for Research Libraries that is frequently mentioned is the ease of access. Many members have found the Center to be user friendly, with far fewer restrictions than are normally found when borrowing from other libraries. In the same article cited earlier, Mr. Boisse says, "The major activity of the staff at the Center is to make that material easily accessible to scholars at member institutions. There are exceedingly few research libraries which are as willing to send rarely held and sometimes fragile material out on interlibrary loan as the Center is."[21]

The Center serves its members by allowing easy access to collections that many research libraries would lend with severe restrictions if at all.

Advantages and Disadvantages of Membership

Membership in the Center for Research Libraries carries with it both advantages and the possibility of disadvantages. The major advantage is the easy access to a wide range of materials. The primary disadvantage is that this access can come at a high cost especially if the services are seldom used. Many libraries have carefully investigated these issues. In this section the author would like to briefly present two case studies and then discuss a recent article which evaluated membership in an in-depth manner.

The first case study is that of Texas A&M University. Texas A&M became the first Texas member of the Center when they joined in 1970. A 1972 article in the *Texas Library Journal* explains that institution's rationale for membership:

> Like others, we reluctantly reached the decision that it simply is not economically feasible for any but the wealthiest institutions to own libraries of sufficient size and richness to provide adequate support for the teaching and research activities of a large general university.[22]

After investigating various alternatives they reached the decision that "[t]he obvious answer was the Center for Research Libraries."[23] In 1972, the second year of membership, an analysis of the borrowing discovered that at a rate of between 175 and 200 items per year the average cost to the university was around $28.00. The authors state that although these costs at first glance seem

> rather high [n.b. remember, this was in 1972] ...[t]hese titles...are

needed very infrequently at Texas A&M, but when needed they are vital. They would likely be very difficult to locate and borrow through regular interlibrary loan channels if the Center did not hold them. For Texas A&M to have acquired a wide enough collection of newspapers, foreign doctoral dissertations, and current journals to have assured a reasonable chance of being able to provide these titles from our own collection when needed would cost us several hundred thousand dollars per year. At this rate our membership is indeed cheap.[24]

The preceding scenario is that of an institution that had carefully examined the costs and benefits of membership and had then concluded that the advantages outweighed the cost. Other libraries have made similar examinations and reached another conclusion. In a 1983 article in the *Journal of Academic Librarianship,* Jay K. Lucker, Director of Libraries at the Massachusetts Institute of Technology, presents the rationale of a library which decided not to join the Center. Throughout the article, Mr. Lucker emphasizes that this decision was made even though he fully supports the Center, and that MIT's decision was economic.[25] He lists three major reasons for this decision. They are:

1. [MIT's] strong dependence upon current scientific and technical literature, especially serials;
2. a long history of collecting in these fields resulting in an extensive collection of backfiles of both major and lesser-used titles; and
3. a general lack of research interests in the humanities and in retrospective collections in the social sciences.[26]

In the case of MIT, the conclusion was that the costs did not justify the benefits.

The September 1988 issue of *College and Research Libraries* presented the findings of extensive research by John Rutledge and Luke Swindler. They examine several arguments which favor membership in the Center.[27] Earlier in this article, I listed the seven advantages of membership in the early days of the corporation as given by Louis Kaplan. The authors of this new article found seven arguments in favor of membership. These new arguments are somewhat different from the earlier list and are loosely summarized as:

1. The obligation to cooperate. The authors believe that research libraries have a duty to cooperate and that CRL is one means of fulfilling that goal.
2. The Library's Library. The Center operates as an extension of your own library. Materials that cannot be maintained locally can be housed at the Center and accessed as needed.
3. Unique Collections and Services. The Center is only as strong as its collections are unique. If materials are easily available through other means, the Center loses a major reason for its existence.
4. The Insurance Policy. The argument is that when hard times hit, the

Center's copy will be maintained even when individual libraries are forced to cancel subscriptions.

5. Cost Avoidance. It is cheaper to buy one copy cooperatively than for many libraries to maintain individual subscriptions.

6. Some Deposit, Some Return. The Center serves a function as a warehouse for little-used materials. The authors view this as not a major argument and say, "If low-use materials can be economically stored on optical discs, why bother to send the paper to Chicago?"[28]

7. Patron Perspectives. The authors found that patron response to the services of the Center was "overwhelmingly positive."

Rutledge and Swindler conclude that: "there can be no universally applicable methodology for evaluating membership in the Center for Research Libraries. Rather, each library must make an autonomous decision, because the tangible benefits for membership in CRL are highly situation dependent."[29]

Alternatives

When the Center for Research Libraries was established, it was in many ways pioneering large-scale library resource sharing. In the world of the late 1980s, there are several other examples of types of resource sharing that some libraries are finding attractive means of cooperation. In some cases, these may have replaced membership in the Center; in others, they provide an additional service.

Some examples of these are local cooperation in collection development such as the Research Triangle Libraries Network, local or regional shared remote storage facilities, such as the California Regional Storage Facilities, the emergence of national networks, such as OCLC and RLIN, and local or regional networks, like Illinet Online in Illinois, which provides a statewide union catalog using records from the statewide OCLC archival tapes. There are also many printed union lists of holdings, frequently on the local or regional level. Some are comprehensive, others are subject based.

All of these types of activities combine to offer the librarian a wide variety of options. Sometimes they provide direct competition for the Center such as when a group of local libraries agrees to a cooperative collection program, or when they build a shared regional housing facility. In other cases, they can complement the Center for Research Libraries, and, in some instances, the Center has capitalized on this situation. The inclusion of the Center's holdings in various online databases is a prime example of this cooperation. Every library needs to carefully analyze the various options available to them. Sometimes membership in the Center for Research Libraries can provide access to unique materials needed by a library's patrons. In other situations, a library may find that the needed resources are available elsewhere, with reasonable restrictions, and at a lower overall cost to the institution.

Conclusion

The Center for Research Libraries provides one effective method of maintaining a collection of materials that are seldom used but that are nevertheless of value to researchers. From its beginnings as the Midwest Inter-Library Center, to its present status as a national institution, it has striven to provide access to valuable resources. It continues to face challenges on several fronts. Primary among these challenges are two: the potential for losing membership as libraries continue to weigh the costs vs. benefits in periods of fiscal constraints; and the increasing ease of locating alternative sources through the use of national utilities such as OCLC and RLIN.

I would like to conclude this article as I began, with a quotation from Joseph A. Boisse. Concluding his remarks at the New Orleans Conference he says: "If the Center did not exist, academic librarians would try to establish it right now."[30]

Bibliography

Many articles have been written about the Center for Research Libraries. This bibliography in not totally inclusive, and excludes many news reports and articles that essentially duplicate existing information. It is meant to provide the reader with a list of important publications concerning the Center and its programs, and should be useful to those wishing more detailed information.

In July 1988, just prior to the annual meeting of the American Library Association, the Center for Research Libraries Interlibrary Loan Officers Advisory Panel, and the Collection Development Officers Advisory Panel presented a program devoted to the Center for Research Libraries Programs and Services. The stated purpose was to disseminate information about CRL's collection, its role in resource sharing and access to the collection.

Library Acquisitions: Practice and Theory devoted several pages of its 1988 volume to a transcription of papers presented at that program. These combine to present a snapshot of the current status of the Center. These articles are:

Linda A. Naru, "Transforming Concept into Practice: How Collection Development, Interlibrary Loan, and Reference Staff Utilize the Center for Research Libraries," *Library Acquisitions: Practice and Theory* 12:397-398 (1988).

Joseph A. Boisse, "CRL Membership: the Library Director's Perspective," *Library Acquisitions: Practice and Theory* 12:399-402 (1988).

Sheila Dowd, "Major Collection Components and Policies of the CRL," *Library Acquisitions: Practice and Theory* 12:403-405 (1988).

Virginia Boucher, "Bibliographic Access to the Center for Research Libraries' Collections," *Library Acquisitions: Practice and Theory* 12:407-410 (1988).

Christopher B. Loring, "Maximizing Use of the Center for Research Libraries Through Interlibrary Loan; CRL as the Lender of First Resort and Other Strategies," *Library Acquisitions: Practice and Theory* 12:411-414.

Carolyn Mateer, "The Role of Public Service Librarians in Promoting Use of CRL's Collections," *Library Acquisitions: Practice and Theory* 12:415-418.

Recommended Readings

Ray Boylan, "The Center for Research Libraries," In: *Encyclopedia of Library and Information Science*, ed. Allen Kent, New York: Dekker, 1983.

Ray Boylan, "Serial Publications in the Center for Research Libraries," *Serials Review* 5:79-82 (January/March 1979).

Ray Boylan, "Scholarly Citadel in Chicago: The Center for Research Libraries," *Wilson Library Bulletin* 53:503-506 (March 1979).

Maurice Glicksman, "Some Thoughts on the Future of the Center for Research Libraries," *Journal of Academic Librarianship* 10:148-50 (July 1984).

Information Systems Consultants Inc., "Options for CRL: A Preliminary Report to the Membership, Governance, and Fees Committee: Final Report," Bethesda, Md., Information Systems Consultants, 1984.

Louis Kaplan, "The Midwest Inter-Library Center, 1949-1964," *Journal of Library History* 10:291-310 (October 1975).

John Rutledge and Luke Swindler, "Evaluating Membership in a Resource-Sharing Program: The Center for Research Libraries," *College and Research Libraries* 49:409-424 (September 1988).

Donald B. Simpson, "Center for Research Libraries: Meeting the Opportunity to Fulfill the Promise: a Symposium," *Journal of Academic Librarianship* 9:258-69 (November 1983).

John B. Smith and Hung Chih Ye, "The Center for Research Libraries –Experience of the First Texas Member," *Texas Library Journal* 48:224-26 (November 1972).

Sarah E. Thomas, "Collection Development at the Center for Research Libraries: Policy and Practice," *College and Research Libraries* 46:230-235 (May 1985)

Gordan Williams, "The Center for Research Libraries: Its New Organization and Programs," *Library Journal* 90:2947-51 (July 1985).

The Center for Research Libraries also publishes items containing information of interest. In addition to the wide range of bibliographies and other handbooks that are available, the Center regularly publishes some items. These include:

Center for Research Libraries, "Annual Report," Chicago, The Center, 1965-present.

Center for Research Libraries, "Newsletter," [irregular], 1965-1980. This publication has been continued by "Focus on the Center for Research Libraries" [bimonthly], 1981-present.

Notes

1. Joseph A. Boisse, "CRL Membership: The Library Director's Perspective," *Library Acquisitions: Practice and Theory* 12:399-402 (1988).
2. Donald B. Simpson, "Center for Research Libraries: Meeting the Opportunity to Fulfill the Promise: A Symposium," *Journal of Academic Librarianship* 9:258-269 (November 1983).
3. Ibid. p. 258.
4. Louis Kaplan, "The Midwest Inter-Library Center, 1949-1964," *Journal of Library History* 10:291-310, (October 1975).
5. Ibid. p. 292.
6. Ibid.
7. Ibid. p. 299.
8. Simpson, p. 259.
9. Ibid.
10. Linda A. Naru, "Transforming Concept into Practice: How Collection Development, Interlibrary Loan, and Reference Staff Utilize the Center for Research Libraries," *Library Acquisitions: Practice and Theory* 12:397-398 (1988).
11. "Board's Planning Conference Focuses on Membership, Finances," *Focus* 8:1 (March-April 1988).
12. Sheila Dowd, "Major Collection Components and Policies of the CRL," *Library Acquisitions: Practice and Theory* 12:403-405 (1988).
13. Ibid. p. 404-405.
14. Sarah Thomas, "Collection Development at the Center for Research Libraries: Policy and Practice," *College and Research Libraries* 46:230-235 (May 1985).
15. Ibid. p. 231.
16. Ibid. p. 233.
17. John Rutledge and Luke Swindler, "Evaluating Membership in a Resource-Sharing Program: The Center for Research Libraries," *College and Research Libraries* 49:409-424 (September 1988). [The citation is found in their reference number 33 on p. 423.]
18. Joseph A. Rosenthal, "Toward a Viable Program for CRL—Back to Basics," *Journal of Academic Librarianship* 9:268-269 (November 1983).
19. Virginia Boucher, "Bibliographic Access to the Center for Research Libraries' Collections," *Library Acquisitions: Practice and Theory* 12:407-410 (1988).
20. Ibid. p. 409.
21. Boisse, p. 401.
22. John B. Smith and Hung Chih Ye, "The Center for Research Libraries—Experience of the First Texas Member," *Texas Library Journal* 48:224-6 (November 1972).
23. Ibid. p. 224.
24. Ibid. p. 226.
25. Jay K. Lucker, "A Nonmember's Point of View," *Journal of Academic Librarianship* 9:264-265 (November 1983).

26. Ibid. p. 265.
27. Rutledge and Swindler, p. 411-417.
28. Ibid. p. 416.
29. Ibid. p. 421.
30. Boisse, p. 402.

The Economics Behind Resource Sharing: Implications for Collection Development and the Future of Libraries

Diane J. Graves
Acquisitions Librarian, University of Illinois at Chicago
and Yvonne L. Wulff
Assistant Director for Collection Management, University of
Michigan

In the NASIG proceedings issue of *Serials Librarian*, College of Charleston's David Cohen writes, "...libraries, which we all readily recognize as the institutions that bear the stewardship responsibility for information, have only a limited (and perhaps diminishing) role for organizing, controlling, and delivery of information among scholars."[1] This article will explore how and why the role of academic libraries is diminishing in the minds of our clientele, and consider how alternative attitudes about resource sharing might return libraries to the forefront of the information field. The authors will consider how collection development traditions may change, and how that change will affect resource sharing successes or failures and ultimately the success or failure of academic libraries in higher education.

Cooperation among libraries both within type and in multitype consortia has been the topic of numerous scholarly journal articles, papers presented at professional meetings, and contributions to collections such as this one. Most authors cite rising materials costs as the incentive to cooperate. Nevertheless, a look at the numbers reveals trends that indicate not only rising materials costs, but a burgeoning proliferation of materials to purchase. The Faxon Company, which has maintained statistics from its database since 1974 has found, for instance, that:

- The number of fulfillable journal titles rose from 38,079 in 1974 to 104,714 in 1989; an increase of 66,635 or 175%.
- The number of journals which were introduced and have subsequently ceased, suspended, changed title or outright failed between 1974 and 1989 is 79,612.
- In 1989, approximately 152,370 other titles (gray literature, newsletters, and other pieces of serial information) were being acquired by libraries and tracked on Faxon's Linx systems. Thus, the total number of active serial titles in the Faxon database in 1989 was 257,084.
- The average price per serial title paid by college and university libraries in 1979 was $50.11; by 1989 it had risen to $125.87. Scientific and tech-

nological libraries (such as Illinois Institute of Technology) pay an average of $234 per serial title per year.
- The average price for foreign titles has risen from $41.34 per title in 1976 to $143.09 in 1989.[2]

Meanwhile, Cohen found that, "...in the sciences alone, [researchers] generate two articles per minute each day—well over 1,000,000 articles per year."[3]

Similarly, the 1989/90 *Bowker Annual* reveals pricing and publishing trends in the book and non-print arenas. While the number of titles published dropped from 52,637 in 1986 to 47,489 in 1988, the average price per volume rose from $32.43 in that period to $38.39.[4] And new demands have been placed on materials budgets in the forms of online database searching and the acquisition of CD-ROMs, which now number over 200,[5] and average between $1,200-5,000 each.

No library can afford to acquire even half of all published material, both in terms of cost, and the investment in space and personnel time required to process and provide access to a burgeoning quantity of information. Meanwhile, faculty members often rank the library low on the scale of valuable information sources[6] and argue that libraries' holdings, particularly in journals, are insufficient. An average size library at a college or university may subscribe to anywhere from 3,000 to 10,000 journal titles, a fraction of the nearly 260,000 possible acquisitions cited above.

Is the faculty concern really for more adequate materials budgets or different collections policies? Or is the average professor disgruntled because he must leave his cozy office on a blustery day to cross the quadrangle to the library, where he encounters difficulty locating the desired material? Is he told that to obtain the piece, he will endure a 10-14 day wait for interlibrary loans to acquire it or alternatively, a three-hour drive across the state to large university XYZ to procure it sooner?

Technologically, libraries occupy a potentially advantageous position relative to information provision. The availability of sophisticated telecommunications networks, including those carrying data as well as telefacsimile transmissions, enables libraries to send information easily from one location to another. In a recent *Library Journal* article, New York Public Library Director Richard DeGennaro writes:

In the future, the size of a library's collection of conventional materials will matter far less than it does now. The question is no longer how many volumes a library has, but how effectively the library can deliver needed resources from a wide variety of sources to users via the new technology. The emphasis is shifting from collections to access. The new information technologies are democratizing the availability of research resources.[7]

Despite libraries' ability to transmit and acquire information with ease, traditions in the way we conduct business on a daily basis tends to reflect more the scenario of the disgruntled professor in the car en route to another university than the democratic picture painted by Dick DeGennaro. The democratizing factor may indeed come from without the library establishment, and ultimately eliminate the need for libraries to create resource sharing agreements for anything but historic print material.

Electronic mail, the linking of national and international networks, and the successful distribution of microcomputers into academic offices and laboratories has created a rift in the patterns of communication within collegial groups. Traditional communication patterns among scientists, for example, include informal networks (phone, mail) which precede formal communication of research results (seminars, conferences, journals). The addition of the new communication tools may result in fundamental changes in the old patterns.

A librarian at a major Ivy League university shared the observation that many of the tenured faculty have circumvented traditional means of information sharing, and in effect "publish" all of their work on networks such as BitNet. They no longer see the need, from a professional standpoint, to participate in the chain of scholarly publishing. That route is not yet available to junior faculty or graduate students, and may not be adopted widely in the humanities, but its emergence suggests that further changes lie ahead.

The for profit sector recognizes the value placed on speedy information transmission and is working hard to identify products and services to fill emerging needs. The challenge for librarians involved in collection development and resource sharing will be to exploit those information resources which supplement and enrich campus resources. When services are marketed directly to users, the library will still be the court of last resort for training, trouble-shooting, and locating that part of the written record which is no longer supported by IBM, AT&T, or the other major corporations now anxiously seeking new markets for information and their networks. As Nancy Evans writes, the challenge in this new environment "is to arrive at a reasonable and equitable selection of information sources available at no additional charge to users."[8]

In a free market economy such as this one, vendors and publishers, and purveyors of networks and telecommunications services in particular, have every right to identify and pursue a potentially hot market and redefine formulas and collection building. If libraries wish to remain a central part of the information chain, they will have to accomplish two goals:

1. Create and implement effective means for patrons to locate access to information, whether at the local institution or elsewhere.

2. Develop resource sharing methods that are inexpensive to the end-user, convenient, and require minimal effort on his or her part. Eliminate as many barriers between the user and the information as possible.

If academic libraries in particular can become truly user responsive, they will maintain their position as key players in the information world. Nevertheless, traditions die hard, and the desire and even incentives persist to collect for ownership as much as possible. As part of the observation of its 50th anniversary, *College and Research Libraries* reprinted an article first published in 1965 entitled, "Quantitative Criteria for Adequacy of Academic Library Collections," by Verner W. Clapp and Robert T. Jordan. This "reprint of a *C&RL* classic" argues that academic library collections can and should be measured quantitatively, not simply using subjective qualitative criteria.[9] In a brief foreword, 1989 *C&RL* editor David Kaser states that the piece was selected for reprinting because it launched the now well-known "Clapp-Jordan formula," and because the "paper should be remembered as a landmark contribution to the literature of academic librarianship."[10]

The bottom line is that much collection building in the past 25 years has focused on numbers, and it continues to do so partly because of tradition and inertia, and partly because of user expectation. Technology notwithstanding, libraries and their parent institutions prefer to own, not share. It is the sheer prohibitive numbers of publications available as much as budget restrictions, that cause libraries to seek cooperative agreements now. Our lack of success in this venture could have enormous impacts on the profession of academic librarianship, particularly if users begin to obtain their information through alternative means. The day could arrive when university administrators question the value of an enormous investment in personnel and physical space that is the library, particularly if the library is performing functions which are no longer demonstrably useful to the university community.

Despite the need to consider new means for accomplishing library goals, there are external forces discouraging libraries from seeking access alternatives to mass acquisition of materials. Chief among these is the accreditation system. Also products of tradition, accreditation standards often reflect a strong bias toward the physical location of resources in an institution's library. Online access, interlibrary lending agreements, and membership in consortia rarely qualify a library in the minds of accreditation officers. Perhaps one role of collection development professionals will be to educate accrediting agencies about the economics of collecting versus providing access to sources through alternative, non-print means.

Cornell University's Ross Atkinson has proposed that libraries rethink the way they approach collection development in the future. He states that libraries in academe have five basic functions to fulfill: notification, documentation, historical, instructional and the bibliographical "metafunction."[11] Atkinson argues that rather than attempting to define library purchases by using "core" and "non-core" distinctions which are muddy at best, each bibliographer might consider reviewing materials published in a given subject area as they fall within the five functional categories. A collection developer could consider the needs of the clientele, and consider where the emphasis should fall: is this a journal-dependent discipline which requires access to current journals and not much historical or monographic material? Is it a social science discipline which needs access to raw data in the form of unpublished documents? Is the curriculum emphasizing instruction—is this a service department providing background education for specialists in another field?[12] Atkinson continues with a comment on the role of resource sharing in such an arrangement:

> Cooperative collection development could also benefit from a method that bases cooperative agreements upon functional categories. Certain types of sources and many notification sources cannot be shared effectively among institutions, but must be owned.[13]

Atkinson feels that cooperative collection development and resource sharing have never been particularly successful. He notes that, "the first decade of *College & Research Libraries* contains several calls for improved cooperation in the development of library collections. The arguments and the recommendations presented in those articles are not at all unlike positions still taken today, which is evidence of how modestly we have progressed in this area."[14]

But the technology provides libraries with the same tools for rapid transmission that it offers the private sector. Twenty years ago, there were fax machines and telephone lines. Now we have "flat bed" fax equipment and high speed data transmission lines. Soon, the process that creates microfilm for preservation will create an electronic "copy" for whatever purposes users can invent. With the catalogs and indexes on line, we can identify a source and its location. When the information can be detached from its source, transformed for transmission, reconverted upon delivery, and used with no significant loss of content along the way, resource sharing takes on new dimensions. Collection development and public service librarians can join forces to define what will be owned, leased, borrowed or paid-on-demand.

Academic libraries are sitting at a crossroads that may well define their existence and raison d'être in the coming century. If librarians work with their faculty clients and the university administrators who control their budgets, as well as external groups such as accrediting agencies to re-educate them about the role of libraries in the information chain, libraries will not only survive but flourish. Collection development officers will likely play a pivotal role in the re-education process, in part because of their stronger ties with faculty and administrators, and also because their jobs will be among the first to demonstrate radical change.

Conversely, if libraries choose to cling to the status quo, thinking of collection development only in terms of acquiring print material and eschewing resource sharing alternatives, the academic librarian may find herself managing only undergraduate reserve collections and huge archival storage facilities for historic information and rare books, while the corporate sector provides the service that the academic research community needs. The challenge will be to effect a smooth transition from the current to the future, ascertaining that the print-dominated functions which libraries currently perform continue until it is time to make the break to new means of information provision. Most likely, it will be decades before a full transition is complete, and in the meantime, librarians will have to ride two horses. As one librarian wrote, "The future of college and university libraries will depend largely on the commitment of librarians and educators to resource sharing and the provision of traditional as well as innovative services in a network environment."[15]

Notes

1. David Cohen, "Scholarly Communication and the Role of Libraries: Problems and Possibilities for Accessing Journal Articles," *Serials Librarian* 17:3/4, 43 (1990).

2. The authors wish to thank Robert Davidson of the Faxon Company for providing current, unpublished data for the article.

3. Cohen, "Scholarly Communication," p. 43.

4. Chandler B. Grannis, "Book Title output and Average Prices: 1988 Preliminary Figures," in *The Bowker Annual: Library and Book Trade Almanac 1989-90* (New York: R. R. Bowker, 1989), pp. 424-469.

5. Margaret Morrison, "The Promise of New Technology," in *The Bowker Annual: Library and Book Trade Almanac 1989-90* (New York, R.R. Bowker, 1989), p. 79.

6. Cohen, "Scholarly Communication," pp. 43-44.

7. Richard DeGennaro, "Technology and Access in an Enterprise Society," *Library Journal* 114:4, 42 (October 1, 1989).

8. Nancy Evans, "Development of the Carnegie Mellon Library Information System," *Information Technology and Libraries*, 8:2, 116 (June 1989).

9. Verner W. Clapp and Robert T. Jordan, "Quantitative Criteria for Adequacy of Academic Library Collections," *College and Research Libraries* 50: 154-163 (March 1989).

10. David Kaser, "Fiftieth Anniversary Feature—'Quantitative Criteria for Adequacy of Academic Library Collections': A Reprint of a *C&RL* Classic," *College and Research Libraries* 50: 153 (March 1989).

11. Ross Atkinson, "Old Forms, New Forms: The Challenge of Collection Development," *College and Research Libraries* 50: 508 (September 1989).

12. Atkinson, "Old Forms, New Forms," pp. 514-515.

13. Atkinson, "Old Forms, New Forms," p. 515.

14. Atkinson, "Old Forms, New Forms," p. 511.

15. Plummer Alston Jones, Jr., "The History and Development of Libraries in American Higher Education," *College and Research Libraries News* 50:564 (July/August 1989).

How Can We Improve Resource Sharing? A Scholar's View

Michael Carpenter
School of Library and Information Science
Louisiana State University

In the best of all possible worlds, all materials germane to a scholarly project would be in a scholar's own library, and if not there, at the institution closest to the scholar. But this is not the best of all possible worlds. Some materials are unique, and others scarce. Some of these materials are scattered among different libraries. Even in a world characterized by plentiful financial resources, sharing of materials among different libraries would be necessary.[1]

Unfortunately, frustration and wasted time are the hallmarks of resource sharing for many a scholar who needs to use materials found in several libraries. Frustration arises both from the inability to locate libraries housing needed materials, and from time wasted in what often becomes an impotent effort to see the materials. The arrangements for resource sharing are often elaborate, but essentially misdirected. The reasons for this failure are found in goal displacement, improper discretionary behavior, insufficient education of library managers, and conflicting visions of the mission of libraries.

Many writers have discussed the "library without walls." As the fable of such a library goes, because we have online databases capable of displaying the holdings of all libraries, a library collection is not confined to a single building or a single campus alone; now it is available to the nation or even the world. The difficulty with this fable is that catalog access alone to the resources of other libraries is not the same as physical access. If significant hurdles or prohibitions are put in the way of the user, the library without walls is little more than a reverie. And yet, a catalog describing the resources of other libraries is a *sine qua non*, a necessary, but not sufficient, condition of effective resource sharing.[2]

To demonstrate that the library without walls is substantially more myth than reality, and to make an effort to change the myth into reality, I will first examine a real-world case of the use and frustrations of resource sharing, then discuss the lessons this case has for libraries, and finally propose a scheme to encourage the sharing of research library resources.

The Case of Charles Coffin Jewett:
The Frustrations of Using Resource Sharing

As we examine the utility of resource sharing among libraries, it would be remiss not to recall the career of Charles Coffin Jewett (1816-1868).[3] In several of his writings, Jewett states a concern in the 1840s and 1850s about the lack of true research library resources available in the United States. He intended to deal with the problem by making the Smithsonian Institution the national library. Instead, at the instigation of Joseph Henry, he devoted time and even personal funds to the somewhat more limited project of creating a national union catalog.[4] One of the reasons for the national union catalog scheme was to permit the loan of books from library to library as well as to allow extracts to be copied from books to order. I became interested in Jewett because of my interest in the connections between his and Panizzi's cataloging rules. When I failed to find any correspondence between the two, I started to look into Jewett's career; as I investigated the archival material, I found a substantial amount of material scattered widely throughout various libraries. There is no central supply of Jewett material because of one cardinal fact: The administrative offices of the Smithsonian, which might have been expected to hold that material, suffered a fire in 1865 from which very little survived, and no Jewett manuscripts whatever. Therefore, if one is interested in Jewett, one must rely heavily on the sharing of resources among many libraries; Jewett corresponded with many people.

In the following study of my experiences with the resource sharing arrangements of American libraries, I have identified some of the thirty-eight libraries I used with pseudonyms, so that they may remain anonymous. Their identities are unimportant for the lessons I intend to draw about resource sharing in general, and my interest is not to criticize or appraise the actions of named individuals or institutions, but instead to demonstrate the general principles of resource sharing as I have found it practiced in today's research library environment.

I started my study with the references at the end of Joseph Borome's biography, *Charles Coffin Jewett*.[5] Although Borome states that "time has dealt harshly with the manuscript letters of Jewett,"[6] Borome's references were a beginning. I wrote various libraries in an effort to obtain photocopies of Jewett manuscript material. Most responded, sometimes quickly, others in a leisurely fashion, and one not at all. What I was able to find was substantially more material than Borome uses.

I found the papers of one of Jewett's most voluminous correspondents, Henry Stevens, scattered in three different libraries across the country, A, B, and C. When I visited library A, which has the biggest holding of Stevens material, I found a strange restriction; a reader can have up to 200 sheets issued from any one collection, while any more copies have to be made on microfilm. This rule applies to individual collections of any size in the library.

In library B, the Stevens material pertinent to Jewett is scattered among three separate collections. Some of library B's Stevens material was acquired long before that owned by library A. Library B's holdings of Jewett and Stevens materials are not reported in either the *National Union Catalog of Manuscript Collections* or any online database. I was able to learn of it only through a catalog of the library's holdings which I had seen by chance.

The indexing of library A's collection contains no reference to library B's collection of Stevens material.

Library C made photocopies of the Jewett materials in its Stevens collection and sent me the bill. Library C later acquired another collection containing Jewett letters; fortunately this collection was reported to the *National Union Catalog of Manuscripts* a few years after it had been purchased, and I was able to use the newer materials, too.

Library D never responded to any of my letters; library D has at least two documents cited by Borome. No catalog of library D is available. Library E holds an unknown, but significant, amount of Jewett material. Because this material is in the library's archives, I had to obtain permission to use it. Doing so took over four years of correspondence. It is not clear that I saw all the Jewett material library E possesses when I visited it. I believe the staff is not aware of the extent of Jewett material in the library.

When I visited library F, the librarian personally brought me the material. The librarian also discussed the available Jewett material as well as any scholar could. The library even provided free photocopies of the material.

Library G has a policy of permitting no more than twenty photocopies per day of any material in the library. It also has a most intimidating copyright release form, which, among other things, states that copies made to order are only lent to the scholar, and the library has the right to approve any use made of the text of materials in the library prior to their publication.

The collections of library H are constantly growing and being cataloged. At library H one need only use a coin-operated photocopy machine. A guard checks all photocopies to ensure that they have the name of the institution on them; this mark is made on the paper by the photocopy machine. Researchers must use only paper the library provides specially for the taking of notes.

Library J has the reputation of being an extremely prestigious library. No photocopies are made without a lengthy application being filled out and returned with a check, which includes a substantial handling fee, prior to the work being done. The application form for photocopying materials in this library also contains a clause requiring the library's prior approval for any publication relying on (not necessarily quoting) material in the library.

The manuscripts reading room at library K was remodeled just prior to the introduction of portable personal computers and thus, unfortunately, has only two or three electrical outlets in the center of the room. The library contains a highly miscellaneous collection of Jewett manuscripts. Photocopy service is available during weekdays only, with walk-up service available for the library's highly specialized reference collection. For rare book and manuscript material, photocopying is available through a rather simple written request form; coin-operated photocopying is not available. One condition of being a reader in the library is that the library requests it be notified of any publications resulting from use of its collections. These publications are indexed to the materials in the library, thus permitting scholars to examine the views of other writers on a particular document. It should be noted that only accredited scholars are allowed the use of library K's collections.

Library L was most kind in permitting my representative to search the archives for information on Jewett; it did not even require a written statement from me. Its staff tried to find information for my representative so that she did not even have to search the catalog.

Library M has been a source of material not only on a photocopy basis, but also as a source of books borrowed on interlibrary loan. It sent photocopies of manuscript material located through the *National Union Catalog of Manuscript Collections*, and billed me after sending them.

Library N had a strange response to my inquiry about its contents; its representative said that although it is a private institution, it could not bar my visit because its building was constructed with the aid of Federal funds. Although I did not have to use the library's special collections department, the library is well stocked with printed materials relevant to the life of Jewett.

Library O had a single item relative to Jewett, for which a full catalog entry had fortunately been entered into OCLC. The curator of the special collections department graciously sent me a free copy of the letter, which has been most useful in tracking down one of Jewett's aborted projects. This aborted project was a second edition, otherwise unknown, of Jewett's *Notices of Public Libraries in the United States,* the first attempt at arriving at an inventory of American library resources.

Sometimes resource sharing must be done on an international basis. A crucial article was published in a French periodical in 1845 from which Jewett clearly obtained his idea of a catalog composed with the aid of movable stereotyped entries. Because the title of the periodical was common to several published in mid-nineteenth century France, I had to track down a clear description of the periodical in a detailed bibliography. I found a bibliography of nineteenth-century French periodicals in library P. Using the description in that bibliography, I tried to obtain the article through interlibrary loan.

Library Q claims to hold a microfilm copy of the journal; library Q returned my requests unfilled on two widely separate occasions, saying that, in spite of the OCLC entry describing issues of the journal, replete with a citation to the bibliography listing, it did not have any issues of the journal in question in the film they had.

Later I lost the photocopy of the bibliography. When I became affiliated with Louisiana State University, I had to borrow the bibliography on interlibrary loan to photocopy the entry once again. Then I thought I would be able to find a copy of the periodical. The library of Louisiana State University does not have a copy of a French union list of periodicals.

The British Museum catalog contains a blind reference to a periodical with the required name, but the main entry is not present in the catalog. In 1988, I visited the British Library and satisfied myself that it did not have the periodical in question. However, the British Library does hold a copy of the French union catalog of periodicals, a catalog which is not widely held in

American libraries. In any event, because it is a reference book, it cannot be borrowed. Only in the catalog's section on additions and corrections was I able to find a reference to the periodical. Runs of the periodical, which proved to be a newspaper, could be found in two French libraries. The LSU Library was able to acquire a photocopy of the article from French library S. Acquiring this copy took at least four months. The document is clearly the source of Jewett's ideas of a stereotyped library catalog and its employment as a national union catalog. Some of Jewett's writing is a direct translation of the French.

While working at library K one day, I came across the 1918 *Handbook of Manuscripts in the Library of Congress*. Opening this catalog by chance, I found a description of a manuscript relating to Jewett's rules in the Library of Congress (LC). Later, while visiting LC, I tried to locate the document in the printouts of the Manuscript Division's collections. The document was not there. Dimly remembering the earlier catalog, I asked for a copy and found the document I desired listed therein. It is a set of galley proofs of Jewett's rules in a much earlier state of the text than had heretofore been available. Jewett directly quotes Panizzi's rules. It is also possible to verify from the same galley proofs that Jewett did not directly borrow from an earlier state of Panizzi's rules.

As the above story indicates, research can sometimes be frustrating. But it doesn't have to be made unnecessarily difficult through what appear to be misdirected policies. In the next three parts of this paper, I will attempt to systematize my experiences, analyze them in terms of a set of generalizations which I shall call *laws of resource sharing*, and finally suggest a remedy to make resource sharing work for, rather than against, scholars.

Three Types of Resource Sharing

There are three types of resource sharing, upon all of which I have had to rely. The first is the admission of a travelling scholar to a library other than the one with which he or she is affiliated. The second is through provision of a substitute for the original material, usually in some sort of photocopy form, to that scholar. The third is through provision of the desired materials by direct or indirect loan to a scholar at a distance. In this paper, I shall examine all three.

A private library generally has no legal compulsion to open its doors to users not affiliated with the institution. And even those institutions that do allow the public to come inside and examine materials do not have to lend materials to or allow copying by members of the outside public. What, then, compels libraries under no legal mandate to allow use of their resources by others? This is a central question to be answered by such constructs as the "academic community" or the "community of scholars." Whether or not those high-sounding terms are honored in reality, there are sufficient restrictions on the use of library materials to cause a scholar to question the reality underlying the concepts.

Contrasted with the dream of resource sharing of materials from diverse, unique, distinctive collections is the actual nature of collection policies. The collections of large libraries are becoming increasingly uniform. As financial resources dwindle, only core, instructional materials are purchased. So-called research materials receive lower priority, not only for purchase, but also for cataloging. Since most departments have their counterparts on other campuses, with counterpart curricula, core instructional collections are becoming more or less identical from campus to campus.

The first type of resource sharing to be examined here is the actual visit to a library other than a scholar's home institution. Typically, the scholar visits the department of special collections to examine material unique to that library. It is not often that a scholar visits a library to use its general collections, unless it holds a highly specialized reference collection supporting a substantial core of manuscript and early printed material.

The working conditions for a scholar travelling to another library's manuscript collection are generally not conducive to high productivity. Typically, the special collections area opens later than other parts of the library and is rarely open in the evenings or on weekends. With such short library hours, the conscientiously working scholar is beset with nonproductive hours that cannot be devoted to the project at hand.

Often libraries have not put enough information into the database (for instance, OCLC or RLIN) to permit an accurate estimate of what materials they have that are relevant. So, when the researcher arrives, after having paid for a non-refundable, fixed-stay airline ticket, he or she finds that the library has at least twice what the staff mentioned on the telephone when the researcher was checking the information provided by the online database or union catalog.

The contrast between the promise and the reality of the physical surroundings is striking. Many departments of special collections have beautifully panelled walls. Yet, many of those beautiful facilities do not allow the use of portable computers or tape recorders in the taking of notes. When the researcher photocopies pencilled notes during the day, he or she is sometimes met with staff comments about the evil effects of photocopying machines on old-fashioned scholarship. At some libraries, the exit door is even locked from the inside in contravention of the state fire code.

To illustrate the contrast between physical beauty and excellent working conditions, I would note that one of the best places for a scholar to work is at library T where the physical conditions are aesthetically terrible. Free-standing gray-painted steel shelves with naked archival boxes fill the room. Steam pipes are overhead. The fluorescent light is dreary. But one can work easily and efficiently. Intellectual access is carried down to the level of folders in the archival boxes. Photocopying is easily accomplished by taking the document to a coin-operated machine. Microfilming of folders is available provided one has identified them—an easy task, since several editions of the guide to the collections have been published in inexpensive microfiche. All this produces an excellent research atmosphere.

The second kind of resource sharing is through the provision of a substitute for the material, usually through photocopying. The photocopying I required was of unique materials. It became impossible to travel to thirty-plus libraries to examine a few pieces of manuscript material in each. Even when one can visit the library, photocopying provides the ability to take notes rapidly and accurately from unique material. Unfortunately, with respect to resource sharing through photocopying, the following observations have to be made:

1. The photocopying policies of many libraries need reexamination. For example, the complexity of forms one must complete for a simple photocopy or microfilm can be astounding. The form used by the British Library, requiring signatures from a reference librarian, a representative of the conservation section, another representative of the photographic department, along with a signed copyright declaration, probably contributes substantially to the extraordinarily high costs charged by that institution. Many American libraries have forms just as imposing as those of the British Library. On the other hand, there are a few libraries whose special collections departments seem to take very little interest in the minutiae of recording the numbers of photocopies and completion of complex applications, and simply allow the reader to use a coin-operated machine without supervision.

2. Many libraries require the user to sign a statement stating that he or she will return the copies to the libraries after the study is finished, the copies being only lent to the reader. With respect to the vast majority of research materials, the point of this procedure seems unclear. It can intimidate users for no apparent reason. It is also most likely legally invalid, and difficult to enforce.[7]

3. Many libraries require users to sign some sort of copyright agreement for the favor of using any and all materials in their special collections departments, but not in their regular collections. Again, the reasoning behind the form is never made entirely clear. Frequently, rights are claimed by a library far in excess of what a reasonable interpretation of copyright laws would require for unpublished materials.[8] For example, the library often takes the right to approve research papers based on materials in their collections prior to publication. Such a clause appears to be an attempt at censorship.

4. Finally, library photocopying policies can become a means of frustration. Generally libraries will not lend volumes of periodicals. However, citations from the nineteenth and earlier centuries are often insufficient to provide accurate identification of the page numbers or titles of articles in pre-twentieth century periodicals. Incomplete citations make photocopying requests difficult to fill by the lending library. A scholar is thus frustrated; the volume which would contain the title or page

numbers is not available, and the lending library will not photocopy the desired materials without a full citation. The information cannot be obtained without a direct visit, or without cooperation from a specially hired searcher, an additional expense for the researcher.

The third type of resource sharing, and generally the best known, is interlibrary loan. The main observation I make here is that the types of material that evidently cannot be borrowed, no matter what the intended use, can be astounding. Unborrowable types of material are also not specifically stated in interlibrary lending codes, but instead are set forth in a particular library's random policy which is often not available to the potential user or his or her library's interlibrary loan office. In short, the effect can be capricious. For example, it is hard to obtain copies of genealogies, whole volumes of periodicals, unusual reference books, etc., but there is no written document stating any policies on the matter.

Having discussed some of the frustrating aspects of resource sharing, I shall generalize and provide descriptions of some of the fundamental regularities underlying the above phenomena. Where there are regularities in behavior in social arrangements, laws descriptive of that behavior can be stated. The following is an attempt to list those laws.

Laws of Resource Sharing

The majority of materials in an academic library are held in common by a majority of academic libraries. This observation, or first law of resource sharing, stems from the fact that new materials for undergraduate collections for such core majors as English literature, chemistry, philosophy, and biology, do not in general vary widely from library to library.[9] Even for the greater portion of graduate course work, the nature of newly acquired materials does not vary widely from library to library. It is of only so-called research material that collections are likely to be unique among academic libraries. Most interlibrary codes recognize this fact when they prohibit borrowing by undergraduates.[10]

The first law recognizes that there is a large body of material for which it is unnecessary to have elaborate interlibrary lending procedures. Additionally, resource sharing of this material is positively harmful; its withdrawal by outsiders can work hardship on the instructional staff, as materials used in teaching must be readily available. With respect to the so-called common core of a collection, every academic library, even a research library, is fulfilling the role of a formal educational support center.[11] But there are other roles a large library must fulfill. It must be a library of reference for its community, however the community is defined. For this purpose, the library buys a core collection that is easily identifiable and held in common with a majority of academic libraries. But, the final role, that of a foundation for research, is the one in which no library can be self-sufficient. Although a wealthy library can collect current published materials comprehensively, such a library cannot provide a comprehensive collection of retrospective materials.[12] Some source materials will always remain outside the research library's reach.

It would appear that one remedy for the unreachable primary resource is informing others that the material exists. Unfortunately, a second law comes into play here.

The more important the material for a new subject, the less likely it is to have been cited, used, or even cataloged. If the subject is indeed new, the basic material is unlikely ever to have been used or cited, unless it were in a substantially different context. Clearly, no subject cataloging will have been provided for the material. More importantly, descriptive cataloging is provided for manuscript and rare book material only on a haphazard basis. If it has been cataloged, an entry for it will probably not be found in the online databases. Very few manuscript material entries are found in OCLC.[13] Unprocessed arrearages are often as big as or bigger than the processed portion of a library's collections. For example, the Library of Congress now has an arrearage larger in bulk than the processed manuscript material in its collection.[14]

Some administrators claim that there is no need to catalog special collections materials because no one ever asks for them. The absurdity of this argument is clear; if no one knows about the material, no one will ask for it. The fact that the argument is often taken seriously and the resources available for cataloging library materials are reduced indicates that the library has made a policy judgment that much material which is zealously guarded is not worth the dollars it takes to catalog it, even on a collective or archival basis. Such a policy judgment seems to be a case, not of managerial discretion, but of discretionary behavior. Discretionary behavior, which is defined as a manager's deciding to make a policy for personal reasons unrelated to the organization's goals, runs counter to the research library goal of the dissemination of knowledge.

It is strange that holdings information is provided to the library community for material which will generally not become the subject of a resource-sharing arrangement, namely the core collection, while material important to the foundation of new investigations cannot be used on a shared basis because no other library knows of the existence of the material.

A corollary, third law is: *As the supply of catalogers declines, the amount of unique materials rises. Access will become indefinitely postponed for many materials.* One way of remedying the problem of cataloging arrearages is to request a grant to do the cataloging. The library then hires a cataloger for the term of the grant. This solution is not practical. Given the well-documented shortage of catalogers, mainly those catalogers who are willing to lead a vagabond life are hired; they are typically those catalogers who are unable to maintain a full-time job, whether from personality difficulties or from lack of competence. Even so, grants do little more than support the cataloging of specific blocks of material. They do not fund the processing of the massive arrearages of materials that have built up in recent years; to catalog them will require a systematic long-term effort. Perhaps the remedy is to create an incentive to provide intellectual access to unique materials.

One approach to identifying materials is to state that a library collects with a certain degree of intensity in a given subject area. The theory is that if a scholar knows that a particular library collects comprehensively in a given subject area, then the library will likely contain unique materials. The problem is that although a library may claim that its collections in a given area are comprehensive, a subject-oriented approach assumes that library materials pertain to one subject only.

Library administrations appear to think that there are no other ways of dividing subjects than shelf classifications. Unfortunately, as catalogers are aware, library classifications disperse material on a subject through several "disciplines" which are the basis for assigning classification numbers. Furthermore, many library materials are cross-disciplinary in nature. In fact, many of Jewett's materials are classified in both Q and Z. An approach to collections which assumes that library materials have a single subject would therefore seem adequately rebutted. Nevertheless, a few years ago, members of the Research Libraries Group (RLG) started the Conspectus On-line program to assess strengths in various areas of collecting.

Aside from the notorious lack of uniformity in assigning degrees of collection intensity, there are serious objections to using the conspectus in the context of resource sharing.[15] The subject divisions used in the conspectus were created from an unsystematic abridgment of the Library of Congress classification scheme. Books which are found in cross-disciplinary research are not properly accounted for in the scheme. More importantly, for purposes of interlibrary loan, specifically identified materials are what is called for, rather than subject collections. Additionally, minimally cataloged materials will not be found in the conspectus.[16] It is the non-core materials that will be the object of much resource sharing. The conspectus simply misses the issue. Thus the fourth law states: *The categories in the RLG Conspectus are inappropriate measures of the strength of collections in a given area, and do not address the scholar's needs.*

A fifth law follows: *The majority of new scholarly work will require access to several libraries because the material is widely diffused among libraries.* This law was certainly confirmed in the Jewett case. No library can collect all retrospective material, including sources, for a new research topic when the material required for the research is old.

The sixth law of resource sharing states: *The more important a printed book is for a historical study, the less likely it is to be available for resource sharing.* Everyone knows about the obvious case of incunabula being unavailable for interlibrary loan, even though they may be key documents for a research project. But there is another, less-obvious class of materials that is essentially outside the scope of resource sharing. Although there is no written policy on the matter, one evidently cannot borrow a genealogical work for work on a historical personage. My university's interlibrary loan office tried to obtain one genealogy from fifteen different libraries, noting on each request that the borrower needed the work for scholarly and not genealogical research. Each time it failed. Of course, RLG's interlibrary lending code refers to conditions imposed by a lending library, but contains no general mention of genealogies.[17] Evidently, the RLG agreement is not all that it seems. It is supposed to stand for a broadened version of resource sharing, for libraries who are members of the club: true research libraries. In fact, it turns out to be something else.

Research libraries are supposed to be part of the academic community, the community of scholars. However, the reality indicates that, with respect to sharing of resources, not all materials are considered resources to be shared with other members of the academic community. That there is also a social stratification with respect to sharing of resources is seen in some of the provisions of the RLG manual. Some of the institutions are libraries "of last resort," or libraries to which application should be made only after other libraries have failed to provide the desired material. Among these are the New York Public Library and the library of the American Antiquarian Society.[18] Other libraries are in a class of overburdened "Last Resort Net Lenders," libraries that have been net lenders, or libraries that have lent more than they have borrowed, within the Research Libraries Group and now wish to be treated for a time as libraries of last resort.[19]

Some of the libraries of last resort restrict the photocopying of materials they will physically lend to another library. Why this should be so, when the library is willing to lend the book, is unclear. It may be that there is some moral virtue to transcription by pencil. The British Library's policy of making a negative microfilm and selling a positive copy to the reader makes sense. The book is filmed only once, and copies of its contents are indefinitely available.

Along with the stratification of research libraries, we can find a seventh law: *The more prestigious the institution, the more restrictive the conditions are for use of its materials.* The only exception to this law of which I am aware is the Library of Congress. There are some libraries that a scholar cannot enter without having completed a Ph. D., or a book-length study, in the field under investigation. There are other libraries that permit only a small number of pages to be photocopied on any one day. The library's purpose for these rules is unclear; what *is* clear is that the practice has the effect of enforcing a long stay by the scholar, or else discouraging scholarship altogether.

A corollary is to be found in libraries that essentially forbid photocopying of any sort on the grounds that photocopying ruins the books as physical objects. Such libraries may insist that a special library worker wearing white gloves turn the pages. The very act of exposure of the book to light for reading, of course, can be expected to put more strain on the permanence of the paper than can any amount of properly handled microfilming.

Here, I would suggest an eighth law: *Preservation is often an excuse for making the material useless.* The love affair with the physical object must be conquered if meaningful preservation of the text is to be accomplished.

The physical object, especially if it is already fragile, will not last for much longer, regardless of the vain wishes of descriptive bibliographers. The curators of the material should, however, ensure preservation of the text through some sort of photographic or machine-readable reproduction.

If the objective of the library is to preserve the text, to pass it down through the ages, then the attitude of total resistance to photocopying held by some libraries must be overcome. Furthermore, the photocopies must be widely diffused. Time will certainly ensure the destruction of unique photocopies. Accidental destruction, unforeseen exogenous occurrences like war, flood and fire will surely someday deny us the physical object. To attempt to defeat the processes of time by deliberately making documents inaccessible is doubly destructive. For doing so effectively denies knowledge of the documents to the present as well as to the future. It may be time to rescue documents from such "preservation."

Libraries which only "lend" photocopies are clearly guilty of goal displacement; when asked about the policy of only lending photocopies that the reader had paid for, librarians from two different institutions stated that the objective of the policy was to preserve the "value" of the documents that had been photocopied. What maintaining the unique status of a document has to with the dissemination of knowledge is obscure.

Laws such as the eighth and last one above indicate that access to materials may be denied to the scholar for reasons extraneous to research. There is a capricious element to a scholar's access to shared resources. However, many academic writers on the subject of resource sharing have stated that the extent of the library's physical collection is not important. What counts is availability of collections. As mentioned above, they have often referred to the new situation as the "library without walls." However, it needs to be stated here that: *The library without walls is a myth. Access to materials delayed, restricted, or made subject to capricious factors, is access effectively denied.*

To generalize further: *Library policies on resource sharing are but an outgrowth of the organizational culture of a particular library.* The petty behavior described above, as well as the wise policies, the fact that some librarians have become retentive, that others have come to worship physical objects to the exclusion of their contents, while yet others have maintained a service orientation, believing that books are for use, are but expressions of organizational culture in a library.

Organizational culture is the sum of shared beliefs, attitudes and values of the members of an organization. It is manifest not only in their actions, but also in the stories they tell, the rituals they perform. Organizational culture is a product of the rewards and penalties enforced by management. As an example, a library will perceive itself as research-oriented if management insists on publication as a requirement for usage. In the absence of formal management directives, organizational culture can be set by the informal organization of a particular institution. A well-known example of culture being set by an informal organization is seen in the post office: postal workers will soon ostracize a co-worker who exceeds the quota which management has set, in spite of the best efforts of management to get workers to surpass their quotas.

Legends about stolen materials are often manifestations of an organizational culture that is highly aware of physical security. The ritual of not allowing readers to turn pages by themselves is the result of oft-repeated stories of torn books. Luxuriously appointed surroundings can set the organizational tone for an institution that will see a reader as a source of trouble, an annoyance, a possible destroyer of books.

We need not accept the organizational culture given us. We can change culture. This we can do by providing an incentive to change. It is a cardinal maxim of personnel management that people do not in general act irrationally. Seemingly irrational behavior is generally caused by badly designed compensation structures or other stimuli. People respond, not necessarily to the true needs of the organization, but to what they perceive will cause them to advance within the organization. The good news is that we can change those stimuli.

Toward Improvement in Resource Sharing: Competition among Libraries

I propose a means of changing the inappropriate behavior on the part of library personnel by adding a new stimulus, that of competition among libraries. If research libraries are supposed to fuel research, then it is time to measure how well they do, not through an indirect substitute or proxy, such as the number of books, but through the publications their collections engender. This measure will also test for the true effect of resource sharing.

One way of evaluating library effectiveness may be to encourage writers of journal articles to give credit to the libraries whose resources they have used. If such a citation index were then extended to these acknowledgments, there could be a quantitative measure of effective library resource sharing.[20] Instead of so-called tonnage models of library rankings, similar to what we have in the statistics compiled by the Association of Research Libraries, which rely on budgets, numbers of titles, volumes, and journal subscriptions, we could see how well the collections are actually aiding scholarly research, the ostensible aim of research libraries.

The library citation index system would be somewhat similar to that now employed by citation index services. One difference would be that the affiliation of writers would be identified so that libraries could compare the amount of help they give faculty members from their own institutions with the help they give others.

It may be objected that the citation index for libraries will demonstrate that personal collections, rather than library collections, are at the base of much research. Would this be a shame? Imagine if the main resources available to writers in science and technology were not long runs of journal subscriptions, but instead preprints, reprints, and handouts. It would demonstrate that there is a viable substitute for multi-thousand dollar journal subscriptions. It might even obviate the need to devote an ever-increasing share of a library's budget to just a few journal subscriptions.

The acknowledgment index would also encourage competition among libraries to develop and catalog unique collections that can in fact be shared with other libraries instead of the homogeneous policy of research collection development we are now seeing. National coverage of so-called esoteric materials would be increased, perhaps to the detriment of the traditional core collection materials.

Libraries could become aware in some quantitative sense of how much their collections aided the academic community as a whole, compared with service to their own faculties. Because of the relatively small number of researchers, libraries would find that the only way of raising citation counts would be to develop collections different from those of other libraries. Because of the variety of research projects undertaken throughout the nation, it is doubtful that libraries would compete among themselves to acquire the same unique material. Increased interlibrary access to the materials would provide an additional incentive for cooperative acquisition agreements for source materials.

In order to ensure that the library citation index operates efficiently, it may be necessary to establish a policy at each library participating in resource sharing arrangements requiring that credit be given to the library in any publication based on materials, published or unpublished, furnished by that library. Libraries would have an interest in establishing this policy to ensure that they are cited. Users of material obtained through interlibrary loan are notified of the identity of the lending library through the band placed around the book's cover or by rubber stamps or other indicia on photocopies. Since participating libraries are also heavy purchasers of citation index services, they can ensure that the indexing will be done.

A final remark about library citation indexes needs to be made. One often used means of determining use of collections is to keep a register of visitors to a collection. Libraries also maintain records of the destination of photocopies and materials sent out on interlibrary loan. These are output measures, and, as such, do not measure the amount of publication activity, the only tangible measure of research, that has originated from their collections. Furthermore, output measures are subject to distortion; a library administration might decide to ease up on restrictive policies to show its funding authorities that use has increased. Or they could place an attractive exhibit within the restricted area and collect the signatures of visitors in that fashion. In either case, there would be no demonstrable increase in research activity. It is to measure research activity that the statistics are kept. Far better would be to use the citation count.

Paradoxically, through competition among libraries, we can ensure cooperation and sharing of resources. Through that competition, we can help the scholar do research. The academic community or community of scholars will benefit greatly from competition among libraries. For what more could one wish?

Notes

1. The topic of resource sharing impinges closely on those of collections management, broadly construed, and the provision of intellectual access to materials to be shared. For that reason, much of what I discuss will be concerned with cataloging priorities as well as with what ought to be collected by libraries.

2. One can imagine a world in which a potential user would have to write every library to enquire if that library had the item wanted. Such a method was envisioned by Panizzi when he was denying the utility of printing the British Museum catalog. See Great Britain, Commissioners Appointed to Inquire into the Constitution and Government of the British Museum, *Report of the Commissioners Appointed to Inquire into the Constitution and Government of the British Museum, Together with Minutes of Evidence* (London: Her Majesty's Stationery Office, 1850). The problem is the amount of time a search would take.

3. This paper does not pretend to be an analysis of interlibrary loan traffic. Specifically, I have not surveyed the subject matter of materials shipped from one library to another. It is solely a set of reflections on my own experiences.

4. The history of Jewett's project has never before been fully recorded. Suffice it to say that one of the results of my investigation, "Charles Coffin Jewett (1816-1868): A Reappraisal" (forthcoming), is that Jewett got the idea of a national union catalog from a Frenchman, the Chevalier de la Garde de la Pailléterie, as early as 1845. In a letter he wrote to George Perkins Marsh in August 1854, shortly after his termination at the Smithsonian July 10, 1854, Jewett unequivocally states that the work on the stereotyping project and the union catalog was Henry's way of keeping Jewett so busy that he would not have time to make the Smithsonian a national library.

5. Joseph A. Borome, *Charles Coffin Jewett.* American Library Pioneers, VII. (Chicago: American Library Association, 1951).

6. Ibid., p. 174.

7. According to Section 108 of the 1976 Copyright Act, a copy of previously published material must become the property of the user.

8. It is not even clear how cautious a library should be about copyright matters relating to unpublished materials created prior to the middle of the nineteenth century. Although some librarians note that section 303 of the 1976 Copyright Act copyright protection is afforded for materials created prior to 1978 at least until 2003, and, under the proper circumstances until 2028, the real effect of the 1976 act was to eliminate the perpetual protection afforded to unpublished materials under the common law as provided in the 1909 Copyright Act. In either case, the descendants of the author have copyright in the material. But there is a substantial question as to the identity of the claimants when well over a century has passed since the creation of the material. Also, there is the very real question as to the damages available to a claimant when the material has lain unpublished for such a long time.

9. I owe this observation to Harriet Rebuldela, Head of the Acquisitions Department of the Library at the University of Colorado, Boulder, during a conversation in May, 1988. She should not be held responsible for the use I make of it. Even if exact editions of materials are not duplicated, the canonical works are.

10. Of course, it is possible that an outstanding undergraduate honors thesis could be written which would require access to material beyond the basic core.

11. See Charles R. McClure et al., *Planning and Role Setting for Public Libraries:*

A Manual of Options and Procedures (Chicago: American Library Association, 1987), especially page 28. The discussion of roles in general holds true for academic libraries as for public libraries.

12. One can conceive a library that sets out to obtain copies, at least in photographic form, of everything ever published, or ever collected in manuscript form. For all respects except those requiring physical or descriptive bibliography, this library would be a universal repository. Given the amount of uncataloged material in existence, the chances of success for this repository are distant. The so-called library without walls will founder on the problem of lack of intellectual access. It will also not be equivalent to the universal repository because of the lack of ready physical access, at least in the foreseeable future.

13. The printed *National Union Catalog* volumes, especially for pre-1956, are generally the only accessible location information for much early twentieth-century and nineteenth-century printed material. It is simply not found in OCLC or RLIN. Nor have the vast majority of entries in the *National Union Catalog of Manuscript Collections* been converted to OCLC or RLIN form.

14. Library K, on the other hand, is a rarity; it catalogs its manuscripts individually and has no more than a thirty-day queue. Living without an arrearage is possible.

15. The only real verification device has been found to be standard bibliographies of certain subject fields. Even this device rests on questionable assumptions:
    1. It is questionable whether any bibliography is truly exhaustive.
    2. Bibliographies take a long time to be compiled, and some fields develop differently through the years; their canons may change through time, thus vitiating claims made by a given bibliography.

16. Current minimal-level cataloging standards call for no greater detail in the subject approach than the first letter of the appropriate Library of Congress classification scheme to be applied to a call number. Subject headings, as well as subtitles, which often indicate subject content, are omitted in minimal-level cataloging.

17. Research Libraries Group. *RLG Shared Resources Manual*, 3rd ed. (Stanford, California, August 1987). Note also the same lack of mention of genealogical works in the American Library Association Interlibrary Loan Codes, available as American Library Association, Reference and Adult Services Division, Interlibrary Loan Committee, *Interlibrary Loan Codes, 1980;* International Federation of Library Association and Institutions, Section on Interlending. *International Lending Principles and Guidelines, 1978* (Chicago: American Library Association, 1981).

18. Ibid., p. 30.

19. Ibid., p. 31. Given this supposed problem, I found it surprising that it was quite often the case that materials for my project came from one of the temporary libraries of last resort.

20. I owe the idea of a citation index of libraries used to Joanne Marshall, of the University of Toronto, during a conference in August, 1988. She should not be blamed for the use I make of it, nor for the mechanism I suggest of implementing it.

CD-ROM Projects in Texas Consortia

Pamela A. Zager
formerly Assistant Acquisitions Librarian at
Lamar University Library
Beaumont, Texas
currently Head, Monographs Acquisitions
Iowa State University

Introduction

As societies become more information-dependent, library budgets easily can be exhausted. The impact is real, and our profession, which has always been characterized by the overriding tenet of accessibility to information, is in danger of becoming unable to fulfill that promise. Libraries are faced with the task of ensuring continued and improved information access. Yet it has become evident that the cost of providing traditional library services and collections will exceed the resources that individual institutions are able to commit. Advances in telecommunications and computing technologies have already changed the environment in which libraries operate. Today, there is an interim answer—increased consortia activity facilitated by the use of CD-ROM products, resulting in alternative methods for information delivery.

Resource Sharing

Five commonly acknowledged by-products of resource sharing are:
1. greater user access;
2. improved bibliographic control;
3. coordinated collection development;
4. an aid to preservation and conservation; and
5. increased technological applications.[1]

Information resources needed for study and research are not always available in a single library, particularly in times of economic uncertainty. A consortium arrangement allows users to access the collections and services of all of its member libraries. Libraries are faced with converting cataloging records into machine-readable form for use in whatever form of automation is being employed by the consortium. Programs are devised to coordinate subject analysis and development of each institution's collection. Consultants and workshops can be employed to assist member libraries in an area of pressing need—the preservation of library materials. Finally, as technology continues to develop and is applied in various ways in a consortium setting, user expectations elevate, and libraries begin to realize their true potential as information brokers.

There are certainly valid arguments for using more sophisticated means of information retrieval. Exposing students, faculty and the general clientele to a variety of automated information tools becomes a positive learning experience for all involved. Automation is correctly perceived as something which is done *for* the library user rather than *to* the user.

CD-ROM Union Catalogs

Optical disk technology is a relatively new medium recognized for improving library services. It functions in a viable, economical format with improved high speed search capabilities and high density storage.[2] Librarians are using this technology in virtually every aspect of library operations, from materials acquisition to cataloging to document delivery.

When optical disk technology was introduced in libraries and to the general market, the price was unaffordable for all but a few educational institutions. As prices fell, libraries saw this as an opportunity to facilitate library resource sharing. This relatively new development in resource sharing is a purposeful attempt to meet the objectives regarding information accessibility. Automation merely enhances cooperative activities which have long been in place. Microfiche catalogs, an early and common form of automation, have been replaced in many cases with more sophisticated technology. CD-ROM is the recommended vehicle over microfiche for several reasons:

1. most users do not like to handle and view microfiche because of its limited linear searching capabilities;
2. microfiche equipment cannot be used for other purposes, eliminating the power of the microcomputer to find information;
3. it prevents interaction by the user;
4. many states have established precedents of moving toward electronic catalogs; and
5. publishers have been moving toward compact laser technology.[3]

The positive aspects of automating collections are apparent with CD-ROM technology. Most notable is its large storage capacity. It is an affordable method for providing library services and has a low per copy replication cost for additional workstations, whether they are in-house or in another library. There are no telecommunications costs. It actually improves library services with its design for the end-user requiring minimal librarian intervention. It can utilize sophisticated search options. It is very durable, with only the laser touching the disk. CD-ROM can and does function as a backup catalog, and the database, once built, can migrate to newer and different technologies.

On the other hand, there are drawbacks to this alluring technology.

There is a lack of standardization regarding the types of equipment with which the software can operate. There is also a lack of compatibility between the search strategies used by each vendor. Like any technology, strategic management is required to handle the budgetary commitment. Service and production delays affect the turnaround time in the updating process. Remastering is a repetitive and expensive process. Finally, uncertainty about its longevity is the real risk involved in CD-ROM investment, as it is clearly an interim technology.

The Texas Experience

The mid-80s marked the first grant for use of optical disk technology in a Texas library. The Texas institutions which have participated in CD-ROM union catalog projects since then have had different reasons for using this technology, and they have often had different approaches to implementation. Several CD-ROM union catalog projects in Texas are already in place or in the planning stages:
1. the Association of Higher Education (AHE) project in North Texas coordinates four large libraries;
2. a Houston metroplex consortia, known as Houston Area Research Library Consortium (HARLiC) includes large academic libraries;
3. Brazoria County Library Network (BRAZNET), located in South Central Texas, includes both public and school libraries, all within the same county;
4. the South Texas Union Catalog (STUC) project encompasses many small and medium-sized libraries of all types spread over a wide geographic area in the Southern region of Texas;
5. South and East Texas Union Project (SETUP), is a proposed project to include multi-type libraries, with the exception of large research libraries, from Orange to Brownsville, Texas.

Texas has a number of union catalogs in different formats including microfiche, CD-ROM and online systems. For the purposes of this chapter my research has been to report the experiences of the four active resource sharing groups, as well as the plans for the one proposed project. While certain aspects of each consortium are shared, they all vary in terms of arrangements, products used, funding or accomplishments.

In the past, there has been an absence of one entity to provide strong leadership in the coordination of a statewide resource sharing plan for the automation of library collections. While the Texas State Library has initiated a variety of projects for 1989-93 to enhance resource sharing activities, in reality it has been individual libraries working within the framework of consortia which have made the difference. Geographic enormity and the sheer number of educational institutions in the state are obstacles in achieving one statewide CD-ROM union catalog. The emphasis instead has been on regional efforts. This is set forth in the *Automation and Resource Sharing Plan 1990-93* which states, "that resource sharing in Texas should be built on a foundation of local networks rather than a statewide database beyond that which we already have from participation in OCLC...." As required by law, the State Library has been the administrating body for grant funding of three of the union catalogs now being produced. Federal monies have been channeled through the State Library in an effort to meet information needs statewide.

Association of Higher Education (AHE)[4]

Since 1963, the organization now known as AHE has had a leadership role in Texas and the nation. Two groups, Inter-University Council of North Texas and TAGER Television Network, joined to form the Association for Higher Education of North Texas in 1980. The primary purpose of this not-for-profit corporation is to provide educational support services to the academic community and the private sector in the region. The network consists of nineteen public and private colleges and universities, nineteen private sector corporations, and two public libraries. With this membership diversity, information resources are integrated to strengthen the educational foundation of the area.

The Library Committee, a division of the AHE's Library Programs and Services Department, is committed to library programs, especially to resource sharing. In the 1960s, several services were implemented:
1. a teletype network to determine the ownership of specific library materials;
2. a courier service to transport resources;
3. courtesy cards for interlibrary borrowing.

In the 1970s, the Library Committee formed AMIGOS to bring cataloging resources to Texas and the Southwest, through the Online Computer Library Center (OCLC).

The AHE Library Committee's most recent accomplishment involved testing the use of optical disk technology as a format for a five library union catalog. Baylor University, Dallas County Community College District, Dallas Public Library, The University of North Texas, and The University of Texas at Arlington combined their records to create a union catalog pilot project. AMIGOS provided Library Corporation with databases on magnetic tape to use with the Bibliofile Intelligent Catalog product.

AHE received grant funding for this project from the Texas State Library and Archives Commission. Federal funds made available through the LSCA Title III totaled $128,934 for the grant year 1988. The purpose of this type of grant is to learn as much as possible about creating a public access catalog by using optical disk technology, specifically CD-ROM.

After an extensive evaluation period whereby numerous products and proposals were reviewed, AHE selected the Library Corporation's Intelligent Catalog. This software uses various components of expert systems, hypertext, syntax analysis, thesaurus substitution, and artificial intelligence. It automatically performs dictionary, key-word-in-context, or Boolean searches.

It is user friendly in the sense that the user need not qualify searches. Responding to natural language requests, the software determines the required path by the user's response to basic questions, and provides for an on-screen tutorial. Both headphones and a telephone receiver are available for the user to interact with voice responses from the programmed audio portion of the disk. Additional features include Save Item, Review Log, Make Notes, and Get Advice.

The pilot project catalog contains 1,078,753 bibliographic records of holdings for the five participating libraries, contained on two disks. The union catalog is expected to "expand the availability of resources in this region to education, business, industry, and public users alike. It will also strengthen existing collections and provide more efficient use of public funds in purchasing library collections." Each member library houses a workstation which is available to the public—twenty-three in all.

Some major obstacles became obvious during the grant progression. The MARC record, the standard for bibliographic access, varied with each library. When merging the database records, it was discovered that OCLC/MARC is not the same as NOTIS/MARC, VTLS/MARC, etc. The sheer magnitude of the project was underestimated and caused time constraints forcing AHE libraries to compromise various elements of the location display information.

From everyone's perspective, the learning experience was tremendous despite the problems and frustrations of the project. This was true for all the output organizations—AMIGOS, OCLC, Library Corporation, and AHE. The result was that each participant became better equipped to act as a resource person in building future catalogs. AMIGOS learned a great deal about how to build and merge data from different kinds of databases. Library Corporation simply had never built a database this large, and many of their capabilities were significantly enhanced. This even included the ability to respond to acts of nature, as during the project the Library Corporation building was struck by lightning, forcing the company to start from scratch.

AHE has always been a leader in Texas for using new technology, and is widely recognized in the nation for exercising a leadership role in this area. Even though AHE coordinates the project, the actual leadership comes from the librarians themselves. Overall, the project has been judged a success, and plans are already underway to include additional libraries in the union catalog.

Houston Area Research Library Consortium (HARLiC)[5]

Organized in 1978, HARLiC was created to share the resources of the major research libraries in the Houston area. With its widely diversified industrial and economic base, this library arrangement strives to serve both a highly skilled workforce, as well as delivering major funding to the area. It is governed by a Board of Directors consisting of the library directors of the member institutions. Committees appointed by the Board are active in developing and implementing the projects to further the goals of the consortium.

The eight member library groups of HARLiC are:

1. Houston Academy of Medicine–Texas Medical Center Library;
2. Texas Southern University;
3. University of Houston;
4. Houston Public Library;
5. Rice University;
6. University of Texas Medical Branch;
7. Prairie View A & M University; and
8. Texas A & M University.

All the libraries, with the exception of Rice University's Fondren Library, will contribute their holdings to the database for the CD-ROM union catalog for HARLiC.

The HARLiC card is an example of the many resource sharing services offered by the consortium benefiting researchers and students. Eligible patrons may use this card to access a plethora of collections and services. Other benefits include:

1. the special library collections and the subject area expertise by librarians to aid researchers;
2. the reciprocal borrowing privilege, directly or through interlibrary loan, at no charge;
3. the free courier service that delivers items between libraries; and
4. the cooperative collection development that ensures the book will remain in at least one library.

The consortium has now embarked on a CD-ROM union catalog that will facilitate the aforementioned services. To accommodate the approximately 2.1 bibliographic records, four half Hitachi CD-ROM drive equipment will be used as part of the MARCIVE capabilities. Initially, the CD-ROM union catalog grew out of an idea for a library specific backup catalog using optical disk technology. Many card catalogs were no longer being actively updated, and occasionally online systems go down. This project offers continued development of consortia resource sharing and cooperative collection development and, simultaneously, provides a desperately needed means of back-up.

The CD-ROM union catalog is expected to be a great success. Because the equipment required to run the catalog is defined generically, each library has the option of how many to purchase. It will save the user time and energy by enabling the catalog search process to include several million more items. Perhaps the biggest challenge will be to teach the concept of a union catalog to users who are, after all, accustomed to using only one catalog per library. Because the union catalog will not be integrated with other library functions such as circulation, acquisitions, etc., both extensive signage and bibliographic instruction will be necessary to promote the best usage. Each library has its own bibliographic instruction program and will expand it to include the concept of a CD-ROM union catalog.

After an LSCA Title III grant for a project to link online catalogs of the HARLiC libraries was rejected, the consortium sought funding from the newly created HEA Title II-D directly from the Department of Education. This two-year $100,000 grant was awarded to HARLiC in September 1988.

Brazoria County Library Network (BRAZNET)[6]

BRAZNET is a multi-type library consortium made up of school and public libraries in Brazoria County, Texas. BRAZNET's members are currently using laser disk technology to convert in-house existing shelflists into machine-readable form, thus creating a union catalog of their holdings on CD-ROM. This union catalog was installed in January of 1989 and has already experienced a new release. The network consists of libraries located in Angleton, Alvin, Brazoria, Clute, Freeport, Lake Jackson, Manvel, Pearland, Sweeny, and West Columbia. The school libraries involved are: Alvin High and Junior High, Angleton High, Brazosport High, Brazoswood High, Clute Intermediate, Freeport Intermediate, Harvey Junior High, Lake Jackson Intermediate, Manvel Junior High, and Pearland High School. The library collections range in size from 8,000 volumes to 63,000, totaling approximately 350,000 volumes.

A major stumbling block of the Brazoria County CD-ROM project was the fact that at the outset no library in the county had records in machine-readable format. Their project consisted of a grant to convert retrospectively to MARC format the records of 16 libraries to create a bibliographic utility using a CD-ROM format. A second grant the following year enabled the consortia to add five additional libraries to the network. Prior to requesting funds specifically for optical disk technology, several technologies were investigated, ranging from dial-in access to an online catalog to microfiche. Telecommunications costs, which would have involved services from four different telephone companies, were simply unfeasible. Microfilm records would have been more expensive than creating a database for 350,000 records.

A timely retrospective data conversion project set the stage for the CD-ROM catalog and it resulted in the automated holdings used in a test public catalog, the familiarization of staff to automation (i.e., a CD-ROM bibliographic product), and, most importantly, a means of implementing resource sharing.

CD-ROM was the most affordable method of conversion. General Research Corporation's Laserquest was selected as the source database due to its delivery of a 96% hit rate on samples from shelflists of school and public libraries in BRAZNET. Other databases proved to be more academic library oriented. With the use of Laserquest, BRAZNET members converted entire collections within a year, averaging approximately 50 records per hour. It should be noted that 8 clerks were hired for the data processing, none of whom had previous experience using a personal computer. After 6 hours of training and 8 hours of observation, each clerk worked 4 hours a day to improve accuracy. To facilitate the understanding of the MARC format, a handbook containing the fields used in BRAZNET cataloging was devised by the project coordinator. Each field selected was defined as well as the appropriate subfields. Examples were provided, and punctuation rules from AACRII were set forth. Within a few weeks, clerks had enough knowledge to make uncomplicated original entries.

Prior to the data conversion project, each library had only a catalog with their specific holdings. The lone exception was the main branch in Angleton which had a catalog of all libraries; however, it did not indicate at which branch location the material was available. With this system it was actually easier to find something in Houston than in a library only a few miles away. Patrons tend to think a book is unavailable in the entire system when it can't be found in a branch catalog.

Public school library collections were tested for overlap to determine whether networking could be expected to produce real benefits. Samples were taken from the schools and compared to the BSLS shelflist which revealed the average percent of unique titles to be 57.5%.

An LSCA Title III grant provided $119,775 for the BRAZNET CD-ROM union catalog. Brodart's Le Pac was selected for the actual catalog software. It provides refined and comprehensive searching with authors, titles, subjects, keyword, call number (Dewey in this case), and Boolean. It is designed to be forgiving of spelling errors as well.

Another interesting aspect of the BRAZNET consortium is their inclusion of eleven school libraries. Educators, students and parents have always had access to the public library system. With the establishment of the consortium and the implementation of the shared union catalog, the public librarians will be better prepared to help students and teachers with assignments and questions using the additional and special resources of education libraries. The one potential drawback is that school libraries are closed for the most part during the summer; however, as is apparent from interlibrary loan statistics, there are fewer questions relative to that material in the summer months.

Increased access will improve the value of the different special collections such as the large print book collection of over 800 books which are delivered to homebound residents, as well as the over 1000 Spanish language books and videos provided to the Spanish speaking community.

BRAZNET has current plans to expand to other school districts and a special library. In the future, BRAZNET intends to include all school and public libraries in the county.

South Texas Union Catalog (STUC)[7]

The STUC project is the cooperative effort and culmination of three consortia: PAISANO, Hidalgo County Library System and the Circuit Rider Health Information Service.

The PAISANO Consortium of Libraries was formed in 1985 and has provided the impetus for facilitating resource sharing through projects such as serials union list and a telefacsimile network for the transmission of interlibrary lending. The fourteen members consist of:

1. Bee County Junior College;
2. Corpus Christi State University;
3. Corpus Christi Public Library;
4. Del Mar College;
5. Laredo State University/Laredo Junior College;
6. McAllen Public Library;
7. Pan American University;
8. Texas A&I University;
9. Texas Southmost College;
10. Texas State Technical Institute-Harlingen;
11. Texas State Technical Institute-McAllen;
12. University of Texas Marine Institute at Port Aransas;
13. Victoria College/University of Houston-Victoria; and
14. Victoria Public Library.

Initially, they contacted only the OCLC libraries from Victoria south to Laredo and Brownsville and gained support for a union catalog by eleven libraries. A former director of VC/UHV wrote a grant to create an experimental union list of serials, and included a telefacsimile for interlibrary loan. The next year, continuations were added along with four new member libraries. Once implemented, the fifteen participating libraries' statistics increased dramatically, revealing that more of their information needs were being met within the consortium. Not every library used telefacsimile routinely; yet, for those that did, the delivery time was one day, and this type of delivery accounted for a fair percentage of interlibrary loan activity.

The Hidalgo County Library System was organized in 1972 and supports the sharing of resources in the county by operating a courier service with Pan American University. The members include nine public libraries and four high school libraries.

The Circuit Rider Health Information Services (CRHIS) was organized in 1982 to disseminate information to health professionals. A union catalog includes the holdings of the hospitals and part of the health science collection of the Victoria College/University of Houston-Victoria Library. A medical librarian headquartered in the VC/UHV Library provides literature searches, current awareness services, and document delivery. Membership consists of five medical libraries and VC/UHV.

PAISANO initiated a serials union list which ran for two years until a decision was reached to include monographic holdings in the form of a CD-ROM union catalog. At that time, the other two consortia, Hidalgo County and CRHIS, were brought in to form STUC. An LSCA Title III grant was approved. Fortunately, the cost of CD-ROM has declined so substantially that STUC was able to cover not only the catalog production but equipment as well. Some libraries, mostly hospital and public, did not have records in machine-readable format. The following year, a matching grant from the Meadow Foundation was received enabling libraries to convert and add records to the second edition of the catalog. One reason application to the Meadow Foundation was so successful was the fact that they have previously funded southwest Texas projects aimed at improving information delivery to the Hispanic population.

In August of 1989, thirty-two libraries received the Brodart produced catalog, containing approximately 750,000 records. Some libraries plan to use the union catalog for an opac, ILL backup, and public service tool. The union catalog will be the first resource consulted for interlibrary loan, and will enable the libraries to fill a greater portion of interlibrary needs from regional sources. Since only one third of the libraries in the South Texas Union Catalog project have direct access to an OCLC terminal, the project will ensure equal and timely access to records and materials to all participating members. The development of Brodart's ILL function has been delayed. Future plans will enable the stations to be connected through an electronic mail network, which will make possible direct transmission of interlibrary loan requests.

South and East Texas Union Project (SETUP)[8]

The one project that will come closer to a statewide project than any of the others is the proposed consortium SETUP. Using Brodart, the union catalog will encompass two regional library systems and six consortia, including the East Texas Consortium, BRAZNET and STUC. This project will constitute the most cooperative effort to date in Texas. The two projects mentioned earlier, STUC and BRAZNET, had already selected Brodart's Le Pac catalog. The purpose of SETUP is to combine the two catalogs to form one union catalog, and to include in it additional members such as the East Texas Consortium, the Council of Academic Libraries and Learning Resource Centers, various public libraries in the Houston area library system, and one South Texas system (Harlingen Public) which was not originally included in the STUC project.

It should be noted that the SETUP project is contingent on grant funding. It typifies the sort of resource sharing envisioned by the Texas State Library. The unique feature of the project will be the creation of three subregional ILL networks—Victoria, Lamar and UH–Clear Lake. While each ILL server will poll only the libraries in its sub-region, it will be able to route requests to any library in the union catalog. Restricting the polling to subregions will minimize the costs of communications for each of the server centers.

SETUP hopes to include nearly every academic library from Orange to Brownsville, with the exception of large research libraries. Increased availability of information in these libraries, especially the small public and community college libraries, will be greatly improved.

Commonalities

While all of these projects have varied in some identifiable ways, the shared primary objectives of the CD-ROM projects have been to provide better access to collections as a whole, and to increase consortia activity.

The common purposes of using CD-ROM technology include:

1. to research and demonstrate the feasibility of creating an optical disk bibliographic database with combined holdings;
2. to distribute the catalog to consortia libraries, in some cases even if their holdings are not included;
3. to merge machine-readable MARC bibliographic records of participating institutions into a central machine-readable database;
4. to match and purge duplicate records while including institutional holdings symbols in the union catalog;
5. to encourage collaborative efforts between libraries by increasing the effectiveness of the consortium's membership;
6. to provide increased access to collections of research and instructional learning resources to users throughout a community or geographic location;
7. to establish a user friendly environment whereby search strategy software facilitates search capabilities with Boolean and keyword combinations; and
8. to make effective use of the catalog as a tool for cooperative collection development.[9]

One overriding concern of all the project managers is the communication aspect between library and vendor. The vendor has a product to sell, and the librarian has a specific public service agenda for that product. It is all too easy to get bogged down in the nitty gritty details of trying to customize the product for a particular library. Vendor communication is especially a concern when the technology is new. With user groups, the dialogue will improve and become more focused on important problems such as the standardization of products and price structuring.

With the CD-ROM database investment, it is necessary to consider criteria frequently used to assist in the selection, purchase and management of CD-ROM:

1. Marketplace;
2. Hardware trends;
3. Software trends;
4. Product availability;
5. Product evaluation;
6. Purpose;
7. Goals;
8. Environment;
9. Scheduling;
10. Compatibility;

11. Current costs;
12. Future costs;
13. Completeness;
14. Reliability;
15. Flexibility;
16. Ease of use;
17. Documentation; and
18. Service.[10]

Of these criteria, costs are invariably the major consideration, including the equipment (hardware and software), the processing fees, which include deduping, premastering, mastering, updating, additional copies, and in some cases, cross references, authority control, and subscriptions or service fees.

CD-ROM projects such as those outlined in this chapter are playing an essential role in resource sharing in Texas. While it is recognized that they are only an interim solution to the problem, they are nonetheless filling a real need on a day-to-day basis in an uncertain and demanding economic state environment.

Notes

1. Personal interview with Katherine Pearson Jaycoe, Director, Library Programs and Services, Association for Higher Education of North Texas, 21 July 1989.
2. Andre, Pamela Q.J. "Optical Disc Applications in Libraries," *Library Trends* 37, no. 3 (1989): 326.
3. Epler, Doris M. "Networking in Pennsylvania: Technology and the School Library Media Center," *Library Trends* 37, no. 1 (1988): 47.
4. Jaycoe, loc. cit.
5. Personal interview with Linda Thompson, Assistant Director for Bibliographic Services, University of Houston, 18 August 1989.
6. Personal interview with Steve Brown, Director of Brazoria County Library System, 18 July 1989.
7. Personal interview with Dr. S. Joe McCord, Director of Library Services, Lamar University, 31 May 1989.
8. Ibid.
9. Jaycoe, loc. cit.
10. Cochenour, John and Patricia Weaver "CD-ROM: Practical Considerations for Libraries," *Journal of Library Administration* 9, no. 3 (1988): 62-63.

The Illinois Telefacsimile Network

Carolyn Grangaard Smith
Networking Consultant
Illinois State Library
Springfield, Illinois

Resource sharing and equal access to information are fundamental commitments of Illinois libraries. These libraries are continually searching for new methods of meeting the information demands of their patrons. The library patron of today can be an ubiquitous user of information. The Illinois Library and Information Network (ILLINET) patron has become accustomed to the almost instantaneous access to information available through a myriad of on-line and off-line sources. Time, energy, and money are essential factors to consider in any service and libraries are facing a great challenge in getting information to the patron in an efficiently expedient manner. Therefore, in an effort to meet the challenge of expedient exchange of information, libraries in Illinois tested an alternative to the traditional document and information delivery systems. The telefacsimile network of ILLINET was created.

History of Telefacsimile Transmission

Telefacsimile transmission, better known as fax, is the ability to send and receive hard copy images over telephone lines. The technology has been in existence for many years. The basic principles of facsimile transmission were set forth by a Scottish clockmaker and inventor, Alexander Bain. In 1843, he developed a device which could send an electric current over wires and reproduce the motion of a pendulum. This was the beginning of facsimile.

The technology and equipment have grown more sophisticated over the decades since Mr. Bain's invention, but the basics of the technology remains the same. A telefacsimile machine operates on the concept of scanning an original copy and distinguishing between black and white areas on the page. The more typical telefacsimile machine scans a document one separate page at a time. The machine is capable of scanning and transmitting printed pages, handwritten copy, pictures, and drawings. Currently, fax machines can scan directly from a bound book or transmit from a computer terminal. The information scanned is translated into electrical pulses, with each pulse varying in intensity based on the image scanned. These pulses are then transmitted over telephone lines to a receiving machine. This machine translates the electric pulses back into dots which reproduce the original image. This image will be printed on paper, correct in the position and shading. Thus, the result is a nearly instantaneous transmission of information from one location to another.

Facsimile transmission has been in use for many years. The government, the military, and the press were early users of this technology. Libraries began experimenting with telefacsimile in the 1960s. During this decade, the Group I machine was the standard in fax technology. It was not uncommon for a Group I machine to take up to six minutes in transmitting a single page. Initially this new found mode of communication was not widely accepted by librarians. Libraries felt the technology was impractical; transmission was slow, copies were typically low quality, and the equipment was cumbersome, unreliable, and expensive.

Technology continued to improve and the Group II machine was introduced in the mid 1970s. Although this machine reduced the transmission rate to three minutes per page, fax still did not gain widespread acceptance in the library community, primarily because it was considered too slow and cumbersome. As a result, fax was typically used to transmit interlibrary loan requests. The actual document was still delivered by conventional methods.

It wasn't until the advent of the Group III machine in the early 1980s that the technology answered the need of libraries for a rapid, efficient, and cost-effective means of information and document delivery. The Group III machine is compact and easily installed into any standard phone jack. It is able to transmit a page in under one minute and copy resolution and quality is greatly improved. The relatively low cost of a Group III machine makes it feasible equipment for libraries with even the smallest of budgets.

ILLINET

With the advent of the Group III machine, Illinois libraries began to look at the feasibility of a fax network.

Interlibrary cooperation has long been a way of life for Illinois libraries. The Illinois Library and Information Network (ILLINET) is the voluntary working partnership of all types of libraries throughout the state. It is the framework supporting networking activities which take place amongst Illinois libraries. Currently, two thousand four hundred and twenty-one multitype libraries are participating members of ILLINET.

The Illinois State Library monitors funding of ILLINET. Eighteen regional library systems serve as the traditional hubs of ILLINET and the initial contact points for Illinois school, academic, public and special libraries. Through their membership in ILLINET, each member library has access to an expanded universe of unique, varied, and readily available resources. In addition to the regional system, there are seven designated Research and Reference Centers which handle interlibrary loan and information requests. Resource sharing is the joint commitment of every member of ILLINET.

Resource sharing is enhanced in Illinois by a number of major components of ILLINET. The Illinois State Library brokers OCLC services to Illinois libraries through ILLINET/OCLC. Currently, there are over three hundred libraries which are participating members in the ILLINET/OCLC network. A subsystem of OCLC which is unique to Illinois is Serials of Illinois Libraries Online (SILO). SILO is the most inclusive multitype, online union list of periodical holdings in Illinois libraries. Over 600 libraries are currently participating and have access to nearly 300,000 OCLC Serial Control Subsystem local data records.

ILLINET Online (IO) is a computer based library network which allows access to the collections of over eight hundred Illinois libraries. Through computer lines, any one in the state has immediate access to information regarding the holdings of these participating libraries. IO's two linked components, LCS (Library Computer Service) and FBR (Full Bibliographic Record), provide libraries with circulation, interlibrary loan, and catalog support services.

A final major component of ILLINET is the Intersystem Library Delivery Service (ILDS), funded and monitored by the Illinois State Library. ILDS delivers materials which have been requested through interlibrary loan. The system provides 24-hour delivery to over 2,000 direct drop-off points throughout the state.

Libraries in ILLINET use these data bases, union lists, and delivery services to locate and deliver materials which answer the information needs of library patrons around the state.

Libraries in Illinois have maintained a national leadership role in multitype library networking and resource sharing. In their commitment to this role, members of ILLINET are continually seeking methods which better utilize existing resources and deliver information more expeditiously. With the improvements in telefacsimile technology, it appears that fax could become a viable complement to the existing delivery service.

Illinois Fax Experiment

Illinois began its experiment with fax in 1983. At that time, seven libraries in Western Illinois which had a tradition of resource sharing, submitted a proposal to the Illinois State Library outlining a project which would improve document delivery amongst multitype libraries using facsimile transmission. These libraries realized that resource sharing is greatly facilitated when bibliographic access and systems of delivery are prompt. Any enhancement of the delivery system which would allow rapid same-day delivery of information would increase client satisfaction. The library would be able to directly contact the source holding the desired information and receive the information back in a most efficient manner. No longer would these libraries be limited to search and borrowing strategies based on the routes of a delivery system.

The Illinois State Library has had a long commitment to improving the equitability of access to information for its citizens. Programs such as the Intersystem Library Delivery Service (ILDS) are proof of dedication to the idea that both the smallest rural area as well as the largest metropolitan are entitled to an efficient delivery service. When these libraries approached the State Library with the fax project, it saw the potential for a viable complement to the standard delivery system which was already in place. The project was funded through a Library Services and Construction Act (LSCA) Title III grant. The ILLINET telefacsimile network was born.

The seven institutions which were members of this infant network warrant mention for their farsighted efforts in developing the project. The original participants were: Carl Sandburg College, Galesburg Public Library, St. Mary's Hospital and Galesburg College, Western Illinois Library System, Monmouth College, and Western Illinois University. Margaret A. Wainer, who was the Assistant Dean of Learning Resources Services at Carl Sandburg College, was the director of this original project.

During the first year of the project, these seven libraries experimented with various aspects of fax service, including transmission of interlibrary loan requests and the transmission of full documents. Statistics were kept in the areas of requests received and sent, turnaround time, cost per transmission, and time and cost comparisons between various types of delivery methods. These statistics showed that fax transmission was a viable alternative to traditional delivery methods. Turnaround time clearly demonstrated that fax was the most expedient method by which to send requests and deliver documents. Facsimile costs, although slightly higher than traditional delivery methods, were judged acceptable, considering the rapidity with which a document could be placed into the hands of a patron.

Foremost in the conclusion of the project was patron satisfaction. The final report stated "Fax created a level of expectation and enthusiasm among patrons regarding information services prompting a redefinition of services and service levels..."

Based on the success of the first year, the Illinois State Library funded an expanded project the following year. During this second year of funding, the infant fax network in Illinois grew to twenty-two multitype libraries including the Illinois Research and Reference Center (IRRC) at the University of Illinois.

The four permanent Research and Reference Centers and the specially designated Special Resource Centers are an integral part of the interlibrary loan network in Illinois. These centers handle the information and author/title requests that cannot be filled on the local or system level. The second year project proposed to test the feasibility of fax technology at the Research and Reference Centers in ILLINET. Fax, along with OCLC, mail, and the LCS component of ILLINET Online, was tested as a method for transmitting interlibrary loan requests. The method proved successful and plans were made to install telefacsimile equipment in the remaining Research and Reference Centers in Illinois.

Expansion to Health Science Libraries

By the end of the second year of the project, the fax network had expanded to nearly 30 machines. The Illinois State Library funded the grant for a third year through LSCA Title III monies, with the emphasis being shifted to the area of health-science information and resources.

Testing had shown the Illinois State Library that the largest category of unfilled information requests amongst ILLINET libraries was in the subject area of health science. It was anticipated that by extending the fax network to include selected medical schools and health-science libraries, access to health-science resources would be expanded and the number of unfilled requests lowered substantially.

The Illinois State Library, working closely with the Greater Midwest Regional Medical Library Network (GMRMLN), chose 27 system libraries, medical schools, and health science libraries as participants in the third year of the project. Fax equipment was also installed in the remaining Research and Reference Centers in ILLINET. The fax network had now grown to over 75 institutions.

For the health-science libraries, use of the fax system was limited to the transmission of requests. The exception to this was the delivery of a document in response to an URGENT or RUSH request. As agreed upon by participants, URGENT requests were for emergencies of a "life or death" nature and required a response within four hours. RUSH requests received an answer within 24 hours.

The inclusion of these medical resources in the fax network proved its value by cutting unfilled health-science information requests by more than 7 percent at the close of the grant year. This initial three year project was the basis of the fax network in Illinois. This pilot program proved to the library community in the state that telefacsimile transmission was a viable complement to traditional delivery methods. The technology was cost effective, simple to use, efficient, and widely accepted by both librarians and patrons.

Further Expansion of the Network

The potential of the fax network was just beginning to be realized. Based on the positive results of the initial project, the Illinois State Library committed itself to the further expansion and development of the fax network. Fax technology had proven itself valuable as an alternative to traditional document delivery methods and as an acceptable means of transmitting interlibrary loan requests. The Illinois State Library was now committed to exploring the possibility of utilizing fax technology in such innovative projects as: developing resource sharing on a regional basis, conducting coordinated collection development programs, and assisting remote rural libraries gain more equitable access to other resources.

In the early stages of the development of the network, the strategy of the Illinois State Library was to fund projects which would provide the basis of the network. With early LSCA projects, the emphasis was on equipment purchase and telecommunication costs. The idea was to aid libraries in purchasing the equipment which was necessary to build the foundations of the network. The State Library stipulated that any equipment purchased through grant funds must meet Group III specifications and be compatible with the Group II technology. However, the Library avoided recommending any particular make or model of telefacsimile equipment. This would allow the individual library the flexibility of choosing equipment which would meet its specific local needs.

As the network expanded, the State Library shifted some of its funding emphasis away from the basic "equipment purchase" grant. Projects which used fax technology in innovative programs were funded such as the "Multitype Interlibrary Loan PC/Fax Interface Program", funded in 1988-1989. In this project, nineteen multitype libraries investigated PC/Fax interface technology. During the course of the grant, interlibrary loan requests were generated on a PC and then transmitted via phone lines to a receiving fax machine which would print a hard copy of the request. A second part of the project analyzed the feasibility of scanning an article by fax and transmitting it to a receiving PC where it was stored on disk or printed. Some problems were encountered during the project. Participants agreed that the technology of the PC/Fax board had not reached the stage of development necessary for the easy and efficient PC/Fax interface needed for interlibrary loan transactions.

The Illinois State Library has recommended that fax be tied to other projects in the state. Excellent examples of this are the number of mini-consortia which have developed around shared resources through the OCLC/SILO project. As stated earlier, SILO is the union list of periodical holdings of ILLINET member libraries. Through SILO, libraries have immediate access to information regarding the periodical holdings of other libraries. By using fax technology, requests for articles and the delivery of the desired document can be accomplished in minimal turnaround time.

By the beginning of fiscal year 1989, the Illinois State Library and the Illinois State Library Advisory Council (ISLAC) determined that the fax network was well established in Illinois. Through LSCA projects and the ever-growing number of libraries who purchased fax equipment with their own resources, the fax network had grown to over 600 institutions. As a final incentive to libraries, the State Library offered matching grants to libraries for the purchase of fax equipment. Through these Title I and Title III grants, over 200 libraries added fax equipment to their facilities. Again, the individual applicants were allowed flexibility in choosing their equipment. The State Library asked only that the machines be Group III, be housed in the library, and be able to receive transmissions twenty-four hours a day.

Fax in Interlibrary Loan

The current status of the ILLINET fax network stands at over 900 participating libraries. Heaviest use of the fax network continues to be the area of interlibrary loans. Libraries within ILLINET use the technology to fax interlibrary loan requests, transmitting requests directly to the holding library, and thus circumventing the more traditional hierarchical lending routes. Additionally, an increasing number of libraries are also using fax technology to deliver the requested materials. Length of article, "needed-by" dates, and costs are all factors which are taken into consideration before transmitting the document.

The fax network has changed the borrowing patterns of libraries in ILLINET. Statistics indicate that borrowing is shifting to a horizontal level (i.e.: intrasystem local library to library and intersystem local library to library) rather than adhering to the traditional borrowing strategies, (i.e.: local library to system headquarters to Research and Reference Center). Libraries are more readily requesting materials directly from a holding library, having discovered that patron satisfaction is greatly increased through the one-day delivery of information available via fax.

Fax technology has become an integral part of the every day operation of the Research and Reference Centers throughout the state. These centers receive thousands of interlibrary loan requests monthly via fax. The requests which are handled by the Research and Reference Centers normally arrive through the hierarchical routes, coming from system headquarters or in some instances, individual libraries. However, the fax network has altered the way in which the Research and Reference Centers respond to these requests. Whenever possible, these centers will respond by sending a document via fax directly to the requesting library. The Research & Reference Center at the University of Illinois at Urbana also utilizes fax to send negative responses to interlibrary loan requests. With the prompt receipt of a negative response, the borrowing library can immediately try other search strategies to obtain the materials requested by a patron.

Others Uses of Fax

The library community in Illinois has discovered that fax technology is not only limited to interlibrary loan. Fax technology is being used to facilitate reference service. Many reference materials are extremely expensive and it is virtually impossible for one library to hold every needed reference title in its collection. Through the fax network, libraries are cooperating in the coordinated development and use of these reference materials. The fax network allows one library to almost instantaneously request and receive needed information from reference materials held by a cooperating fellow library.

ILLINET libraries have experienced the growth of reference service direct via fax from patrons' homes or offices. Libraries receive reference questions directly from a patron through a traditional method, such as the telephone. The library can then respond by sending the requested information or document directly to the patron via telefacsimile transmission. Thus, the formal fax network amongst ILLINET libraries is informally extended to include the patron at home or in the office.

Fax Protocols

The ILLINET fax network, with its many applications, has developed through the cooperative spirit of participating libraries. Urged by the Illinois State Library and supported by funding for equipment and innovative projects, the network nonetheless was the result of grass-roots support for the technology.

There had been no attempt by the State Library to develop formal protocols and policies while the network was in its developmental stages. Not wishing to impede the development of the network, the State Library offered guidance and parameters for the purchase and use of equipment only. This "hands-off" attitude was instrumental in the success of the network's development. The lack of formal protocols and policies encouraged cooperative efforts between libraries. These libraries were free to develop resource sharing schemes based on their unique situations, taking into account the needs and requirements of their individual institutions and patrons.

Some protocols and policies have been developed amongst defined groups of libraries. In most fax projects, protocols were developed as guidelines for participants. Due to the very nature of the majority of their information requests, libraries in the Greater Midwest Regional Medical Library Network (GMRMLN) adhere to a set of guidelines for fax transmission. A number of the multitype library systems in Illinois have also developed protocols for the interstate use of fax. The Illinois Interlibrary Loan Code, formally adopted by the state in 1988, covers fax transmission by defining it as a form of specialized delivery. But none of these established protocols address transmission outside of their particular interest groups. They rarely address the issues which arise when looking at fax transmission between different types of libraries, across system boundaries, etc.

With the ILLINET fax network well established in Illinois, the library community has indicated that now is the time to explore the feasibility of establishing fax protocols and policies on a state-wide basis. In response to the library community, the Illinois State Library and the Research and Reference Center Advisory Committee sponsored the ILLINET Fax Conference in September of 1989. Over 150 librarians came together to voice their concerns and opinions about the current needs and future demands of fax technology in libraries. As a result of this conference, the State Library has appointed a Task Force to formulate protocols and policies in regard to fax transmission among ILLINET libraries. These guidelines will interrelate and complement both the Illinois Interlibrary Code and the national guidelines being developed by the Reference and Adult Services Division of the American Library Association. These protocols will provide minimal guidance and will strive to ensure the continued smooth operations of the fax network as it grows and expands. The promotion of resource sharing among network participants will be the major objective of the protocols.

Continued Commitment to Fax

The continued commitment to the fax network by ILLINET libraries and the Illinois State Library has been evidenced in many forms. In 1988, the Northern Illinois Learning Resources Cooperative, a consortium of community college and academic libraries in Illinois, conducted a study which resulted in "A Functional Plan for an Illinois Library Telecommunications Network." This plan outlines the requirements for a statewide electronic network which would provide for the transmission of high-quality voice, data, and video signals amongst libraries in Illinois.

The Illinois State Library publishes the "ILLINET Directory of Library Telefacsimile Sites in Illinois." The primary purpose of the directory is to facilitate the sharing of information resources by Illinois libraries. The publication, updated yearly, lists the participating libraries in the ILLINET fax network, providing address, name of contact person, telephone and fax numbers.

Conclusion

The ILLINET fax network has been an overwhelming success. The experiment began in 1983 with seven initial participants. In 1989, the network stands at over 900 participants and is still expanding. The network was developed with a great deal of financial support and encouragement by the Illinois State Library. But controls and guidelines were kept at a minimum so as not to inhibit the use of the network, nor to intimidate the new user of the technology.

In retrospect, very few problems were encountered during the development of the network. Those problems which did arise were usually in the area of equipment. As the technology improved, these problems were eliminated.

With the network now firmly established, the support by the Illinois State Library will shift. There is no longer a need to provide support for the purchase of the equipment to build the network. Emphasis will shift to support the technology as it is used to promote resource sharing, urge coordinated collection development, and provide equitable access to information. Protocols and policies will be developed to assist the continued smooth operation of the expanding network. The potential of the fax network is overwhelming.

Yet as priorities change and the network expands, the fundamental premise of the network remains the same, to provide a feasible complement to traditional delivery methods which will enhance the conveyance of needed information into the hands of a library user.

METRO Collection Inventory Project: A Conspectus Case Study

Suzanne Fedunok
Assistant Director for Resource Development
Columbia University, NY
for the METRO Collection Inventory Project Task Force

A donor called the METRO office recently because he wanted to donate his extensive collection on photography to an appropriate library in the New York City area, and as a newcomer to the city he did not know which libraries had good collections on this subject. METRO was quickly able to provide him with a list of those libraries with research level collections. He indicated he would also like to make a financial contribution to one of these libraries.

A graduate student at the City University of New York needed help compiling a guide on English and American literature collections in the New York City area for new students. He got in touch with METRO for a list of libraries in the city with good collections and for advice on how to describe library holdings. METRO gave him information, and the guide is such a success it has been reprinted.

At a reception to welcome the incoming president of a local college, the librarian was able to give a detailed on-the-spot analysis of the strengths and weaknesses of their seventeenth century French literature collection because she had just completed a collection assessment for METRO. The college president was very impressed.

Those are a few examples of how the METRO Collection Inventory Project is benefiting libraries and clients in the the metropolitan New York City area. This chapter gives an account of the precursors and genesis of the METRO project and a detailed history of the project to date.

I. Background

Alaska, New York, Illinois, and Minnesota have evolved multi-type library consortia that include school libraries. The New York Metropolitan Reference and Research Library Agency, commonly called "METRO," is an organization of 230 institutional members forming a regional, multi-type library information network across metropolitan New York cities. Library members include public libraries, special libraries of all sizes, school libraries, small, medium and large academic libraries, and research libraries. Now in its twenty-fifth year, its programs are structured around collection development, bibliographic control, bibliographic access, lending and direct access, reference, brokered services, professional support, and information exchange. The goal of all METRO activities is to expand the services member libraries can offer their users.

Ongoing resource sharing activities include the creation and maintenance of a Library Services and Construction Act-funded union list of serials, group discounts on library materials purchases, administration of applications for New York State Coordinated Collection Development Aid, and the development of a coordinated collection development plan for all participants. The METRO Collection Inventory Project is a creation of the Resources Development Committee of METRO. The Resources Development Committee appoints a task force of eight members each year to plan and direct the inventory project. METRO provides a staff liaison person, and clerical and database support. The parent committee also oversees a cooperative film acquisitions program, a government documents discussion group, and a cooperative acquisitions program for expensive items.

In order to understand the background and potential of the METRO Collection Inventory Project for resource sharing, it is useful to know something of its national and regional forerunners. METRO sees its program not as an isolated effort but as part of a growing national, even international, movement to use a common instrument and a common language to define and record collection strengths. From the assessments, information is gathered to inform the consortium's resource sharing activities. As the momentum has grown, the various projects have borrowed from and built upon each other. Libraries and consortia beginning collection assessment projects today can easily take advantage of the considerable amount of documentation available in the literature and in the notebooks and training materials prepared by their predecessors. Most of Section I (below) and part of Section II are taken mainly from prepared remarks given at a panel called "Know Your Collections: Assessing for Sharing" given by METRO Collection Inventory Project Task Force members Patricia Young (City University of New York), Lynn Mullins (Rutgers), Joan Grant (New York University), Rhonna Goodman (METRO), and Susan Vaughn (Brooklyn College) at the 94th Conference of the New York Library Association at Lake Placid in October, 1987.[1]

Research Libraries Group

It is appropriate to begin a history of the current collection assessment projects with a discussion of the work done by the Research Libraries Group (RLG). RLG is a consortium of major research libraries which formed a partnership to find cooperative ways of addressing the challenges presented by sharing and preserving resources. Although there is no exact chronological progression from one project to another, the strong influence of the RLG experience can be seen in a number of the other programs. The background is covered in an article by Nancy E. Gwinn and Paul Mosher entitled "Coordinating Collection Development: The RLG conspectus."[2] In 1980, the program committee for RLG's Collection Management and Development Committee (CMDC) voted to develop a collection development policy statement for the consortium with the ultimate objective of developing an "eventual national research resource collection" held by its members and the Library of Congress. Paul Mosher, then collection development officer at Stanford and co-chair of CMDC, wrote the proposal to guide the project. His report became the basis for the RLG conspectus, the instrument used by RLG to record and collate detailed information about its members' collections.

Conspectus

The conspectus is a detailed listing of subjects based on the Library of Congress classification system. In choosing LC for the format of the conspectus, the CMDC acknowledged that while the LC system is imperfect and not even universally used, it is the best system in existence for describing collections. The group collection assessment project depends on having a common framework and the LC classification is as close as libraries come to a universal language. While the approach in the conspectus to interdisciplinary fields and area studies has changed somewhat over the years, basically the document is arranged in twenty-four divisions by LC classification, with almost 500 sections divided into a grand total of over 6,000 subjects. Libraries rate both current and retrospective holdings in each subject according to a 0 (out of scope) to 5 (comprehensive) scale. The conspectus is available via RLIN in an interactive online database, so that areas not juxtaposed in LC can be pulled together for an area such as medieval and renaissance studies. Online the conspectus can also be sorted by any grouping of the participating libraries. This feature facilitates cooperative collection development activities in regional groups.

Benchmarks have been developed for a number of subjects to help libraries choose the appropriate collection level. These supplementary guidelines show the percentage of materials a collection should contain in order to be rated at a certain level. For instance, the supplemental guidelines for the Medical and Health-Science conspectus state that a level three collection will have at least 25% of the English language titles indexed in *Index Medicus* in addition to major reference tools, significant indexing and abstracting services, and a broad selection of major textbooks, monographs, and government documents.

The collection assessment data submitted by the libraries is analyzed by the CMDC Conspectus Subcommittee. That group identifies those subjects that are collected at a research level by two or fewer members. These subjects are considered "endangered." The subcommittee first considers whether or not a research collection within the membership is necessary. If it is, they may ask a library to accept a "primary collecting responsibility" (PCR) for that subject by maintaining their collection at the 4 or 5 level, or by upgrading from a lower to a higher level. Accepting PCR responsibility is always voluntary; the intention is not to dictate local policy.

Verification studies are another feature of conspectus maintenance. They are random samples of standard bibliographies searched by the participants as a test to see if the collection level codes have been applied consistently and well. Results of the searching are compared to see if, for instance, the libraries who rated their collections at level three had similar coverage of the subject. The results show that libraries were using the codes consistently, and, if anything, have tended to undervalue their collections.

North American Collections Inventory Project (NACIP)

In 1981, a task force of the Association of Research Libraries (ARL) concluded that an inventory of collection strengths was essential for cooperative collection development, and that the RLG conspectus was an appropriate tool to use for that purpose. Since there is considerable overlap in membership between RLG and ARL, a good many members were already well involved in this effort. In 1981-82, these assumptions were tested by five non-RLG libraries. The conclusion of the test was that ARL should proceed with the conspectus document, but that there was need for detailed instructions, training, and documentation. Three Indiana universities began the project in the pilot phase, and it was expanded to include all interested ARL libraries. Now the effort is international, with the participation including the Scottish National Libraries, major research libraries in the United Kingdom, and libraries in Sweden.

Canadian Association of Research Libraries

ARL has worked very closely with the Canadian Association of Research Libraries known as CARL. That organization is developing a database for a Canadian inventory of research collections. CARL has adapted the NACIP materials for such things as expansions for Canadian history and literature. They have set up six regional working groups to coordinate the assessments and provide support systems and an opportunity for peer review.

Alaska

A similar, yet very different, effort got under way in Alaska in 1982. The objective of analyzing strengths for purposes of resource sharing was the same, but the libraries involved differed in size and type. This project, which was funded by grants from the state library, included academic, public, special and school libraries. Dennis Stephens, describing Alaska as a resource-poor state, has said that the collections of the state, taken as a whole, would make one medium-sized university research collection.

The emphases in the Alaska program were to train librarians for collection development policy formulation and collection assessment, to coordinate efforts with projects outside of the state, and to develop the Alaska conspectus. The project was designed with the help of Paul Mosher, who went to Alaska in 1982 to serve as a consultant. He recommended that they write standardized collection development policies, survey their holdings, and prepare individual conspectus analyses for each collection, conduct collection development institutes, and set up a cooperative purchase program.

Pacific Northwest

The Alaska experience served as a model that was further refined for use in a regional effort for the Pacific Northwest. This project was begun by LIRN (Library and Information Resources for the Northwest), funded by the Fred Meyer Charitable Trust of Portland, Oregon. In 1984, a LIRN Resource Assessment Group began work. It is composed of librarians from universities, community colleges, corporations, state colleges, and public libraries. The states included in this effort are Alaska, Idaho, Montana, Oregon, and Washington. What is most interesting about the Pacific Northwest experience is the way they have built upon the RLG. Alaska has worked to organize a project that is feasibile and productive for libraries of various sizes and types. The assessment approach they use is flexible to accommodate the wide range of libraries and information resources in the Pacific Northwest. Libraries can choose among three levels of detail, and collections may be assessed at one or any combination of levels.

Each level is an increasingly detailed breakdown of Library of Congress classification (with Dewey conversions) for twenty-four major divisions. For smaller libraries and general collections, the twenty-four divisions may be most appropriate. For libraries with larger collections, the 489 categories of the next level, which is comparable with the National Shelflist Count, may be more useful. Libraries with comprehensive or research orientations or special libraries may need the full 6,000 subjects of the ARL/RLG conspectus project. In some cases, a combination of these levels may be best— using the detailed subjects for one or two strong subject areas and the more general categories or divisions for others. The training done by the LIRN project is also notable. During a four-day workshop, 28 regional resource people were trained. Then those people returned to their home states and conducted twelve two-day training workshops to which each library was invited to send a representative.

New York

In 1981, the New York State legislature appropriated 1.3 million dollars to be distributed through the state's regional multi-type library agencies, of which METRO is one, to academic libraries of all sizes. The requirement for receipt of the funds was that each agency prepare a coordinated collection development plan for that region. In New York City, the area served by METRO, which is the largest of the agencies, a survey was taken of collection strengths and weaknesses. The resulting "plan" consisted of a list of subjects based on the LC classification and of collection strengths using the ALA collection level codes.

The first Coordinated Collection Development Aid (CCDA) report sent to the state in 1982, reflected the diversity of the libraries within ME-

TRO receiving this funding. It also exemplified the many problems faced by the region in discussing collaborative collection development. A chart appended to the report—subject strengths by institution—measured two feet by seven and a half feet. It contained 326 subject terms compiled directly from CCDA applications, with little or no editing. Since no guidelines were given to applicants, there were many nonstandard terms: college education, medieval studies, history—medieval aspects, design firms, legal medicine, and technology in advertising. There were terms lumped together such as "Anatomy and physiology" or "Theory and composition (music)" instead of "Composition (Music)" and "Music—Theory." There were reversed terms that were really phrases, such as "Economics of education" instead of "Education—Economic aspects," and "Linguistics, applied" instead of "Applied linguistics." Both "Vision" and "Physics" were on the chart, but they did not appear anywhere near "Bibliographies—Vision" and "History of physics."

The collection levels also generated some concern. Six out of sixty-one libraries ranked their law collections at a research level, which is defined to include pertinent foreign language materials and older material retained for research. These were possibly accurate levels, but the Resources Development Committee must have wondered at the same ranking for City College, John Jay, Brooklyn Law School, Columbia, Fordham, New York University, Pace, and Yeshiva. Similarly, four libraries rated their education collections at the research level, and only two reported such a collection in Spanish literature. This lack of uniformity, and uneasiness about communicating in the same language about collection levels prompted the METRO Resources Development Committee to form a task force in 1984-85 to review the CCDA applications for uniform use of LC subject headings. In the summer of 1985 letters were sent by the task force to appropriate CCDA applicants to notify them of changes in subject terminology made on their applications. In that same year, the committee sent a revised CCDA plan to the participating members and to the state. The chart was now a 31-page computer-generated appendix of 281 LCSH terms that included LC classification. [See Figure 1]

At the same time, to foster a greater awareness of the collection levels that were being assigned, the task force planned a one-day workshop to discuss the use of the ALA guidelines. Constance McCarthy, at that time Collection Management Coordinator at George Washington University, spoke on assessing collections using the ALA guidelines. In the afternoon, small discussion groups were organized both by size and type of library and on specific subject areas. This small group method, in a workshop setting, has characterized the project ever since.

The success of those small group discussions encouraged METRO to consider a larger, more standardized project based on the Pacific Northwest model. The committee was not entirely satisfied with the CCDA coordinated collection development plan even after revision. It had imposed some LCSH terms on the plan, some non-LCSH terms persisted, and there was still doubt about the validity of some of the collection levels reported.

The common thread running through these projects is the body of

```
                         CCDA 1986
                        Subject List

    Colleges                          LC              Level
                                 Classification


**  SOCIAL SERVICE
    FORDHAM UNIVERSITY              HV 1-696            B
    HUNTER COLLEGE                  HV 1 -696           C1
    MERCY COLLEGE                   HV 1-696            B
    YESHIVA UNIVERSITY              HV 1-696            B

**  SOCIOLOGY
    COLLEGE FOR HUMAN SERVICES      HM                  D
    FORDHAM UNIVERSITY              HM                  B
    MERCY COLLEGE                   HM                  B
    NEW SCHOOL FOR SOCIAL RESEARCH  HM                  C

**  SPANISH LITERATURE
    BROOKLYN COLLEGE                PQ 6001-8929        B
    FORDHAM UNIVERSITY              PQ 6001-8929        C1
    IONA COLLEGE                    PQ 6001-8929        C1

**  SPECULATIVE PHILOSOPHY
    BROOKLYN COLLEGE                BD                  C1

**  SPEECH
    CUNY GRADUATE CENTER            QP 306              C1
    SUNY/ DOWNSTATE MEDICAL CENTER  QP 306              A
    TEACHERS COLLEGE/COLUMBIA       QP 306              B

**  SPORTS MEDICINE
    NEW YORK COLL.OF PODIATRIC MED  RD                  C2

**  SUBSTANCE ABUSE
    COLLEGE FOR HUMAN SERVICES                          D
    MOUNT SINAI SCHOOL OF MEDICINE  RC 563-568          C1

**  SURGERY
    MOUNT SINAI SCHOOL OF MEDICINE  RD                  B

**  TAXATION
    NEW YORK LAW SCHOOL             HJ 2240-7  5        B

**  TEACHING-AIDS AND DEVICES (PRESCHO)
    BANK STREET COLLEGE             LB 1043             C1

**  TECHNOLOGY
    CITY COLLEGE                    TA 1-TK 9971        B
    ELIZABETH SETON COLLEGE         T                   D
    WESTCHESTER COMMUNITY COLLEGE   T-TX                C1
```

Figure 1.

principles that stood behind the initial RLG work: the use of a standardized tool to share information on collection assessment for the purpose of making cooperative agreements work. The achievements of North American Collection Inventory Project and Pacific Northwest showed METRO that beyond the theoretical commitment to collaborative resource sharing, flexible, well-documented materials had been created to open the arena of collection assessment to many kinds of libraries. Libraries could use the previously established framework and yet tailor their work to serve their own individual needs, while at the same time, the assessments could be used as a basis for collaboration.

II. Proposal

Shortly after the revised New York regional cooperative collection development plans were put into place in conformity with the requirements of the Cooperative Collection Development Act, another METRO resource-sharing program called CAP (for "Cooperative Acquisitions Program") came under scrutiny by a METRO Resources Committee task force. Since 1972, the program has been in existence as a mechanism for the shared purchasing of fairly expensive research and reference materials. METRO members who wanted to join CAP contributed a small percentage of their acquisitions budgets for the purchase of materials that, though jointly owned, would be deposited in a library that had a known strength in that particular discipline. Multiple copies of some major reference works were also purchased for placement in a number of smaller libraries, but for the most part, the titles acquired through CAP were fairly learned, expensive materials. Suggestions for the particular titles to be purchased came from the various libraries that participated in CAP.

In the early years of CAP, government monies were added to the member contributions, and the available funding was fairly substantial (some $215,000, for example, was available during the first five years of the project). In essence, what CAP participants were really doing was trying to map out the collection strengths in the region, gather suggestions for new titles, purchase them, and place the titles in the various institutions in the best way it could. They were trying to do this, however, without the benefit of firm data on the existing strengths of the different libraries.

The task force report, submitted in the spring of 1986 to the METRO Resources Development Committee, addressed complaints about CAP. Among these were that it no longer met the needs of METRO libraries, that materials acquired were too esoteric for some members' constituencies, and that only a small number of libraries with strong collections benefited from the program. There were objections to the criterion that if an item were already in the region it would be ineligible for group purchase. Others felt that CAP materials deposited in libraries geographically distant from their own collections made the materials, for all practical purposes, unavailable to their readers. In addition, actual monies available to the program had dwindled and were inadequate to support major purchasing.

The task force believed there might be a connection between the excitement that the cooperative collection development plan was generating—with its specification of subject strengths among academic libraries, and the availability of state funds—and the difficulties that CAP was experiencing. A task force member had just returned from a LIRN meeting and spoke to the others about the LIRN project. The task force began to think of the many ways that the region could benefit from a similar collection assessment project and how a database of collection levels could be an effective tool for a more sophisticated kind of resource sharing that would assist libraries of all types and sizes with planning. It recommended that CAP continue and at the same time that the METRO Resources Committee plan a collection assessment project for the METRO region. The implications of such a framework for long-range collection planning and resource sharing were quite exciting to contemplate. To quote from their report:

> A standardized, broad-based collection assessment program will give the region's libraries more direction and information in planning for the development and effective management of the various collections. It will also provide the necessary groundwork for more effective regional cooperation. It is envisioned that a collection assessment plan will make the collection patterns in the region known to all libraries and facilitate the development of a database that identifies collection strengths in the region...

> *The advantages to member libraries are:*
> - a clearer and more complete profile of subject-by-subject levels within the various collections
> - a basis for the more selective development of subject collections
> - improved communication with other libraries engaged in the same assessment process
> - enhanced professional skills in systematic collection development
> - additional management tool to adapt collections to changes in institutional mission, programs, or user patterns
> - an additional database for internal analysis for developing acquisition policies, plans, priorities, and strategies
> - additional data for resource sharing and collection development arrangements with other libraries.

> *The advantages to the METRO region are:*
> - patterns of information resources in the region comprehensively displayed
> - subject collections identified in greater detail resulting in referrals of readers to collections in closer proximity and reduction of the burden on larger collections
> - libraries able to coordinate their purchasing power with other libraries when desired
> - non-print resources more widely known.[3]

The task force felt that completion of an assessment project such as the one undertaken in the Pacific Northwest would enable libraries in the New York metropolitan region to tell if there were any serious gaps in coverage of the subjects important to the region, and for libraries who receive state money to coordinate expenditure of the Cooperative Collection Development Act funds to assure that all necessary current publications in the subjects they selected were being purchased.

III. Implementation

The Resources Committee and the METRO Board of Trustees approved the CAP Evaluation task force recommendation which would permit participating libraries to manage collections and plan for their development in a new way. Funding was provided for the METRO Collection Inventory Project to begin a pilot phase starting in the fall of 1986. A committee of six librarians, called the Collection Assessment Task Force, was appointed to plan for the initiation of a collection assessment program.   Some twenty-one libraries were invited to participate in the pilot program, representing the various academic, research, special and public libraries — large and small — that typified the METRO membership. Participating libraries ranged from the Fashion Institute of Technology to Columbia University and the New York Public Library, from the American Museum of Natural History to Mercy College and the Newark Public Library, each with its own traditions of handling selection and collection management.

A big advantage of the LIRN program was that it was designed for a diversity of libraries, and that it offered the flexibility for participating libraries to decide how deeply they wanted to assess its holdings in the twenty-four broad subjects (called "divisions") of the conspectus. The worksheets designed by LIRN also offered flexibility in terms of the availability of worksheets using either Dewey or LC classification schemes. Three subjects were chosen for analysis in the initial phase: art and architecture, chemistry, and education. These were selected to represent the humanities, sciences, and social sciences, and because RLG supplemental guidelines were available for those areas. The task force changed its name from Collection Assessment Project to Collection Inventory Project to avoid confusion with the ongoing CAP program.

In June of 1987, the first training workshop was held. The purpose of the training was threefold: to provide participants with the tools and skills necessary to help them make professional judgments of the strengths of their collections, to introduce a common tool and language, and to provide training in how to use the conspectus. At the same time, care was taken to emphasize that the conspectus is not an end in itself, but a tool to move the libraries involved toward collaborative collection development projects.

The workshop was designed and led by two consultants, Anthony W. Ferguson (Columbia), and Joan Grant (NYU), who had received training in the conspectus methodology. They were supported by task force members who served as discussion leaders. In preparation for the workshop, the task

METRO COLLECTION ASSESSMENT PROJECT
CONSPECTUS CODE EXERCISE

Let's suppose your library has already recognized the value of
completing the Conspectus and you and/or your student assistants have
reviewed specific areas of your education, chemistry and art and
architecture collections through scanning the shelflist, browsing what
is in the stacks and reference collection and looking at cataloging
statistics and approval plan vendor management reports for what is being
added. Perhaps you have even checked some key bibliographies for those
fields. Now you are ready to begin assigning values using the attached
"Definitions of Collecting Levels".

To help prepare you for the workshop we would like you to role play and
provide Conspectus codes for each of the following situations. Moreover,
we would like you to jot down a record of any problems or concerns you
encounter as these will be discussed in small group settings.

1. Conspectus Line No. EDD048 History of Education - China (LC class LA
1150-1154)

Situations

a. The shelflist revealed ten inches of cards for this range of
    call numbers. Imprint dates on these cards indicated 25% were
    published since 1975, the remainder extend back through the
    1800s. About one-half of the cards are Chinese imprints. The
    shelflist and browsing of the shelves revealed a wide variety of
    research level monographs, many education journals both in
    English and Chinese, and the reference collection seems well
    developed both with specialized education reference works and
    more general bibliographical tools. A check of bibliographies
    in five books, dealing with the subject indicated the library
    had 85% of the English works and 50% of the Chinese works.

                 Your rating: Current Collection _____
                               (What the collection is like the
                               day you look at it.)

                               Acquisitions Commitment _____
                               (The kind of collection you are now
                               building as evidenced by current
                               acquisitions patterns.)

b. The shelflist indicated only five books, all published since
    1980, one a Chinese work on audio-visual teaching, three on
    elementary education, and one about the experience of Chinese
    students in America.

                 Your rating: Current Collection _____

                               Acquisitions Commitment _____

                 Written by Anthony W. Ferguson

Figure 2.

force created a manual[4] by revising the LIRN manual for local use, and modifying it to include the newly revised ALA collection levels and RLG supplemental guidelines. Each attendee was asked to complete a conspectus code
exercise in advance to introduce them to assessment techniques and the inter-

pretation of collecting levels. [See Figure 2]

At the beginning of the workshop, participants were asked what their expectations of the training were, and they responded with a list of questions they hoped to answer during the day:

- Is it worth it?
- What are verification studies?
- What sampling techniques can be used to do assessments?
- How are the RLG benchmarks devised?
- What if you do not have the resources to do an assessment?
- What if your collection uses a special classification system?
- What is the relationship between RLG and the METRO data?
- How does the conspectus handle cross-disciplinary subjects?

At the end of the day this list was reviewed. The agenda, which comprised one full day's activities, included lectures, exercises, and small group discussions. First, the program was put in context by giving an overview of the METRO project and the other programs from the ARL, Alaska, and the Pacific Northwest; then the conspectus format and definitions of collecting levels were reviewed in some detail. A small group discussion of a "homework" assignment designed to stimulate thinking on the definitions of the levels was followed by an explanation of the advantages and disadvantages of various collection assessment techniques.

The Collection Inventory Project is based on collection-centered assessment, and emphasizes various assessment techniques such as examination of pre-existing data, list checking, shelflist examination and measurement, and shelf scanning. A second small group discussion focused on identifying some of the internal uses of the conspectus, such as training staff in assessment techniques, improving communication with faculty, providing information for curriculum changes and accreditation reviews, etc. Finally, the participants were given some suggestions on ways to plan and organize their work for the conspectus project. These basic steps were:

1. Determine which sections you will complete and do all of them to educate selectors, analyze the collection, and develop an important planning aid;
2. Identify who will be responsible for each division of the conspectus, and if possible create a team which can divide up the work, interact with each other, and keep the group on the right track;
3. Develop and use a schedule for completion of the project. Round up support from administration to do the work involved, with the advice that it seems to take about 2-3 days of solid, concentrated effort to do a division, depending on the length of the division, amount of clerical support, selector's knowledge of the collection, etc.;
4. Provide training and support by reviewing the definitions, practice exercises, etc.
5. Provide adequate staff resources, perhaps in the form of students to measure shelflists, check lists, do RLIN or OCLC searches, etc.;

6. Do the work.
7. Understand the background first: become familiar with collection policy statements, curriculum descriptions, interests of library users, history of the development of each collection, etc. For the assessment itself:
   a. Gather sufficient information about what materials are/were collected, material not collected, how current is the material;
   b. Use tools to assess collection such as supplementary guidelines, examination of the shelves, compare shelflist count with national shelflist count universe, check lists and bibliographies, consult with experts in the field, examine how materials are acquired (approval plans, foreign vendors, buying trips, title by title, etc.), and how much money is committed to the area.
8. Monitor the project by giving the team progress reports and intermediate deadlines and also bring the group together regularly to review results, discuss problems and receive encouragement;
9. Review the results with library administration;
10. Submit results to METRO. [See Figure 3]

Workshop participants were given four months to complete the worksheets for the three assessments, which were due to the METRO office by the end of September, 1987.

Six weeks later, a follow-up workshop was held to give participants the opportunity to share the experiences, successes, and problems they had

Division: PHILOSOPHY AND RELIGION			Library: Date:			By:	
LC CLASS	LINE NUMBER	DIVISION, CATEGORIES and SUBJECTS	COLLECTION & LANGUAGE CODES				COMMENTS
			CL	AC	GL		
	PAR000	PHILOSOPHY AND RELIGION					
B1-68	PAR001	Philosophy - Periodicals, Societies, Congresses					
B69-789	PAR001.5	Philosophy - Hist & Systems, Ancient - Renaissance					
B108-626	PAR002	History & Systems, Ancient					
B530-708	PAR003	History & Systems, Alexandrian & Early Christian					
B720-765	PAR004	History & Systems, Medieval					
B740-753	PAR005	Arabian, Moorish & Islamic Philosophers					
B755-759	PAR006	Jewish Philosophers					
B756	PAR007	European Philosophers					
B770-785	PAR008	History & Systems, Renaissance					
B790-5739	PAR009	History & Systems, Modern (1450/1600-)					
B840	PAR010	Philosophy of Language					
B2750	PAR011	Kant					
	PAR012	Religious Existentialists					
BC	PAR013	Logic					
BC131-135	PAR014	Logic - Symbolic & Mathematical					
BD	PAR014.5	Speculative Philosophy					
BD100-131	PAR015	Metaphysics					

Figure 3. The METRO Conspectus Worksheet

encountered. The group broke into small groups by subject so that there could be substantive exchange on assessment problems unique to the various subject divisions of the conspectus. The groups were asked to discuss a list of questions, and each group appointed a reporter who summarized the discussion at the end of the meeting. The seven discussion questions were:

- At what stage are you in the project?
- What techniques work for you?
- What major problems are you facing in doing the assessments?
- Can the group members suggest solutions?
- Whom have you involved in the work?
- How much time is it taking?
- What are you finding out about your collection?

During July 1989, METRO sent Rhonna Goodman, METRO staff liaison, to the Pacific Northwest to interview the LIRN staff in order to better understand the administration of the project. Because of a grant from the Fred Meyer Charitable Trust, the PNWCD (Pacific Northwest Conspectus Database) had a four-fifths time senior level professional librarian managing the project, Peggy Forcier, and a full time administrative assistant.

PNWCD had developed excellent project management techniques which could be replicated at METRO. The decision was made to purchase their software, and the data management side of the project was launched. One of the staff members reviewed the data on the worksheets provided at the training session, supervised inputting into the database, and started working on reports. Participants could request at no cost any or all of a series of reports generated from their data once it was input. Samples of these reports were distributed at the follow-up workshop. [see Figure 4] All but three libraries submitted data to the project.

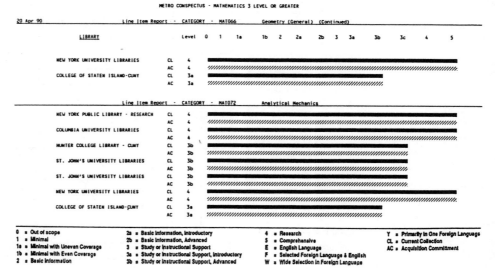

Figure 4.

In dealing with the worksheets, the METRO office compiled a list of common problems encountered in inputting, and the task force decided to give more time to instructing participants on how to fill out the sheets at future workshops. The need for some kind of common language of standard abbreviations became obvious as the intern struggled to get the most information possible into a comments field. This led to the creation of another task force of five librarians which created a thesaurus of abbreviations. In their report[5] they encouraged use of the comments field for further details on collection levels, justifying decisions, and noting exceptions. The comments field can be used to indicate strengths and weaknesses, particular formats and special collections, and policies that cut across division levels. The report noted that comments are particularly useful on multidisciplinary subjects. [see Figure 5]

The Collection Inventory Task Force also realized that one of its roles would have to be to review all of the worksheets for obvious inconsistencies and to get back in touch with those libraries that seemed to be out of line in their evaluations. This led to the creation of a series of assessment validation forms by the task force in the spring of 1989. The validation forms are still being tested by the committee. [see Figure 6]

At the end of the pilot project year in May of 1987, the task force reported to the METRO Resources Committee. Its justification for the project changed slightly, in that mention of CCDA funding was replaced by a more general statement that the objectives of the project were to:

1. Improve the management of collection building and coordination by supporting regional assessment and a database that shows the location and level of subject collection in the METRO region. Assist more effective buying in the face of rising demands and stable or declining budgets for library collections;
2. Assist with cooperative collection development and resource sharing agreements that will selectively coordinate collection growth and strengthen the combined subject resources in the region.

This report cited the importance of publicizing among METRO members the value for resource sharing of the conspectus-based collection inventory project effort. It stressed the need to further publicize the reports and use of the database being created at the METRO office.

In 1985, the New York City School Library System, which includes almost 1,000 schools, implemented a cooperative collection development program, as mandated by New York State for regional school library networks. The program began with a conspectus-like exercise for the schools in the system, but difficulties arose in assessing collections using the subject headings of the METRO tool and the definitions of collection levels. A database of the holdings of the school libraries was created called Metropolitan Interlibrary Cooperative System (MILCS). There is now a network linked by a newly-created interlibrary loan system.

Up to this year, emphasis was put on access to enhanced "special collections" in selected schools in the system. In 1989, the system hired an

COLLECTION INVENTORY PROJECT

THESAURUS

ABSTRACTS	abs
ACTING EDITIONS	act ed Plays with detailed production information. See also prompt bk
ACQUISITION	acq
ADEQUATE	Do not use
ALMANAC	almanac
ALTERNATIVE LITERATURE	altern lit Published works that contrast with the mainstream cultural, political and social press. See also resist publ
ARCHIVAL	archival
ARCHIVES	arc
ART ORIGINALS	Use art
ART REPRODUCTIONS	Use art
ART	art Includes original art, prints and reproductions.
ARTEFACTS	Use realia
ATLASES	atlas A volume of maps, plates, engravings, tables, etc. with or without descriptive letterpress. (ALA)
AUCTION	auction Example: Auction cat
AUDIO TAPE	Use tape
AUDIOVISUAL MATERIALS	AV
AUTOBIOGRAPHY	autobiog Includes diaries, confessions, memoirs and other personal narratives.
AVERAGE YEAR	av yr Example: av yr 1966
BANNED BOOKS	Use censored
BIBLIOGRAPHY	bib
BRAILLE	braille
CATALOG	cat
CD-ROM	cd-rom
CENSORED	censored
CENTURY	c Example: 19-20th c
CIRCULATING	circ
COLLECTION	coll
COMPACT DISC	cd
COMPLETE	compl

Figure 5.

outside consultant to make recommendations on how to improve implementation of the goals and objectives of this resource sharing effort. As part of the response to this report, the New York City schools are now planning assessments based on curriculum mapping techniques to see both how well their system of interlibrary loan access to the special collections is working, and to test the effect of an increased emphasis on how well the more typical middle and high school collections meet curriculum needs. METRO is consulting with the system on these assessments.

In 1986, three school districts in Westchester County, inspired by

METRO COLLECTION INVENTORY PROJECT

VALIDATION FORM FOR EDUCATION DIVISION CONSPECTUS

INSTITUTION _____

LIBRARY _____

HIGHEST DEGREE GRANTED IN EDUCATION _____

ASSESSMENT LEVEL _____

Please give all available figures for the following:

Number of serial titles _____

Current subscriptions to titles listed in: No. of titles _____   %

Education Index _____ _____

Current Index to Journals in Education _____ _____

Social Sciences Citation Index _____ _____

Katz, Magazines for Libraries _____ _____

Percentage of titles for which holdings are complete or nearly complete _____ %

Do you subscribe to the full ERIC? Yes/No

Number of monographic titles _____ and/or volumes

Holdings of titles listed in: No. of titles _____

Woodbury's Guide to Sources in Education _____ _____

Encyclopedia of Educational Research _____ _____

Number of titles _____ and/or volumes _____ held in audiovisual and other media

Do you provide on-line or CD-ROM access to ERIC? Yes/No

Percentage of the collection in foreign language _____ %

Percentage of the collection with copyright in the last ten years _____ %

Funds allocated during last and current budget years for:

	Last	Current
Serials	$_____	$_____
Monographs	$_____	$_____
Audiovisual and other media	$_____	$_____
Database searching	$_____	$_____

Number of titles added to the collection in last budget year _____

What selection tools/methods do you use regularly?

Do you use an approval plan for education? Yes/No
If so, describe your profile.

List any special collections.

Completed by _____   Date _____

Figure 6.

BOCES Collection Level Indicators
for Evaluating School Library Collections

COLLECTION LEVEL INDICATORS

CODE	LABEL	DEFINITION
0	Out of Scope	Library does not collect in this area.
1a	Minimal Level	Few selections; unsystematic coverage; some core works.
1b	Minimal Level, Even Coverage	Core works; basic authors; Spectrum of views presented.
2a	Basic information	Current and classic materials which introduce and define subject and reflect diversity of types of information available elsewhere (dictionaries, handbooks, periodicals, bibliographies). Supports basic level of instruction.
2b	Augmented information	Collection which maintains depth as well as breadth; classic, critical and bibliographic tools.
2c	Study Level	Collection of primary materials, specialized monographs to argument a level 2b collection. Supports advanced level placement courses.

Figure 7.

the conspectus effort, started to work on a redefinition of the assessment levels so as to better describe collections in their school library systems. Indeed, the RLG supplemental guidelines were seldom written with smaller libraries in mind, and the chair of the Research Libraries Group CMDC Conspectus Task Force encouraged METRO, at this time, to try to develop its own supplemental guidelines, both to foster the project, and to enhance the documentation for other libraries involved in the national effort. Francene Costello, of the Southern Westchester Board of Cooperative Education Systems (BOCES) School Library System, worked with the METRO library school intern Carol Selzer on this project, which culminated in an assessment tool for the subject of economics in school libraries. [See Figure 7]

In planning for "Phase II" of the project the following year, the task force decided to select three more subjects, and to invite the original pilot project libraries, plus an additional twenty libraries, to attend a second training session. In the meantime, the pilot project libraries received proof reports of their data from the assessments of the first three subjects. These reports went to participants in July 1988, along with samples of other kinds of comparative reports for their information. [See Figure 8]

A second training workshop was held in March 1988, and the sub-

25 Jun 89   Line Item Report - CATEGORY - ART250   Photography   Page 1

LIBRARY	CL	AC	GL	COMMENTS
BROOKLYN COLLEGE LIBRARY - CUNY	3aE	3bE		775 titles (LC); 5 current periodicals.
LAGUARDIA COMMUNITY COLLEGE-CUNY	1aE	3 E		83 titles + 8 ref. + 7 periods. about 30 new titles on order.
MERCY COLLEGE LIBRARY	3bE	3bE		Strong in technique and individual photographs.
NEW YORK BOTANICAL GARDEN LIBRARY	1aE	0		
COLUMBIA UNIVERSITIES LIBRARIES	3 F	3 F		Artistic aspects only,early serials, tech.manuals, etc. Epstean Coll.Rare Bk. & Manuscript
CITY COLLEGE - CUNY	3	3		
FASHION INSTITUTE OF TECHNOLOGY	2a	2a		
HUNTER COLLEGE LIBRARY - CUNY	3a	3		No current subscriptions to photographic journals.
AMERICAN MUSEUM OF NATURAL HISTORY	3aE	3		
MARYMOUNT MANHATTAN COLLEGE	1aE	1a		
ST. JOHN'S UNIVERSITY LIBRARIES	1bE	2bE		Emphasis is on creative photography which is collected at a 3a level.
NEW YORK UNIVERSITY LIBRARIES	1 E	2 E		
WAGNER COLLEGE LIBRARY	2bE	2b	2b	247 titles, 6.23% of art coll.; most published in 1970s and 1980s.
YESHIVA UNIVERSITY	1aE	1aE		
NEW YORK INSTITUTE OF TECHNOLOGY	3 E	3 E	3 E	349 tls. From gen. works to applied photography, lighting and cinematography
MANHATTANVILLE COLLEGE	1b	1		Book collection well distributed but almost no journals.
SUNY AT PURCHASE	2bE	2bE	2bE	
ST. VINCENTS MED. CNT. OF RICHMOND	0	0		
COLLEGE OF STATEN ISLAND-CUNY	2aE	2aE		150 + 10 + 15
MANHATTAN COLLEGE-CARDINAL HAYES	1 E	1 E		17 titles.

Line Item Report - SUBJECT - ART250.5   Photography (General - includes History & Science)

LIBRARY	CL	AC	GL	COMMENTS
BROOKLYN COLLEGE LIBRARY - CUNY	3a	3b		225 titles (LC).
COLUMBIA UNIVERSITIES LIBRARIES	3 F	3 F		
CITY COLLEGE - CUNY	3b	3		
FASHION INSTITUTE OF TECHNOLOGY	2bE	2bE		Primarily history.
HUNTER COLLEGE LIBRARY - CUNY	3	3		Adequate visual resource represenation.
AMERICAN MUSEUM OF NATURAL HISTORY	2bE	2		
ST. JOHN'S UNIVERSITY LIBRARIES	3aE	2bE		
NEW YORK UNIVERSITY LIBRARIES	2 E	3 E		
SUNY AT PURCHASE	2bE	2bE	3aE	3" + selected per
COLLEGE OF STATEN ISLAND-CUNY	2aE	1bE		30 titles

0 = Out of scope	2a = Basic Information, Introductory	4 = Research	Y = Primarily In One Foreign Language
1 = Minimal	2b = Basic Information, Advanced	5 = Comprehensive	CL = Current Collection
1a = Minimal with Uneven Coverage	3 = Study or Instructional Support	E = English Language	AC = Acquisition Commitment
1b = Minimal with Even Coverage	3a = Study or Instructional Support, Introductory	F = Selected Foreign Language & English	
2 = Basic Information	3b = Study or Instructional Support, Advanced	W = Wide Selection In Foreign Language	

Figure 8.

jects chosen were library science/national bibliographies, French language and literature, and mathematics/computer science. A $40 charge had to be made to fund continuation of the project, but this included initial training for up to three additional staff members, a new program for Advanced Collection Assessment Training in May, worksheets, manual, and proof and comparative reports. Added to the agenda of the second workshop were two reports from Brooklyn College and the Fashion Institute of Technology libraries, which were in the pilot project, to explain their experience of the assessments and to reassure and encourage the new participants.

The third collection inventory workshop took place in February 1989, and twenty-one new institutions were trained. This brought the total number of participating institutions to sixty. Subjects assessed this time were religion, biological sciences, and English and American literature.

In May of 1988, the project managers from twenty-five participating libraries met. Although the meeting was initially planned to cover advanced collection assessment training, other issues having to do with the continuation of the project took precedence on the agenda. Joan Neumann, the Executive Director of METRO, told the group that METRO was concerned that the program lacked broad support in the METRO community at large, and she mentioned two negative factors that could prevent its continuation: the METRO office could no longer underwrite the cost of report generation, and collection assessment projects consumed much staff time, especially in the smaller libraries in the consortium. She urged participants to put in writing how the project had helped them in their services. An article appeared in the METRO newsletter[6] in which Brooklyn College, Columbia University, the Fashion Institute, Hunter College, Manhattan College, St. Vincent's Medical Center, and the NYU-Bobst Library contributed information. These libraries reported that

the conspectus had already been used in their institutions:
  • to highlight where resources should be used,
  • to be the core of a collection development policy statement,
  • to serve as the basis of an approval plan profile,
  • to support grant proposals,
  • to review the levels with faculty members,
  • to document a preservation master plan,
  • to support budget requests,
  • to help with new serials decisions,
  • to respond to new programs and new courses,
  • to make special librarians more aware of the scope of collections outside their sphere.

It was clear that additional funding had to be found if the METRO Collection Inventory Project were to continue. A successful grant proposal for a New York State LSCA Title III grant was written by Rhonna Goodman, the staff liaison from the METRO office, to fund four activities in 1988-1989:

1. a series of seminars with at least five libraries already well into the assessment process to develop a model for long-range collection management plans for their institutions;
2. a two-day seminar for members of the Collection Inventory Project;
3. the appointment of three consultants to Collection Inventory Project participants to help them to structure, set up, and implement a collection management and assessment program for their institutions;
4. at least two pilot groups of libraries were to be contacted by another consultant to develop formal resource sharing agreements based on their assessment activity.

The seminar series was held from December 1988, through May 1989. Readings on collection assessment, collection policy statements, book selection, serials selection, budget preparation/weeding/gifts, and preservation were assigned in advance, and discussion held on problems and successes in applying the concepts and techniques to their own institutions. After the last session, the participants were to write reports outlining how comprehensive collection management programs might best be established at their libraries.

The Collection Assessment Institute was held in June 1989. The first day was devoted to client-centered assessments and covered user surveys and interviews, adapting collections to changes in user patterns, use of statistics, and use studies. The second day was devoted to collection-centered assessments, and covered preservation, list making and checking, citation studies, statistical profiling, and condition surveys. Nationally recognized experts Paul Mosher, Jutta Reed-Scott, William McGrath, Howard White, Anthony Ferguson, and Barclay Ogden spoke, and the agenda included small group discussions and "fill in the blank" kinds of exercises on the topics that the consultants could use to measure the degree to which basic concepts were learned, and to facilitate the incorporation of these concepts into library operations. There was also a presentation about formal, written resource sharing agreements in the METRO context from CIP task force member Lynn Wishart and a discussion of how assessment fits into a collection management plan from Joan Grant.

The three consultants divided up the list of sixty participants in the Collection Inventory Project according to type of library, and contacted them to arrange consultations following the Collection Assessment Institute. They devised an "evaluative checklist" for the consultations which included:

- review conspectus worksheets,
- get comparative reports from METRO, and look for likely areas for collaborative collection development projects,
- review internal use of the conspectus,
- go over the elements in a comprehensive collection management program and explain how the elements are integrated,
- ask the client to think about how local conditions would shape the general scenario described,
- critically evaluate their library's approach.

Finally, the consultants worked on how the conspectus process helps in a comprehensive collection plan. In the last quarter of 1988, a consultant was appointed to work with libraries which were potential participants in formal resource sharing and collaborative collection development agreements. Before contacting libraries, the consultant reviewed not only their completed conspectus data, but also published information about the libraries and their parent institutions, such as that found in annual reports and college catalogs. The consultant recognized that factors important to libraries considering formal agreements included: bibliographic and physical access to external collections; institutional commitment; and trust in the continuation of cooperative agreements. The consultant began contacting individual libraries and library consortia in the winter of 1988 to suggest ways to use conspectus data as the foundation for cooperative agreements.

Because some METRO libraries already had informal resource sharing or cooperative acquisitions agreements in place, in addition to widespread participation in several METRO consortial agreements (such as a delivery system and an on-site use system), in the summer of 1989, the consultant surveyed the sixty participating libraries to gather data about their existing cooperative agreements. The consultants planned to use this information in conjunction with data derived from the conspectus to stimulate the development of formal agreements. The task force recognized that formal resource sharing and collaborative collection development agreements could, in part, strengthen existing informal agreements and build bridges where none had existed.

The initial stages of METRO's efforts saw only polite acknowledgment. Bilateral agreements, and those agreements made among an affinity group of libraries or existing network membership, seemed to evolve as byproducts of those relationships, not from METRO encouragement. Libraries seem to expect METRO to offer incentives to cooperation in the form of additional funding, which METRO is unable to offer. The task force expects interest in cooperative agreements to rise after more collections are assessed and more consideration is given to the potential for improved access to information.

IV. Experiences and Conclusions

While our broad goals have not changed, the way the project is administered has evolved over the past three years. We are still in the midst of the project, in terms of the subjects to be covered and agreements on resource sharing to be reached. As Lynn Wishart (Cardozo Law), one of the consultants, pointed out, while the conspectus provides libraries with a common tool that may lead to resource sharing, librarians have never flocked to register major cooperative agreements in writing. She cited several obstacles to collaborative collection development:

- need to share bibliographic data
- need for efficient document delivery
- need for continuous presence of widespread trust that all partners will maintain their commitments
- user attitudes toward dependency on other collections
- tradition and history; i.e., lack of funds, fear on the part of larger libraries that they will be over-used
- legal and administrative problems with parent governing bodies about ownership and access to materials.

None of these obstacles is insurmountable, however, and we have found ample evidence in the consortium of an interest and commitment to the effort, particularly since obstacles such as the lack of a common database and slow interlibrary loan turnaround have been largely overcome.

We would have to admit that the project requires staff time, especially to input and manage the database and reports. We have become more pragmatic in our approach and more realistic in our expectations as to the extent libraries may be able to participate in the project and how much can be expected from the METRO office. Schools and special libraries have been among the last to join the project, and they have sought modifications in the amount of work involved to do the assessments, and revised conspectus definitions and worksheets to suit their special collections. Basically, volunteers do the work involved.

METRO opted for a phased-in approach to resource sharing, one involving a limited number of in-depth assessments by a few volunteer libraries, moving from assessments to agreements. It has taken three years to cover nine of the twenty-four subject divisions. To encourage libraries to do more subjects faster would mean they would not have done them as well, or had much time to master collection assessment skills.

Having gathered what is now a critical mass of data on nine subjects, the effort is to use that data for resource sharing, and to add more subjects of interest to the consortium. In other words, we firmly believe there have been many benefits to participants and to METRO from the pilot project on, even though we are just now beginning to see the fruits of our labors in collaborative collection development.

Without the projects that preceded and inspired it, the METRO Collection Inventory Project would not have been possible, but we have not just copied these projects. The project is now doing original "home-grown" work to advance it—new supplemental guidelines, new and quicker methods of verification of collection levels, and new training tools. Libraries tend to fret overmuch about documenting the collection levels, especially at first, and the task force is exploring ways to make filling out the conspectus less time-consuming to get broader participation from consortium members. Groundbreaking work is underway to bring school libraries into the conspectus for the first time, and we hope the work done already by some of the METRO school librarians will be useful to other consortia. Similarly, some other METRO documents such as the validation forms and thesaurus of abbreviations may be useful to those outside the METRO consortium.

Members of the METRO Collection Inventory Project have tried to expand their horizons beyond the consortium both to learn and to teach, and always to convey their enthusiasm and commitment—in their report about the pilot project at the conference of the New York Library Association, at ALA NACIP meetings, and to state and regional groups. By its second year, the list of similar projects had grown to include the Boston Library Consortium, Illinois Statewide Cooperative Collection Development Project, Network of Alabama Academic Libraries, the North Bay Cooperative in California, the South Central Research Library Council in New York, as well as NACIP, RLG, CARL, Alaska, and LIRN. The METRO project also contributed documentation to the Association of Research Libraries Spec Kit on "Qualitative Collection Analysis: The Conspectus Method."[7]

In describing this largely volunteer-run, conspectus-based project, we hope to inspire others to undertake collection assessments and to participate in the national resource sharing and collaborative collection development efforts. We think it is well worth the effort.

Contributors

We would like to list the people who have served on the METRO Collection Inventory Project Task Force over the years: Linda Dickinson (Hunter), Suzanne Fedunok (Columbia), Suzanne Garrett (SUNY Purchase), Mary Giunta (Barnard), Rhonna Goodman (METRO), Joan Grant (NYU), Robert Kenselaar (NYPL), Thomas Lucas (NYPL), William Monroe (NYU), Lynn Mullins (Rutgers), Anthony Warren (NYPL), Harry Welsh (Manhattan College), Judith Wood (Fashion Institute of Technology), Susan Vaughn (Brooklyn College), Lynn Wishart (Cardozo School of Law), Patricia Young (CUNY).

Notes

1. New York Library Association, 94th Conference (Lake Placid, N.Y., October 23, 1987). "Know your collections: assessing for sharing," a panel discussion given by METRO Collection Inventory Project Task Force members Patricia Young, Lynn Mullins, Joan Grant, Rhonna Goodman, and Susan Vaughn. (unpublished)
2. Nancy E. Gwinn and Paul Mosher, "Coordinating Collection Development: The RLG Conspectus." *College and Research Libraries.* 44 (1983): 128-140.
3. New York Metropolitan Reference and Research Library Agency (METRO). Resources Development Committee. Cooperative Acquisitions Task Force. Report submitted to the Resources Development Committee, May 6, 1986. 5 pp. (unpublished)
4. New York Metropolitan Reference and Research Library Agency (METRO). Resources Development Committee. Collection Assessment Task Force. METRO Collections Inventory Project Manual. METRO Miscellaneous Publication No. 32. New York: New York Metropolitan Reference and Research Library Agency (METRO), 1987. 68 pp.
5. Linda Dickinson, et al. METRO Collection Inventory Project Thesaurus. New York: New York Metropolitan Reference and Research Library Agency (METRO), 1988. 7 pp. (unpublished)
6. For Reference from METRO. No. 186 (July/August 1988): 4-5 .
7. Association of Research Libraries. Qualitative Collection Analysis: The Conspectus Method. Spec Kit #151. (Washington, D.C.: Association of Research Libraries, 1989).

Bibliography

Association of Research Libraries. Qualitative Collection Analysis: The Conspectus Method. Spec Kit #151. (Washington, D.C.: Association of Research Libraries, 1989).

Dickinson, Linda et al. METRO Collection Inventory Project Thesaurus. NY: METRO, 1988. 7 pp. (unpublished).

For Reference from METRO. No. 186 (July/August 1988): 4-5.

Gwinn, Nancy E. and Paul Mosher. "Coordinating Collection Development: The RLG Conspectus. " *College and Research Libraries.* 44 (1983): 128-140.

New York Metropolitan Reference and Research Library Agency (METRO). Resources Development Committee. Collection Assessment Task Force. METRO Collections Inventory Project Manual. METRO Miscellaneous Publication No. 32. New York: New York Metropolitan Reference and Research Agency (METRO), 1987. 68 pp.

New York Library Association, 94th Conference (Lake Placid, N.Y., October 23, 1987). "Know your collections: assessing for sharing," a panel discussion given by METRO Collection Inventory Project Task Force members Patricia Young, Lynn Mullins, Joan Grant, Rhonna Goodman, and Susan Vaughn. (unpublished).

New York Metropolitan Reference and Research Library Agency (METRO). Resources Development Committee. Cooperative Acquisitions Task Force. Report submitted to the Resources Development Committee, May 6, 1986. 5 pp. (unpublished).

Resource Sharing - New York State

Deborah K. Jensen
New England Regional Representative
Faxon Company

The concept of resource sharing among academic institutions in Western and Central New York State took an aggressive and ambitious turn in December 1966. It was at this time that library representatives from Cornell and Syracuse Universities, the University of Rochester, and the State University of New York at Binghamton met to address areas of mutual concern. They also discussed possible cooperative solutions and efforts. The State University of New York at Buffalo became part of this group shortly thereafter, and the organization became known as the Five Associated University Libraries (FAUL). Over the years, FAUL broke new ground in resource sharing, established some workable mechanisms to meet many of its philosophical targets, and left a legacy of cooperation when its objectives were superseded by organizations with broader scopes.

The participants of these preliminary meetings represented the interests of their institutions as well as their libraries. Josiah Newcomb, Director of Libraries, and S. Stewart Gordon, Academic V.P., represented SUNY-Binghamton. Representatives from SUNY-Buffalo were Oscar Silverman, Director of Libraries, and Dr. Robert L. Ketter, Dean of the Graduate School. The Cornell contingent included Dr. Robert Sproull, Academic V.P., and Giles Shepherd, Associate Director of Libraries. The Vice Chancellor for Academic Affairs, Dr. Frank Piskor, and Warren N. Boes, the Director of Libraries, came from Syracuse University. The University of Rochester delegates were Louis E. Martin, Associate Director of Libraries, John Russell, Director of Libraries, and Dr. McCrea Hazlett, University Vice President and Provost.

Although library development was the driving force of this group, they were cognizant that they might also function for developing strategies for sharing other educational resources within the universities.

Long-Range Development Goals

The primary goal of the group was to coordinate the long-range development of their libraries. The common factor in this development was, naturally, resource sharing in all its related guises. The group determined that every library procedure was to be studied in order to meet their goal of providing better service to the academic community and to upstate New York.[1] The Chairman of the Board of Directors of FAUL at the time of its formation, Louis Martin, cited FAUL as one of the first organizations in the country with such a scope of activities.[2]

In August 1967, a constitution and by-laws were drawn up and the Five Associated University Libraries became a formal organization. The administration of FAUL consisted of a Board of Directors of at least ten members with each member institution represented by the chief librarian, or his designate, and the academic vice president, or designate, as *ex officio* members.[3] Four working committees were also set up to focus on Acquisitions, the Budget, State Relations, and Systems.[4] The constitution stated the purposes of FAUL were to:

1. improve and develop library cooperation among the five libraries;
2. work toward a coordinated policy for long-range library growth with:
   a. coordinated acquisitions policies
   b. shared resources
   c. development of compatible machine systems
   d. easy and rapid communications systems among members
   e. provision of shared storage facilities
   f. exploration of other areas of cooperation
3. cooperate with other educational, library and research institutions and organizations inside and outside the geographical area to further the purposes of the association.[5]

Initial steps of FAUL included the presentation of "Talk-Papers" identifying areas of cooperation and action. These were drafted by Giles Shepherd and concerned:

1. optimal exploitation of computers in cooperative library programs
2. experiment in book and reader transportation
3. organizing a compact storage collection of library material
4. coordinating acquisitions policies among large university libraries.[6]

Their initial efforts focused on creating a cooperative computer-based operation. It was decided that the group "should proceed as swiftly as possible to write a proposal which would constitute a study of existing mechanisms or computerized operations such as Talk Paper No. 1"[7] Much of the efforts of FAUL at this time were centered around developing sound policies and procedures for this cooperative operation.

Computerized means for data storage and data transmission were first considered. Following their studies and consultations, the members determined that their primary goal would be establishing a common database and compatible electronic data processing systems.[8] "Database" was defined as:

In the context of the proposed sharing of resources among the Five Associated University Libraries, a database would be the combined stores of the bibliographic descriptions of all five libraries. This database is a prerequisite to cooperative acquisitions, cooperative cataloging, and a common use of the materials owned by the libraries. A central computer store of the bibliographical records of each library should be our goal.[9]

The central database for the member libraries was to be created through the OCLC utility. In fact, FAUL was the first OCLC network in New York State.

The use of the Library of Congress MARC II Format generated considerable discussion. It was recognized quickly that adhering to a standard would effectively allow for the development of compatible systems for participating libraries. On April 25, 1968, the FAUL Board of Trustees adopted a resolution addressing the use of the standard format:

Be it resolved that the Five Associated University Libraries officially adopt the Library of Congress MARC II format for the entry of bibliographic data elements into computer processible form and provide programming support to convert locally produced records into MARC II format, as required.

Be it resolved that F.A.U.L. members may opt to conform to the full MARC II format, a sub-set, or an augmentation of MARC II format specifications, but not conflict with them.[10]

With the decision made for accomplishing their first goal of a shared database, the FAUL members turned their attention to finding sources of funding and providing staff. This focus resulted in a search for a coordinator of library systems. Ronald P. Miller was hired to fill the position and the Office of the Coordinator of Library Systems for FAUL was created at Syracuse University. He served from 1968-71 and was followed by Glyn Evans, 1971-72. To assure the economic base for the group, each library pledged financial support. They also determined that additional funds to address the financial requirements of specific projects would be sought from such external sources as government grants.

Another "Talk Paper" which generated substantial interest addressed coordinated acquisitions policies. A study was made to determine the policies of the libraries with the goal of defining each library's subject area responsibilities for collection development. At the time the study was begun, the libraries informally alerted each other of proposed expensive and unusual acquisitions in order to avoid duplication.[11] The study was completed, but in the following years, little action was taken toward their objective.

Printouts of FAUL holdings were produced, however. Later, Cornell and Syracuse Universities worked together identifying their manuscript holdings. These two universities also joined the shelf list measurement project which is still being used as a collection development tool.[12]

The member libraries established reciprocal faculty borrowing privileges to take optimum advantage of each other's resources. Three of the five libraries had these privileges in place without an imposed fee for service. With FAUL's efforts, the other two members eliminated their charges for this group of borrowers.[13] The faculty now had greater access to a combined collection of approximately seven million volumes.[14]

Journal Access System Information Network Benefits

In the mid-seventies, FAUL became a very active organization and also an influential force in resource sharing. The Journal Access System (JAS) is an example of its endeavors. In response to coping with rising serials costs, cancellations to control acquisitions budgets, and greater user demands on library resources, FAUL took steps to increase their resource access in an expedient, global, and cost beneficial manner. Upon the unanimous recommendation of its Collection Development Committee, the FAUL Board of Directors, in April 1975, adopted a resolution which urged the Center of Research Libraries (CRL) to expand their "Journal's Project Program to include the resources of the British Library, Lending Division (BLLD)."[15] The resolution, a summary of which follows, also formally reiterated FAUL's commitment to cooperative resource access:

> The Board of Directors ... endorses the recommendation ... that we commit ourselves to work with our fellow members and the staff of the Center for Research Libraries to expand the Center's Journals Project into a full-scale national service.
>
> We believe that serials problems within FAUL can be better solved by a large-scale approach rather than a piecemeal approach. The dimension of the problem is sufficiently great to warrant a national plan in which we can effectively participate. We believe that the Center can better serve the academic research community by developing, in consultation with its member institutions and consortia such as FAUL, a growing serials resource with an emphasis on categorical coverage. Our immediate concern is for periodicals in the fields of science and technology ...
>
> As a first step, we recommend that the Center seek to establish an arrangement whereby its member institutions could have full

access to the periodicals held by the British Lending Division.[16]

An information network, the JAS, was formed. The system reached all CRL members but counted FAUL as a progenitor. The program strictly defined the serials it would make available. Concentrating on science, technology and the social sciences, the scope was refined further by stipulating that the imprint data should be from 1970 or later.[17] General goals of the JAS were to provide "simpler and faster access to materials not available in an individual's library collection,"[18] augment the then standard communication methods by establishing an electronic link through TYMSHARE, remove some of the request verification burden from interlibrary loan librarians by streamlining the requirements, and "give more freedom and flexibility in allocating expenditures for serials purchase, thus improving both service and accessibility."[19]

Obviously, this service had a financial impact on its membership. Additional assessments ranging from $1,000 to $3,000 were made on the CRL members. These fees subsidized the free-to-the-requestor photocopying service from BLLD.[20] Savings analysis indicated that at least one library cancelled almost $60,000 worth of scientific journals that amortized the cost of the JAS, while other FAUL libraries used the service to offset the anxiety of cancelling some titles and to help support programs when new journals were not affordable.[21]

Other Joint Programs

FAUL also investigated joint programs that went beyond the confines of library resources. One example of this concerned the potential of establishing a program in area studies which would draw on the strengths of each institution while not requiring each to commit to such a venture resources it did not have. Administrations, faculty, resources, and students would, ideally, be shared. This project did not materialize but the investigation process did highlight strengths and weaknesses that would have to be addressed if a member chose to establish an area studies program independently.[22]

As other consortia became stronger and more effective, the need for FAUL to remain a separate entity gradually diminished. Programs and committee activity slowed down or discontinued as the activities were absorbed by RLG, CRL, and the various regional Library Resources Councils ("3R's"). In December 1983, the Five Associated University Libraries was officially disbanded.

Summary

The consortium came into being at a time when other groups in existence were not yet as effective as the libraries needed them to be. Perhaps it did not succeed at all its endeavors, but it did serve a need and it did leave a legacy of cooperation. FAUL was one of the first to extend beyond the library community and include the entire academic structure of its members to respond to the larger mission of its institutions. It established a basis of cooperation and demonstrated methods achieving this — the medical libraries in the area were strongly influenced by FAUL.[23] With FAUL's requirement for an international rather than a regional approach, and early support of the JAS, it had a positive impact on the development of the national CRL network.[24] Joining other consortia also became cost effective and easier to do since the FAUL members were able to take advantage of each other's existing memberships or to join as a group.[25]

The residual effects of FAUL can still be found in the shared history of these five institutions. The good person-to-person communications that developed among members still fosters some informal collection development projects; in-person-borrowing for faculty is still being reciprocated; the success of other consortia's efforts is enhanced by the past experience of cooperation. These are important results from a pioneering effort which addressed its constituent's concerns, influenced other organizations, and then accepted its demise when other consortia became more effective.

References

Published Materials
F.A.U.L. Newsletter, No. 1 (September 1968). (FAUL publication)

Unpublished Materials
FAUL Constitution, August 10, 1967.

Herling, John P. "Thoughts on a Database for the Five Associated University Libraries," July 28, 1967.

Hussong, Norma Jean. "Report - Five Associated University Libraries (FAUL)," October 1968.

Markwith, Michael. "'We Either Have It Or We Get It For You': An Analysis of the Journal Access System and FAUL's Participation," April 1976.

Minutes of the Five Associated University Libraries, 1967-68.

Report on Second Meeting held by FAUL. Undated.

Interviews with Metod Milac (Syracuse University Library) held in November 1989 and Willis Bridegam (Amherst College Library) held in January 1990.

Notes

1. Norma Jean Hussong, "Report — Five Associated University Libraries (FAUL)," Oct. 1968, p.1.
2. Ibid.
3. FAUL Constitution, August 10, 1967.
4. F.A.U.L. Newsletter, No. 1 (September 1968), p. 2.
5. FAUL Constitution, August 10, 1967.
6. Report on Second Meeting — Held by FAUL. Undated.
7. Ibid.
8. Norma Jean Hussong, p. 2.
9. John P. Herling, "Thoughts on a Database for the Five Associated University Libraries," July 23, 1967.
10. F.A.U.L. Newsletter, No. 1 (September 1968), p. 2.
11. Norma Jean Hussong, p. 3.
12. Interviews with Metod Milac (Syracuse University Library) held in Nov. 1989.
13. Minutes of the Five Associated University Libraries, December 6, 1967.
14. F.A.U.L. Newsletter, No. 1 (September 1968), p. 2.
15. Michael Markwith, "'We Either Have It Or We Get It for You': An Analysis of the Journal Access System and FAUL's Participation," April 1976, p. 1.
16. Ibid., p. 1.
17. Ibid., p. 2.
18. Ibid., p. 3.
19. Ibid., p. 3.
20. Ibid., p. 7.
21. Ibid.
22. Interviews with Metod Milac.
23. Interviews with Willis Bridegam (Amherst College Libary) held in January 1990.
24. Michael Markwith, p. 7.
25. Interviews with Metod Milac.

Collection Analysis and Resource Sharing: the OCLC/AMIGOS Collection Analysis System and the SMU Experience

Carolyn Kacena, Curt Holleman, Roger Loyd, Ann Armbrister, Douglas A. White, and Catherine C. Wilt

In 1989, the AMIGOS Bibliographic Council, Inc., and OCLC, Inc., embarked on a collaborative project to offer Collection Analysis Systems for libraries. This effort brings together the Tape Analysis Service (formerly the AMIGOS Collection Analysis Service) with Collection Analysis CD, a new compact disc tool developed by OCLC.

These services are designed to support more systematic collection building within libraries, providing significantly more multi-dimensional information about the characteristics of collections. Libraries are turning increasingly to unified collection management, focusing expenditures on carefully-formulated collecting policies and demonstrated need. The concept of a self-sufficient collection is being re-evaluated out of budgetary necessity and an emerging view which values ready access to materials as a practical alternative to ownership. The effect on resource sharing efforts can and will be dramatic.

This chapter will describe each component of the Collection Analysis Systems and present a case study of Southern Methodist University's experience with the Tape Analysis Service.

Collection Analysis CD

OCLC/AMIGOS Collection Analysis CD draws on the extensive holdings of the OCLC Online Union Catalog to enable a library to compare its collection development activity against that of peer institutions of similar mission and size. An interactive microcomputer format with a compact disc enables li-

Carolyn Kacena is the Director of Academic Support Automation, Southern Methodist University; Curt Holleman is Assistant Director of Central University Libraries for Collection Development, Southern Methodist University; Roger Loyd is Associate Director of Bridwell Library, Southern Methodist University; Ann Armbrister is the Collection Analysis Systems Administrator, AMIGOS; Douglas A. White is Computer Services Administrative Manager, AMIGOS; and Catherine C. Wilt is Associate Director, Library and Information Services, AMIGOS.

brary staff to conduct analyses locally, independent of the OCLC Online System.

Collection Analysis CD allows a subscribing library to obtain comparative holdings data in statistical form. Holdings data are organized into subject categories based on broad Library of Congress classification or National Shelflist Count divisions; the statistics reveal the extent of overlap, uniqueness, and gap that characterize the library's collection by comparison with that of its peer institutions. The subscriber can also generate bibliographic listings for titles in each subject category.

The context for library analysis is a subset of bibliographic and holdings data derived from the OCLC Online Union Catalog, an international bibliographic database containing more than 20 million unique records. The selective CD database contains approximately 1.6 million abbreviated bibliographic records restricted by publication data to a defined decade. A subscribing library can supplement the peer groupings provided by the CD system with an additional peer group defined by the subscriber.

BCL3 Tape Match

BCL3 Tape Match was developed by AMIGOS and is offered through Collection Analysis Systems as one of two Tape Analysis options. BCL3 Tape Match compares library bibliographic records on magnetic tape against a machine-readable version of *Books for College Libraries*, third edition (BCL3). *Books for College Libraries* was developed as a project of the Association of College and Research Libraries and is widely recognized as a standard listing of recommended titles. BCL3 Tape Match provides a library with a listing of titles held in BCL3 (for which no matches were found in the library's file), and a summary statistical report of match results.

Tape Analysis Service

AMIGOS' role in computerized analysis of library MARC tapes began in 1984, when the network provided an overlap analysis for the Association of Higher Education of North Texas (AHE). This study, based on a model created by the State University of New York (SUNY), analyzed machine-readable holdings of seventeen AHE academic library participants to provide quantitative collection overlap data. The study matched classification numbers in library MARC records against a table of statistical categories based upon an AHE adaptation of the RLG Conspectus.

Upon the successful completion of the AHE project, AMIGOS announced the establishment of its Collection Analysis Service. The Service's goals were to provide computerized analyses of library MARC tapes, supporting customized classification tables and reports. Since the inception of this service, AMIGOS has undertaken collection analysis projects for six resource sharing groups and individual libraries. The data can reveal gaps in subject coverage, collection strengths, and duplication of materials while validating and reinforcing qualitative collection assessments. From this information, resource sharing groups can develop shared programs for collection development, cataloging and retrospective conversion, preservation, and other activities.

Southern Methodist University Tape Analysis Project

Southern Methodist University (SMU) was founded in 1911, by what is now the United Methodist Church; the first classes were held in 1915. It is a private, nonprofit, coeducation institution with emphasis on undergraduate studies. Management of the University is vested in a Board of Trustees of civic, business, and religious leaders.

SMU is one of the largest private academic libraries in the Southwest. The libraries of SMU operate as three distinct units, and also as a federation through the Council of Library Directors. Serving the students and faculties of Dedman College and Meadows School of the Arts, Central University Libraries consist of Fondren, DeGolyer, Science/Engineering, Art, Music, Institute for the Study of Earth and Man, and University Archives. Bridwell Library serves the Perkins School of Theology, and Underwood Law Library services the School of Law.

Although the libraries have their separate identities, services, and clientele, they are partners in an integrated system that provides the best possible information resources in response to the needs of the University community. Economic realities and new technologies necessitate cooperative development and resource sharing. The directors of the University's libraries are pursuing a balance between maintaining traditional library collections and the selective application of today's technology.

Project Purpose

Within the context of SMU's NOTIS system development, conversations were begun with AMIGOS in early 1987 on the use of extracted OCLC records in a collection analysis project. With over 730,000 bibliographic records in machine-readable form by mid-1988, it seemed an opportune time for statistical analysis of the contents of SMU's collections as a basis for future collection development directions. Additionally, as the SMU NOTIS implementation was initiated, valid figures on the overlap between collections were needed as decisions on NOTIS configurations and desired form of the online database were under discussion.

To organize the study, a task force was formed representing all the campus libraries. Mr. Roger Loyd, Associate Director of Bridwell Library, served as Chair. Also represented were the collection development officers of Underwood Law Library, Central University Libraries, and DeGolyer Library; the Associate Director for Technical Services for Central University Libraries; and liaison librarians from the Science and Fine Arts collections. The Director of Academic Support Automation served as the technical project liaison and the Associate Director for Services from the Business Information Center was added later to provide the requirements and input from the business school. A total of ten librarians worked on project planning and organization.

Initial discussions focused on the feasibility of this project. Prior experiences with the AHE Conspectus study met with mixed reviews, and when weighing the costs of a major analysis project, concerns were real. Additionally, the staffing and time implications for incorporating the results and comparing the statistical data with key bibliographies as assessment of the quality of the collections were significant. The anticipation of new directors for Central University Libraries and for Underwood Law Library, the recent arrival of a new director at Bridwell Library, and the new Director of Library Automation meant all campus libraries needed quantifiable measures of the strengths and weaknesses of the collections. Planning for Academic Priorities and Financial Feasibility of future academic plans initiated by the new University President would be fostered in libraries by quantifiable data on the collections. Finally, the regional library planning which AHE represents and the outreach to the greater Dallas "Metroplex" area, which Southern Methodist University's participation epitomizes, would benefit from the project. Assuming availability of at least partial outside funding, it was decided this was indeed the time to embark on this type of review.

Conspectus Outlines Used

Following the decision to proceed, SMU staff met with Ann Armbrister and Douglas White of AMIGOS to review AMIGOS' program offerings. Information was collected on the RLG Conspectus, particularly the *Manual for the North American Inventory of Research Library Collections,* by Jutta Reed-Scott (Association for Research Libraries, 1985). The operational criteria required that this project fit into the regional and national system of analyses and allow SMU full opportunity to share results with other libraries and consortia. SMU staff also needed to be fully conversant with the placement of the technical processing phase in the overall project of collection analysis. The Manual allowed each planning team member to identify the audience(s) for the follow-up processes inherent in the ARL/RLG Conspectus project.

Four possible conspectus outlines were identified: the original AHE outline, the basic RLG Conspectus, various versions of the Pacific Northwest Conspectus, and the Boston Library Consortium Conspectus. These groups approved SMU's use of their earlier outlines of LC classification for the SMU project. SMU's subject specialists reviewed pertinent segments of classification codes with two goals in mind:

1. If no changes were made, would the results be useful within the SMU context?; and,
2. If changes were made, what should they be — combine groups, break them up, redefine break points?

This resulted in a major review of the codes against the latest LC classification tables to ensure that no subject area was excluded accidentally. The group carefully crafted the SMU conspectus using conspectus models from the Boston Library Consortium, Pacific Northwest, and AHE. Generally, the Division level outline was found acceptable, the Category level warranted minimal work to ensure that the sum total of Category-outlined topics matched the Division summary; the Subject level was revised in all areas with extensive reworking needed in Theology/Religion and Law. Every effort was made to eliminate or minimize the number of classification areas which would not fit into one or more of the subject level categories.

A test run was then performed using a 5,500 record sample, which was developed to test each stage of NOTIS implementation. Through this process, it was discovered that the tape analysis software could not process call number ranges which spanned different portions of the alphabet, i.e., LC class ranges C through F for history, or call number ranges where the starting and ending call numbers were not defined to the same level, i.e., S21 – S30.5.

The first problem was solved by defining separate conspectus entries for C-CB, CD-CZ, D-DZ, etc., and assigning them to one class code. The second problem was resolved by modifying the conspectus entry to S21 – S29 and S30 – S30.5. The investigation and implementation of a solution to these problems required approximately six months; however, these changes caused a nine month delay in the project completion.

The sample also revealed call number problems that existed due to: locally-developed classifications outside LC-valid classes; LC call numbers formatted without cutter numbers which could not be retained in the counting algorithm, e.g., the use of dates for constitutions and treaties; and the large numbers of Dewey records without LC-type class number to process. The result was almost 1,000 pages of invalid, miscellaneous, and "no call number" records, which could be used for verification within SMU's NOTIS system once an appropriate LC call number were added to the public catalog after the database was loaded. This report also highlighted a fair number of typographical errors involving lower-case rather than upper-case letters which are likely to appear within NOTIS as errors for correction as well. These results are being factored into the plans for online database editing prior to creation of "smart" barcodes late in the first year of NOTIS use.

Academic Planning

SMU President A. Kenneth Pye appointed two major planning teams in the fall of 1988:

1. The Academic Priorities Task Force: to identify the educational mission of SMU and the changes which would be needed to strengthen the academic programs of the institution;

2. The Financial Feasibility Task Force: to identify the current financial stability, ways and means to ensure a balanced budget, and to develop

realistic proposals for supporting the academic program priorities identified by the first group.

In fall 1989, SMU began a campus-wide review of the proposed academic changes and the financial means to accomplish them. This will become part of the ten-year campus regional accreditation process as well as the
basis for the immediate future at SMU.

The Collection Analysis project results will be used within the libraries to assess the collection strengths in support of new and expanded programs, develop fund-raising packages to assist in major collection expansions, and revise existing policies for programs which are reduced in
emphasis.

Collection Development

The Association for Higher Education of North Texas (AHE) has a history of
creative approaches to cooperation in sharing library resources; in the early
1980s, members of a task force began planning a quantitative study of the
comparative holdings by subject of participating libraries. The members were
particularly struck by the work done by Glyn Evans at SUNY which measured both the total holdings by subject area of compared libraries and the degree to which those libraries' collections overlapped in each category. The
task force decided to break down the RLG Conspectus by Library of Congress call number to define subject areas, and chose the schemes devised by
Mr. Evans for comparing the holdings of the libraries.

Financial limitations prevented the AHE libraries from running comparisons of their complete holdings. With funds sufficient to examine just
two years of cataloging (1982 and 1983), the task force chose to examine only
1982 imprints in our study. The primary reason for restricting the imprint
date to one year was to preserve the validity of the overlap study. If all imprints from the 1970s also had been included, a library purchasing a 1973 imprint during the study could be credited with a unique title, even if each of the
other libraries had purchased the book when it was published.

The two primary purposes of the AHE study were to determine the
nature of overlap among AHE collections and to identify areas of subject
strength. Results indicated that 22% of the books studied were held by only
one library. Another 24% were titles later to be received by other libraries,
and 54% of the books duplicated or multiplied copies already received by
other libraries.

One question that the AHE and other consortia must ask themselves
is: How strong is our joint collecting if all duplication is eliminated? The results of the survey tentatively indicate that the volumes collected by all of the
libraries could be multiplied by 46% to give the total number of different titles collected. Of equal interest was the discovery of where duplication was
the highest. In the social sciences and humanities, duplication was almost
60%; in the sciences and fine arts, it was slightly over 45%. The results of

even though the sciences are the preferred area for cooperation for most libraries.

The results measuring the collecting strength of each institution by subject area were also interesting. The compilation of subject strengths has offered itself as a base for discussions since the survey. AHE librarians have studied how to share collecting responsibilities by assigning subject responsibilities to the library with the greatest strength in the subject area.

Southern Methodist University

At SMU, the Tape Analysis Project analyzed the holdings of four libraries: Central University Libraries, Bridwell (Theology) Library, Underwood Law Library, and DeGolyer Library. The staff was particularly interested in the overlap between Central and Theology in philosophy and religion, between Central and Law in political science and law, and between Central and DeGolyer — which specializes in Western Americana — in Latin and North American history. Overlap was defined as the excess of copies held beyond one copy per title.

In areas where high duplication levels were expected, overlap ranged from 8% in Christianity, to 14% in History of the Americas and in Political Theory. These figures contrasted with overlap results generally from 0 to 3% in the sciences, and from 2 to 6% in the areas of the humanities and social sciences where high overlap was not expected. Such high overlap in Political Theory was not expected; all four libraries collected in that area, causing the high figure. In some areas, overlap was less than expected. Both Central and DeGolyer collect heavily, for example, in the History of Mexico, but the overlap figure was only 11%, due in part to efforts to avoid unnecessary duplication. The study was useful to document that such efforts are working, and in spotlighting areas such as Political Theory, to which no special attention had been given, for future concern.

The aspect of the study which measures holdings by subject area is expected to be very helpful in the refinement of SMU's Collection Development Policy. In some cases, the figures have implied that the collection is stronger than indicated in the Collection Development Policy; in other cases, they have implied the reverse. They, at least, present some indication beyond subjective impression of SMU's areas of greatest strength. In the future, SMU staff plan to compare their results to those of other universities to see which portions of their collection are relatively strong and weak. There are also plans to compare their collecting patterns over the next five years to assess the change from past patterns.

Metroplex Corporate Outreach

SMU is identifying several ways to expand fee-based library services to regional corporations in the greater Dallas "Metroplex" area. Funding from Southwestern Bell Foundation underwrote part of the project; a portion of their funds are to be used to develop a brochure which will identify major scientific and technical subject areas represented within the SMU library collections. The publication may well be expanded to show major collection strengths in all areas or may become a series of focused documents underlying fund raising efforts for the libraries and their collections as well as expansions and underwriting of the NOTIS system hardware.

The North American Theological Inventory

The Bridwell Library is SMU's principal bibliographic resource for the field of religion; it is the library for the Perkins School of Theology, a professional school which prepares individuals for careers in church leadership. The Bridwell participates actively in the American Theological Library Association (ATLA), whose member libraries provide library collections and services at graduate and professional schools of theology in North America.

Since 1985, the ATLA has engaged in a project of cooperative collection assessment known as the North American Theological Inventory (NATI). A committee led by Mr. Michael Boddy, then Theological Librarian at Drew University, analyzed the RLG Conspectus for religion and philosophy as a tool for inventorying theological collections. The committee found the Conspectus methodology to be useful, but found the Conspectus categories insufficiently precise for the sorts of analysis the ATLA members intended. Therefore, the NATI committee drew up revised Conspectus categories, expanding many previous entries so as to make the results more usable while maintaining congruence with the overall RLG Conspectus structure for wider comparisons.

For example, when the NATI committee began work, the RLG Conspectus contained only four categories for the history of Protestant churches [BX 4800-9999]. The committee expanded the number of entries to 33, providing a much more accurate, though still incomplete, list of religious bodies within the Protestant tradition, so that comparisons of collections' strengths and weaknesses could be made. Similar work was done throughout the schedule of LC classifications pertaining to religion, and to a lesser degree, philosophy, especially in LC classes BL to BX. The result was an expansion from 133 to 404 headings in the subjects of philosophy and religion.

The ATLA adopted the NATI project, offered training in the Conspectus methodology through workshops and materials, and urged all its members to analyze and report their collections, following the RLG Conspectus methodology with the NATI categories. To date, about fifty of the more than two hundred member libraries have done so. Results are to be prepared for further investigation by the continuing NATI committee of the ATLA, with a preliminary report to the 1990 annual meeting of the association in June.

In preparing the version of the Conspectus to be used to analyze the SMU library collections' holdings, the SMU committee assigned subject specialties to various staff bibliographers. The religion categories came to Roger

Loyd, who proposed the expansion of the Conspectus version available through AMIGOS by the adoption of the NATI structure for the religion schedule, with minor corrections. The SMU committee agreed, believing that the structure would be of use for its own local project of collection analysis, but realizing the value as well of providing the NATI structure to other libraries wishing to employ a fuller computer-generated analysis of their holdings in religion and philosophy than was previously available. This approach also allowed for full cooperation in the NATI project by the Bridwell Library, and by extension, the other SMU libraries.

NOTIS Database Planning

Early identification of overlap levels between the SMU collections has been important in determining specifications for the NOTIS system. The central system will enable the libraries to retain the autonomy in their collection policies while remaining sensitive to minimizing even further overlapping of collections. Overall, there is 10% overlap between two or more libraries; 610,000 unique titles to the 682,000 records in the consolidated first database processed. This provides some consolation as SMU investigates the storage capacity required within the NOTIS system to support full bibliographic access, including keyword/boolean, for almost 1 million records.

SMU is also reconfirming that significant materials "expected" in the Central Libraries collections will actually be found in the Bridwell Library collections through the accident of funding in the 1950s and 1960s. For example, non-trivial percentages of the unique titles at SMU in literature (6.9%), art (13.1%), and music (3.4%) reside in the Bridwell Library. While generally understood, these apparent anomalies will be part of long-range educational discussions as building renovations, expansions, and collection shifts are contemplated to respond to user requirements in the various schools.

Preservation Planning

SMU plans to work with AMIGOS to test the new software reporting and analyzing library holdings by date and by language. With these additional conspectus reports, particularly those segmenting the library holdings by date, SMU plans to develop long range goals in preservation — identifying blocks within the collections which are prime candidates for deacidification and other potential preservation solutions to deterioration problems.

The collection analysis reports will also be an additional assessment tool with faculty members in developing collection policies in direct support of the academic priorities and the foreign language support necessary and/or desirable for the increasingly international emphasis of the curriculum. A major concern in testing and utilizing new collection analysis software is the accuracy of the language coding for the files and the potential that only a small proportion of the database actually incorporates the optional language field.

Overall, we have been pleased with the first results of the SMU Tape Analysis Project and anticipate that future enhancements will provide the quantitative measures appropriate for the long-range library collection planning for Southern Methodist University.

Project Preparation

Due to the tremendous flexibility of AMIGOS' Tape Analysis Service, much forethought and planning is required to achieve results which will truly meet the library's need. Pre-project planning consists primarily of developing the subject groupings (conspectus file) and selecting report formats.

Development of Conspectus Files

Undoubtedly, the most important element of a Tape Analysis project is the conspectus file which contains all information required to separate library records into subject areas. Entries in the conspectus file contain the following information:

1. *Call number range.* This field holds the call number(s) corresponding to the desired subject area. It may consist of either a range (G-GF) of call numbers or a single call number (SB418).

   Examples: QL921 - QL939 counts all items with call numbers beginning with QL921, QL922, QL923, ... QL939

   SB418 counts all items with call numbers beginning with SB418

   CD-CZ counts all items with call numbers beginning with CD, CE, CF, CG ... CZ

   D-DZ counts all items with call numbers beginning with D, DA, DB, DC ... DZ

   SB counts all items with call numbers beginning with SB

2. *Class code.* Class codes are simply library-defined labels used to identify the subject area being counted.
   Examples: QL921 - QL939   BIO603
   SB418   AGR099
   CD-CZ   HIS000.2
   D-DZ   HIS000.2
   SB   AGR049.5

3. *Conspectus level.* Generally conspectus codes are divided into division, category, and subject levels allowing for report generation at any of the three levels. Conspectus entries range in generality from divi-

sion being the most general to subject being the most specific. This hierarchical structure follows that found in the Pacific Northwest Conspectus.

    a. *Division Level.* SMU defined 52 division level conspectus entries intended to provide general information about the collection. Typical division level codes included: AE-AI (General works), GN-GT (Anthropology), TR (Art), and QH-QL (Biological Sciences).

    b. *Category Level.* Category conspectus entries typically correspond to the next lower level of logical subject grouping. For SMU, category entries were considered subordinate to each division level entry created. Under the division GN-GT, there were entries for GN1-GN48 (Anthropology (General)), GN49-GN300 (Physical Anthropology), GN301-GN699 (Ethnology, Social and Cultural Anthropology), etc.

    c. *Subject Level.* These entries represent the most detailed level of analysis. As with the category level, SMU related the subject entries to the category level entries. Entries such as GN17 (Anthropology - History), GN20-GN21 (Anthropology - Biography), and GN23 (Anthropology - General works) are representative of the detailed analysis that may be performed.

4. *Descriptions.* For the benefit of those to whom the LC call number ranges and the conspectus codes are not meaningful, a free text description of the subject area is included.

Examples: QL921 - QL939   BIO603   Nervous System of Animals.
                SB418   AGR099   Container Gardening.
                CD-CZ   HIS000.2 History.
                D-DZ   HIS000.2 History.
                SB   AGR049.5 Plant Culture.

Tape Analysis Pre-processing

Input data for the SMU project consisted of approximately 732,000 records representing a combination of OCLC cataloging and retrospective conversion. During the first phase, call numbers are retrieved, validated, and upgraded among libraries, and duplicate record resolution is performed for all records within a given library.

    Call number retrieval and validation. The Tape Analysis software retrieves and verifies call numbers, selecting the first occurrence of a call number tag (050, 090, 099). The call number is examined to determine if it meets the criteria for LC call number format. Checks include the following:

The first subfield code, if present, must be ǂa; there must be at least one (1), but no more than three (3) alphabetic characters at the beginning of the number; the first position of the call number must NOT be equal to "I," "O," "W," "X," or "Y;" and, if the call number begins with three alphabetic characters, the first character must be "G" or "K."

If a library record exists which contains only invalid LC call number(s), the contents of the last field upon which verification was attempted will be assigned as call number for that OCLC number. If a library record does not contain a call number, the call number is left blank.

Examples:

090	QC2.F34 1987
090	QC3.G54 1988
050	QC3.G56 1987
Result:	QC3.G56 1987 (first 050)

082	564.56
086	Y4.C56:SRep 43
Result:	No call number (no 050, 090, 099)

099	IO456578
Result:	IO456578 (Invalid)

Call number upgrading. It is imperative that only one call number be used for all occurrences of an OCLC number. Therefore, all call numbers related to the same OCLC control number are reviewed and a single call number is selected to classify those records.

Examples:

First record:	No call number
Second record:	BS87.6.Y65 (090)
Result:	BS87.6.Y65 (No call number replaced by 090)
First record:	IO456578 (Invalid)
Second record:	AS76.23.A7 (090)
Result:	AS76.23.A7 (Invalid call number replaced by 090)
First record:	QC2.F34 1987 (090)
Second record:	QC911.C7 1987 (050)
Result:	QC911.C7 1987 (090 replaced by 050)

Tape Analysis Processing

Call numbers are compared against the conspectus files to determine where the item should be counted. Each bibliographic record will be counted in as many conspectus entries as appropriate. If the call number does not match any existing conspectus entry, the item is assigned to a system-generated "MISC" category. If the record does not contain a call number, it is assigned to a system-generated "NO CALL NUMBER" category.

Examples:

QL926.23.A7	BIO603
DZ87.6.Y65	HIS000.2
CD911.C7 1987	HIS000.2
QL930.9.C8 B78	BIO603
SB418.B6 1976	AGR099, AGR049.5

When this phase is completed, the records are processed to count the number of overlaps within each conspectus entry. Because this process compares across control number and conspectus code, records will be counted more than once if there is overlap within the conspectus codes. For example, if 3 of the 4 SMU libraries held a title classified as SB418.B6 1976, the overlap would show 3 libraries holding 1 title in AGR099 and AGR049.5

Reports

A variety of reports can be generated with the Tape Analysis Service. The following are examples of the five reports generated for the SMU project.

Report A

Library Code		Unique	ISM	ISB	FKS	IUF	Total	Pct. of Library	Pct. of SMU
	CLASS:	ADD000.1	GENERAL				AE-AI		
CNTRL		243	255	5	6	2	255	.052	.036
BRIDWL		35	5	42	2	1	42	.032	.006
DEGLYR		10	6	2	17		17	.029	.002
UNDRWD		5	2	1		8	8	.013	.001
		293					322		.045

NOTES:

1. Pct. of Library. This number is derived from dividing the total column by the number of titles held by the individual institution.
2. Pct. of SMU. This number is derived from dividing the total column by the total number of titles for the study.

Report B

CLASS: ADD000.1   GENERAL   AE-AI

Held by number of institutions:

Library Code	1	2	3	4	Total	Pct. of Library	Pct. of SMU
CENTRL	243	11	1		255	.052	.036
BRIDWL	35	6	1		42	.032	.006
DEGLYR	10	6	1		17	.029	.002
UNDRWD	5	3			8	.013	.001
Total Titles:	293	26	3		322		
Actual Titles:	293	13	1		307		.045

Report D

CLASS: ADD000.1   GENERAL   AE-AI

OCLC NUMBER	TITLE	AUTHOR	ISM	ISB	FKS	IUF	TOTAL
01546097	Centralized information s	Kent, Allen.	X	-	-	-	1
12991874	Diccionario manual; encic		X	-	-	-	1
12991896	Encyclopedie 360.		X	-	-	-	1
12991879	Petit Larousse illustre;	Larousse, Pierre	X	-	-	-	1
12991870	Poole's index to periodic		X	-	-	-	1
04178576	Wellesley index to Victor		X	-	-	-	1
12991833	Wonder world ...		X	-	-	-	1
08556164	index to Appleton's annua		X	-	-	-	1

Report E

INSTITUTION: ISM

CLASS CODE	DESCRIPTION	TOTAL	PERCENT OF COLLECTION
ADD000.1	GENERAL	8	.00
ADD000.2	GENERAL	65	.01
AGR000.1	AGRICULTURE	87	.01
ANT000.1	ANTHROPOLOGY	15	.00
ART000.2	ART	66	.01
ART000.3	ART	3	.00

Report J

INSTITUTION: ISM

CALL NUMBER	AUTHOR	TITLE	OCLC NUMBER
LKDKF	Larousse, Thom	How to manage computer	08761234
6556‡b		Library automation for	12345677
CD‡a34.4		Micrographics : its im	32542133
0L45‡b.R34	Helix, Strom	Mysteries of the holdi	43129992

Technology and Resource Sharing: Recent Developments and Future Scenarios

Marsha Ra
Director, University Library Automation Services
The City University of New York

Part I. Recent History: The 1970s and 1980s

The development and maturation of computer technology coupled with an unabated increase in the cost of library materials provided fertile ground for the growth of resource sharing among American and European libraries in the second half of the 20th century. The amount of resource sharing occurring among libraries took quantum leaps during the 1970s and 1980s, due to the creation and widespread acceptance of computerized bibliographic networks.

Important foundations had been laid during the late 1960s with the creation of the MARC Communications Format. Using this accepted standard format for the coding and transmission of bibliographic information, the major national bibliographic networks, OCLC, RLIN, WLN, and UTLAS were conceived, grew and flourished in the following decade. Libraries joined these networks primarily to automate the cataloging function. An important by-product of cataloging on the networks was the availability of information about the collections of member libraries. The networks soon became known as "utilities" due to their size and the growing dependence of libraries on them, much as individuals and institutions have become dependent on the utilities that supply them power. The majority of libraries used the bibliographic utilities to support wholesale retrospective conversion projects in preparation for in-house online catalogs and circulation systems. These data conversion projects resulted in huge databases spanning imprint years from the beginning of the printed book to the present. Thus OCLC, RLIN and WLN have come to replace the *National Union Catalog* as the primary source of information on holdings in U.S. libraries. The utilities were further enriched by the number of serial union listing projects which proliferated.

After a period of intense rivalry between the two major U.S. bibliographic utilities, RLIN and OCLC, the importance of these growing national databases to resource sharing led to a general acceptance of this bifurcation of the nation's composite bibliographic record. Since the goal of linking these giants was not achieved, it was not uncommon for libraries to belong to one network, but also pay for access to another, so that many libraries now had access to as many as 30,000,000 holdings records. Moreover, there was a good deal of tape loading occurring so that libraries which were members of one utility made their holdings known to members of the other. (For example, New York Public Research Libraries, an RLIN member, downloaded its complete 1.2 million-record machine-readable database into OCLC.)

The richness of the growing computerized bibliographic databases was enhanced by the introduction of interlibrary loan message systems on the utilities. These interlibrary loan modules enabled libraries to satisfy a very high percentage of researchers' needs for materials. In 1989, OCLC celebrated the 10th anniversary of the implementation of its ILL module. OCLC reported that there were 200 libraries using the new module in 1979. Twelve hundred requests were handled during the first month of operation, and approximately 570,000 ILL transactions occurred during the first year. In 1989, the average monthly request rate grew to over 316,000 and the number of participating libraries was over 3,400. During fiscal year 1988-89, 3.8 million requests were processed.[1]

Even very small libraries that could not afford the full services of the utilities were able to participate in computer supported resource sharing through OCLC's Group Access Capability (GAC). Using GAC, small libraries could search the system, view the holdings of OCLC member libraries who agree to participate with them as GAC partners, and request materials. Other solutions employed by smaller libraries as well as smaller networks and consortiums included the use of commercial vendor-supported interlibrary loan services and electronic mail networks. The various specialized library communities, such as medicine and law, also entered into computer-based resource sharing arrangements. Perhaps the most sophisticated and well-funded of these was DOCLINE developed by the National Library of Medicine. DOCLINE offered access to the periodical holdings of all participating medical libraries. Sophisticated software permitted each library to query a custom-tailored hierarchy of member libraries so that the largest of the libraries would not be overburdened.

Another step forward in resource sharing brought about by improved technology was in the area of document delivery. The first telefacsimile machines dated back to the nineteenth century. In the 1960s, 70s and as recently as the early 1980s there were several serious attempts to use telefacsimile transmission for the delivery of periodical articles. These attempts failed because the technology was still too crude. (Equipment was expensive, transmission was slow, copies were unclear, etc.) In the middle of the 1980s, industry acceptance of Group III fax machines capable of transmitting at 9600 baud coupled with a significant drop in the price of the equipment resulted in almost overnight enthusiastic acceptance of fax. In 1989, 77% of all U.S. businesses had installed telefacsimile machines, while 50% of government and education sites had access to fax equipment. It can be assumed that by the mid-1990s the number of libraries using telefacsimile will be as high or higher than the number belonging to a bibliographic utility in the 1980s. So common had fax become that in 1989 the ALA RASD ILL Committee's Fax Subcommittee began work on standards for the use of telefacsimile in interlibrary loan. The National Guidelines will cover borrowing strategies, copyright compliance, formatting of requests, and turnaround time.[2]

Fax was not regarded as the perfect solution, however. Problems still encountered were high phone line charges when fax partners are distant, and the expense of those machines which are best for libraries: machines which permit direct faxing from bound volumes, rather than making photocopies first and then loading the copied sheets onto the fax machine.

Another approach to obtaining the swift delivery of documents in the 1980s was to rely on commercial vendors who offered a combination of online access to periodical indexes with various storage media such as laser disk and cd-rom. An interlibrary loan librarian could search a database online for the desired material. If the material was found, a request for a copy was forwarded to the provider over the electronic network. The provider then produced a hard copy of the article on a laser printer and mailed, express mailed, or faxed the material to the library. The advantage of the laser disk storage medium is that images of illustrations can be retained and reproduced clearly. These document supply services were relatively inexpensive (about $10 per article delivered) and thus might tend to reduce the amount of resource sharing. The cost was little more than the fulfillment charge many private and research libraries levied on their non-reciprocal ILL partners.

II. The Challenges Facing Technology in Support of Resource Sharing in the 1990s

As we have seen, technological innovations in the 1970s and 1980s have brought about an increase in the availability of data, faster transmittal of requests and delivery of materials. Yet there are many challenges ahead. The continued rise in the cost of serials and the resulting cancellation of many subscriptions puts pressure on systems librarians and publishers to devise alternative methods for improved, economically viable yet affordable access to materials.

A problem still far from solution is that of access to the many electronic networks and databases. Access between the major utilities and among the ever burgeoning number of local automated systems leaves much to be desired. The necessity to log onto one system after another in order to search for a item is time consuming and tedious. Many systems of commands must be learned. Some understanding of telecommunications software is required. Moreover, the holdings information contained on the utilities is not entirely reliable for several reasons. First, many libraries have done wholesale retrospective conversion projects from shelf lists without checking the shelves. Thus the networks show ownership of many items which have long since been lost or are in such poor condition that they probably would not be allowed to circulate. Some libraries have used the services of a utility in which they do not maintain membership to create the retrospective file (for example, an RLIN library may contract with OCLC for the provision of retrospective records; an OCLC library may contract with UTLAS). The holdings represented for the non-member library will be unreliable if they are not kept up to date. Lost and missing items are not necessarily deleted from the utility. For these reasons, "hits" may turn out to be ghosts of items once owned.

Not all machine readable records are finding their way into any major utility. A good number of libraries are contracting with commercial firms for retrospective conversion projects are are not tape loading the resulting databases into a national utility. The only access to these holdings is through the local online catalog. The problem of phantom records is being aggravated today as more libraries implement online catalogs. When faced with a choice, most libraries would choose to keep holdings up to date in the local system rather than on the national utility. What is more, a single holding symbol can represent a large library system with branches ranging over an entire county. Information about which branch owns the title may be incomplete or lacking altogether. Such incomplete holding information can cause considerable delays in ILL turnaround time.

One of the recent developments which goes to the heart of the problem of many diverse systems and databases, is the adoption of OSI standards and its initial manifestation in the library world through the Linked Systems Project (LSP).

To the librarian on the line, the very term "Linked Systems Project" evoked dreams of a de facto national database. Soon the interlibrary loan librarian would be able to enter a single search on the network of choice and search the entire national database. An OCLC librarian would have access to the total RLIN database without leaving OCLC and vice versa. These dreams have not been realized. To date, the Linked Systems Project has been standards oriented and its specific applications have not made any apparent impact on ILL librarians. However, the standards which were developed under LSP and the problems identified formed an important foundation for subsequent developments which will have an effect on resource sharing.

The Linked Systems Project was started at the beginning of the decade. The primary participants were the Library of Congress, the Research Library Group (RLG), OCLC, and the Western Library Network (WLN). Although the prime players were thus the four largest networks, the goal as conceived by the LSP participants was to develop standards which could also be used between local systems and the national networks as well as between local systems.

By 1985 the LSP participants had adopted an important telecommunications standard: the seven layer communication protocol known as the Open System Interconnection protocols (OSI) which had been developed by the International Organization for Standardization (ISO). (In fact, not every layer of the seven tier protocol had been approved by ISO by the time the LSP initial applications were implemented. Some variations developed between the LSP protocols and the ISO approved protocols.)[3]

Beyond the adoption of these standards, the specific goals of LSP

were:
1. computer to computer record transfer;
2. the ability to search a target system from one's own system (without logging off); and
3. the transfer of interlibrary loan messages.

Perhaps the most successful application developed was the first: the ability to transfer bibliographic data between utilities as well as between a utility and a local system. However, the specific applications developed do little to support resource sharing. The first implementation of the transfer application was the transferring of authority records between LC and RLIN. The aim was to keep the authority files synchronized in order to support shared responsibility for the building of the Library of Congress Name Authority file under the NACO project.

Today, over 2,000 records pass daily over the LSP link between LC and RLIN. In another transfer application, Geac Computers developed LSP application software to permit New York University to download NYU's RLIN cataloging directly to their local Geac library system. Again, there is no resource sharing aspect to this project. While the technology demonstrated is impressive, it is hard for a librarian whose main interest is resource sharing to become enthusiastic about a system which seems to do nothing more than what is already accomplished with "black box" type interfaces and tape loading. The next stage will see transfer of MARC bibliographic records. Theoretically, RLIN and OCLC could transfer member copy in this way. But even if this were politically possible, it would make little economic sense to duplicate enormous files in this manner. It would be preferable to be able to search without leaving the host system, and this was also a goal of LSP.

LSP applications layer software to permit librarians at the Library of Congress to search RLIN without leaving LC's own Scorpio system was also developed and tested with some success. While LSP protocols enable the search of a target system, they do not guarantee that the search results will match the result which would be expected in the home network. The structure of the target database indexes must be well understood by the searcher. LSP does contain provisions for formulating a search as it would be structured on the target system, but this requires the searcher to have knowledge of how the target system functions and defeats the LSP goal of using searches familiar to the searcher. Other approaches to searching across systems are clearly called for.

In the meantime, some libraries with the need for access to the catalog of a particular "trading" partner have resorted to having extra terminals in-house which access the other library's catalog. For example, Vanderbilt University and the University of Tennessee at Knoxville participate in a joint-use project. They each have set up extra terminals to access the other's catalog. The City University of New York Graduate Center has a special relationship with New York Public Library Research Library. Although CUNY is a NOTIS site, a CATNYP (Carlyle) terminal sits in the Graduate Center library to ease access to NYPL.

In the area of interlibrary loan, The National Library of Canada worked on an interlibrary loan application. NISO is working on a standard for ILL transactions based on this model, standard Z39.63. The elements needed for a standard for ILL transactions are:

1. a definition of ILL data elements, and
2. a definition of the conversion protocols.

X.400 is the telecommunications protocol on which this standard will be built. So far, this protocol has not been generally available in the United States and so very little has been done with implementation of this standard in this country. However, IBM recently announced its first OSI product which is a messaging system for electronic mail and file transfer. The product will utilize X.400. Therefore some movement may soon be seen in the interlibrary loan arena.

The desire to link across networks is not unique to library computing. Universities and government agencies have had links between computer networks for years. These links are based primarily on protocols developed by the Department of Defense in 1969 for its research network ARPANET, and are known as TCP/IP [Transmission Control Protocol/Internet Protocols].[4] In the 1970s the DARPA Internet was formed in response to a need to interconnect different types of packet switching networks. It now consists of more than 300 networks, hundreds of gateways and tens of thousands of host computers. While the library world pursued OSI, there was already a vast TCP/IP network in place. It was assumed that TCP/IP would eventually be replaced with OSI. It now appears that rather than simply replace TCP/IP, it will be subsumed in OSI as the transport layer in the seven layer OSI protocol. Thus the conflict would seem to have been resolved. What has not been resolved is the expense of OSI products and the fact that there is no guarantee that any particular OSI application will be compatible with any other.

Another recent development which will work hand in hand with OSI is the acceptance of a Standard Query Language (SQL) or common command language which each system could theoretically support and which would be used between systems. The need for a common command language was clearly demonstrated in the Linked Systems Project and has been discussed for nearly a decade. Z39.58, the common command language, was approved in 1988. Also approved is Z39.50, the standard Information Retrieval Protocol. Both Z39.50 and Z39.58 are now accepted as an integral part of the OSI application layer. OCLC is using these protocols in its new EPIC service which is a full reference tool. Z39.50 totally circumvents the problem which the LSP project demonstrated: the need to understand the structure of the target system. Z39.50 permits primarily boolean type searching using AND/OR and AND-NOT operators. With the accepted applications layers of Z39.50 and Z39.58, OSI may soon transform resource sharing in the United States.

The development of these standards comes at a time when two paths have converged: that of the librarians and the academic and research computing communities. While libraries were investing time and funds into the growth and development of machine-readable databases on the OCLC, RLIN, while LSP was conceived and implemented, most academic librarians had very little contact with their local campus computer centers. At many universities, computing generally falls into two basic categories: administrative computing (fiscal programs, registration, payroll) and academic computing (support of research and instruction). Libraries fall somewhere in-between. Usually, the first meaningful contact libraries had with their campus computer centers was related to administrative computing occasioned by the need for patron lists for circulation systems, support of fund accounting in acquisitions, etc. But it is in the academic computing environment where interest in the direct provision of information to researchers has emerged. Librarians are finding that their own automation efforts and their role as information providers seem to converge or even compete with the goals of academic computing.

Simultaneous to the developments in the world of library automation, as we have seen, computer networks were being developed to support scholarship and research on campuses all over the country and at government agencies which supported research at various universities. A huge Internet based on TCP/IP protocols developed to support communications, file transfer, and access to supercomputer facilities. Interest in upgrading the NSFNET and NYSERNET backbones to these networks into a new high speed, state of the art network has recently emerged.

As of this writing, scholars all over the country can access more than 60 university library catalogs as well as CARL (Colorado Area Research Network) and RLIN over the Internet without paying communications charges. (The 60 university library catalogs are searchable free of charge. CARL is free except for its Uncover database, a database which includes periodical contents. RLIN also charges scholars for connect time.) OCLC's EPIC database may also become available over the Internet. BRS is committed to an interconnection with the Internet through NYSERNET, the New York State Education and Research Network. The first attempt to list the libraries available on the Internet was undertaken in 1988 and yielded about 20 libraries. The next year a more comprehensive list was attempted. Evidence of the lack of communications between some libraries and their academic computing centers can be found in fact that many librarians do not know that their own online catalogs are accessible in this way. Some libraries, knowing that they are accessible, choose not to answer the call for Internet addresses because they are reluctant to provide unmediated, uncontrolled access to their catalogs.

In the United Kingdom, university libraries have access to a completely free single wide area network, JANET ("Joint Academic Network"). JANET is a node on the Internet used for national and international E-mail file transfer and terminal access. Costs are borne by the Computer Board for Universities and Research Councils of the UK. More than 40 OPACS are accessible over JANET and access to the British Lending Library's services, Blaise-Line and ARTel, a document ordering service operated by Document Supply Center, as well as various free databases, is provided. The University of Sussex Library publishes a directory of the network addresses. JANET participants are now investigating the feasibility of adding databases such as BRS to the services available over its lines.[5]

In the United States, thus far, Internet access to OPACs has been used by scholars who are very familiar and comfortable with computers. At more than one computer center in the United States, faculty have been given seminars and handed out instructions on using the catalogs available on the Internet without consulting the campus librarians. It has also been used by some librarians, but more as a curiosity. At this point, all the Internet accomplishes is a free and simple way to, in effect, dial a series of local databases. There is no hierarchy, no subject directory, no help of any kind to advise researchers on the likelihood of finding desired materials or information in any of the searchable catalogs. None of the OPACs searchable on the Internet supports Z39.50, the Common Command Language. Thus to search each OPAC, new commands must be learned.

From the ILL librarian's viewpoint, the Internet is certainly no improvement on searching the large utilities or the one or two local OPACs of those libraries with which special sharing relationships have been established. A single search of OCLC or RLIN will verify the existence of an item, or bring to light an error in the supplied citation. Much time and effort is thus saved. Furthermore, the utilities support interlibrary loan communications and protocols.

Although searching many diverse catalogs is time consuming, the online catalog is the most reliable source for up-to-date information on a library's collection. However, even as the capability to access OPACs is extended thorough the Internet, access to OPACs may become temporarily restricted because of another development. A recent trend is to load files such as Current Contents, ERIC, the Wilson databases, MLA, etc. into the OPAC so that library users may search periodical indexes online using the same commands they are accustomed to in the online catalog. Unrestricted access, as is afforded by the Internet, exposes the library to contract violations. Most vendors of these files charge based on numbers of terminals accessing the database, or the number of simultaneous users. Software must be available to each local system to limit the files that may be searched. The ability to develop and use such software may depend on the OPAC vendor, the campus computer center, or both. Librarians may not feel they have the finances or the political clout on their campus to insure that such software is in place and may, therefore, wish to place their online systems off-limits to outsiders at least for a while.

Another concern, especially of systems librarians, is that permitting outside access to the library's OPAC over the Internet where there is no control over who comes in, may result in very slow response time. Emory University recently gave its library staff access to RLIN through the Internet. Although Internet access was potentially easier and faster than the modem pool and Telenet access, if only a few people used the Internet link simultaneously, throughput would start to suffer because everyone was using the same

9600 bps connection. The concern is that outside users would clog up and slow down access for campus users who are dialing in from home or office.

Despite shortcomings of the Internet in its present form, it cannot be dismissed by librarians. Over the past two years, Educom's Telecommunications Task Force (including representatives from LC, OCLC, and RLIN) has been meeting to plan the next incarnation of the Internet—a broad band width (T3) Network for Research and Education, NREN. Once such a powerful network is in place, the question of slow throughput will disappear, at least for the transmission of standard text and for the type of transactions which occur now in libraries. NREN is being pursued in Washington as one factor in the campaign to make the United States economically competitive.

Given the high level of interest in the development of the National Research and Education Network and the role the existing networks will play in this resource, it will become as important to librarians as RLIN, OCLC, and LC are today. The Internet as it now exists, and NREN when implemented, provides not only the ability to communicate with hundreds of computers, it also supports file transfer (FTP file transfer protocol). Therefore, it could become an important means for transferring bibliographic information and text such as electronically published journals, etc. Will this be an answer to the staggering costs of serials?

Methods of document delivery supported by technology are far from perfect. The problem is exacerbated by a proliferation of media in which information is stored. An early example of technology getting in the way of resource sharing is the use of microform for back files of journals for space saving or security reasons. With microform there is more staff work required to produce the copy requested for interlibrary loan; reader printers are unreliable; the quality of the copy is frequently unacceptable. In a more recent development, it is not yet clear where "hypermedia" publications containing sound, pictures and text, as well as interactive sections, should fit into resource sharing. Does a library share such materials? If so, what is the method of delivery: does one mail the CD? Will it be possible to send it electronically to a target workstation?

III. The Future of Resource Sharing: Is There Any?

In a paradox typical of technological development, the advent of the computer at first increased the amount of resource sharing that went on between libraries. Now as the technology advances, it will probably make interlibrary loan obsolete within a generation. The goal of computerized information resources which are easily accessible electronically is being pursued by university administrations as well as many librarians. This goal may conflict with the goal pursued by a large part of the library profession. The basic conflict in the two camps is that one group is working toward provision of information directly to the user, while the other group is concerned with improving the mediated services which librarians provide. One assumes a highly sophisticated scholar user; the other assumes that librarians still have a role to play in scholarship and research.

One of the distinctions between the recent efforts to overcome the incompatibilities between OCLC and RLIN, which were at the core of LSP and the impetus behind the Internet and NREN, is the target beneficiaries of the efforts. LSP was directed at librarians. It was a means to improving behind the scenes production work that goes on in libraries. The Internet and NREN are directed at researchers, educators and, perhaps, librarians. Furthermore, the promise of NREN as a vital factor in the on-going economy and the defense of the United States, gives it the hope of having an influx of funds to support it that a library cooperative venture can never dream of realizing. With T3 telecommunications lines, with laser storage, and group IV fax technology, it will soon be possible to send fully digitized files of text and illustrations over the NREN to a requestor's workstation, whether the requestor is a librarian or an individual. The day is not far off when systems will be linked through common communications protocols, and bibliographic and other text files will be searchable by an accepted common command language, over a national education and research network, with fax machines sharing the same common and subsidized communications network. Powerful communications lines will permit the sending of digitized illustrations directly to workstation screens. Resources will be created and shared dynamically without the involvement of librarians.

A critical factor in forecasting the role technology will play in "resource sharing" in the decades to come is the manner in which scholarly information is developed, shared, and transmitted. This is changing so drastically, that it will be a challenge to librarians to find their place in this brave new world of communications and access. Since scholars and writers work on word processors, and publishers use computers for the creation of their products, the electronic database becomes the product. As academics use microcomputers for writing and communicating over networks in the pursuit of research, more scholarly information is in the electronic medium. It seems a natural progression for electronic publishing to proliferate, and, in the academic world, to short circuit and eliminate the incredible expense of publications. If the scholarly community doesn't figure out how to avoid the expense of publications, the publishing world will figure out how to charge for the electronic databases which are becoming more important as a revenue base than print media in some cases. (*Chemical Abstracts*, for example, now finds that cost recovery for the production of their database is found in their electronic product, whereas just five years ago, it was found in their paper product.)

Librarians now expound the view made acceptable by economics that libraries strive to provide access rather than to amass comprehensive collections. But why is a library necessary to provide access when the technology permits access at the scholar's home or office? Rather than the traditional model of researchers using their own library, visiting or borrowing from other libraries over ILL, and then producing a book or article which is transmitted through publication, some envision a network of library and database resources which are held locally and remotely. The researcher uses the same network to access information, share files with colleagues in the production of research, and then publishes the results electronically over the same network. It is to this end that many of the new standards are being developed: not to the end of easy access in and out of each other's OPACs. In addition to Z39.50 and Z39.58 standards mentioned above, the Standard Generalized Markup Language (ISO standard 8879) and NISO Z39.59, accepted by the Association of American Publishers, facilitates the transfer of articles, books, etc. on word processing so that the publishers can avoid rekeying. This is being taken further by TEI, the Text Encoding Initiative at the University of Illinois at Chicago, the goal of which is to flag accurately contents of a document for easy and precise indexing.[6] Standards for storing and transmitting hypermedia are also under development. Eventually, resource sharing in the profoundest sense, may go on in academic communities with little involvement of librarians. Robert L. Parks, director of the Office of Public Affairs of the American Physical Society, testified before a congressional hearing on access to electronic databases:

> We are fast appproaching the day when electronic databases will largely supplant conventional libraries as the repository of scientific and technical information and will become the preferred means by which scientists communicate their findings.[7]

But a role for librarians in the immediate future can be considerable. Ronald F. E. Weissman, Asst. VP for Academic Computing, Brown University, writing about the change in academic computing from programming to the collection and analysis of information:

> The University will increasingly see its role as that of online information provider to aid exploratory learning and research. And providing a rich body of online information will be a growing challenge for academic libraries worldwide, and will foster much cooperation, sharing and joint development efforts between libraries and computing centers. Indeed, the provision of such a data-rich world will make academic libraries significant change agents in higher education, and key to our next-generation technology architecture.[8]

The day may come when libraries as we know them become museums of materials which predate this truly electronic age, and serve as repositories of books for recreational reading. In the meantime, there are issues to be faced relative to the diverging goals of the librarian and the academic computing world. First and foremost is the question of mediated versus non-mediated access. Today's scholar in the United States can access at least 60 OPACs electronically at no cost to him. Some day, he will probably be able to access 1,000. If 1,000 libraries are available, how does he choose and what does he do with the information he finds? A world of information is available to him. What does he do with it? (The possibility of expert systems and knowledge navigators which would let the searcher know the best approach to the subject to be researched is a possibility.)

Of most relevance here to the question of resource sharing as it is today, is the issue of what access to 40, 60 or 1,000 OPACs and bibliographic files really means in the practical sense of getting the material represented by these systems to the user. If I have direct access to the catalogs of Notre Dame, Princeton, Yale, Harvard, Columbia, etc., does this mean I have access to their collections? Does that mean that I know, understand, and accept the carefully negotiated arrangements for economically fair resource sharing that librarians at these institutions have made?

Providing direct access to the "world" is not necessarily desirable. The need for a mediating librarian is seen as necessary not only by the librarians who would mediate, but also by those librarians at the institutions whose catalogs are being accessed by the scholar at his or her workstation. What user will submit requests which follow national interlibrary loan code? Who would be responsible for making sure that the user's own library doesn't already own the item?

IV. Conclusion

For the immediate future, resource sharing and document delivery continue to be enhanced by the evolving computer and telecommunications technology. However, librarians at the institution level should become involved with the research computing community so that they remain a vital part of the delivery of information. Librarians can play an important role in assuring that technology does not lead to chaos, that order is maintained. Librarians may be able to prevent technology from causing major disruptions in our carefully structured resource sharing arrangements while they are still necessary. For the long term, librarians may have to choose between two diverging paths: either increasing involvement in the emerging electronic world of scholarship, bringing their skills and knowledge to this new world, allying with scholars and producers of electronically created and disseminated information; OR, becoming curators in the more traditional type of library. The librarian may also serve as a bridge between the traditional and the new, serving the needs of the less educated by mediating, teaching and bringing them up to a level where they can become part of the electronic age. Whichever path the individual librarian chooses, resource sharing as we now understand it will probably cease to exist.

Notes

1.   Storey, Tom. "OCLC to Celebrate 10th Anniversary of Interlibrary Loan Subsystem," *OCLC Newsletter*, no. 179: p. 8 (May/June 1989).

2. *Library Systems Newsletter* 9, no. 6: p. 49 (June 1989).

3. McCoy, Richard W. "The Linked Systems Project: Progress, Promise, Realities," *Library Journal* 111, no. 17: pp. 33-39 (October 1, 1986).

4. Avram, Henriette. "Building a Unified Information Network," *Library Hi Tech* 6, no. 4 (issue 24): pp. 117-119 (1988).

5. Buxton, Andrew. "JANET and the Librarian." *The Electronic Library*, 6, no. 4: pp. 250-263 (1988).

6. Goldstein, Charles. "Full Text Retrieval from Structured Text," *Bulletin of the American Society for Information Sciences* 16, no. 6: p. 11 (Aug./Sept. 1989).

7. Quoted in Turner, Judith Axler, "Effort to Limit Access to Unclassified Data Bases Draws Criticism," *Chronicle of Higher Education* 33:12 (Mar. 4, 1987).

8. In: *Brown Online*, 2: pp. 3-6 (May, 1989).

The Impact of CD-ROM on Resource Sharing

Marilyn K. Moody
formerly Head, Access Services Department
Parks Library, Iowa State University

The impact of CD-ROM on resource sharing is quite complex and multi-faceted, yet very few librarians have considered this aspect of CD-ROM usage. This is especially ironic when compared to the excitement librarians are showing about the impact of CD-ROM on reference services. In reviewing CD-ROM literature, it sometimes seems that every library which has implemented ERIC on CD-ROM has written an article about that experience. However, the impact of CD-ROM on interlibrary loan services and the broader topic of resource sharing has seldom been mentioned, or has been discussed only in a perfunctory manner.

This chapter reviews several different aspects of CD-ROM and its relationship to resource sharing. While a large part of this chapter is descriptive of the current state of CD-ROM activities, it also discusses the implications for the future. While not attempting to be exhaustive in describing every CD-ROM product or service, it does include examples that are representative of the variety and complexity of the CD-ROM products and activities which have, or will have, an impact on resource sharing.

CD-ROM Union Catalogs

Perhaps the most direct impact of CD-ROM technology on resource sharing has been caused by the birth of the CD-ROM union catalog. In many states the production of these catalogs has been spearheaded by the State Library or State Department of Education, often through the use of LSCA federal funding. Unlike many online systems, public and secondary school libraries have been major participants in the development of these catalogs. Universities, academic libraries, and special libraries have also been involved in union catalog projects. In some instances, catalogs have been developed and used by existing networks or consortia, and in others, they have become the reason for developing a new resource sharing network.

Typically, a CD-ROM union catalog is formed by bringing together the machine-readable records and holdings of the libraries in the project and forming a union listing based on those records. In some projects, the creation of machine-readable records and the retrospective conversion of materials into machine-readable form is also a major component. Although the majority of these projects have worked with monographic print materials, serials catalogs and catalogs of non-print materials are also being produced.

Pennsylvania is one of the leaders in this area with the development of the Access Pennsylvania CD-ROM database. Introduced in 1986 with a database of 650,000 school, academic, and public library records, the union catalog was created as part of a larger initiative to provide access to libraries and information for all citizens of Pennsylvania.[1] The catalog itself is based on Brodart's Le Pac catalog, which has fairly sophisticated search software, including Boolean logic. Although not all of the objectives of the overall ACCESS Pennsylvania plan were realized, the union catalog has been a very successful component of the project. The union catalog has had a dramatic impact on resource sharing, particularly for the school libraries involved with the project. Libraries which had never participated in interlibrary loan now have a system which allows them to determine easily the location of items held statewide. These same libraries' holdings also became accessible to other libraries, allowing small libraries which had never before lent items to become lenders. Shortly after the project began, it was reported that all types of libraries participating in the project had indicated a 68% increase in interlibrary loan transactions.[2]

A similar project modeled after the Pennsylvania model is the MaineCat union catalog developed by the Maine State Library. Using Autographics as their vendor, the database includes 950,000 unique titles with 170 libraries participating in the project. This catalog became operational in December 1988, with 50 additional libraries scheduled to be added as participants in July 1989.[3]

The Missouri State Library has also been involved with a statewide union catalog project using Le Pac software. The first edition included 3 million records from over 200 multi-type libraries. LSCA funding was offered to all tax-supported public libraries in the state to purchase microcomputers, CD-ROM drives, modems, and BiblioFile for retrospective conversion use.[4] The Missouri system uses ALANET as the communication system for its interlibrary loan transactions.

Wisconsin has also developed a system using Brodart's Le Pac software. Their 3.2 million-plus title database is replacing a microfiche union catalog of more than 6,000 fiche. The Le Pac catalog is in the process of being tested at 17 libraries in the state.[5] The State of Kansas has also contracted with Brodart for the production of a union catalog on CD-ROM. Like Missouri, they also use ALANET as a communication medium.[6]

Iowa was one of the first states to develop a CD-ROM union catalog, with the development of its product, the Iowa Locator, in 1986. Sponsored by the State Library of Iowa, the product was developed and produced by an independent contractor, the Blue Bear Group. The third edition of the Iowa Locator, released in October 1988, included more than 5 million unique titles.[7]

The State of Nevada used General Research Corporations' LaserGuide system to implement a statewide union catalog. The system includes more than 1.2 million holdings with 60 workstations installed in public, academic, and state government libraries. This catalog is used not only for statewide resource sharing, but is also used by smaller libraries as their local in-house catalog.[8]

The State Library of Louisiana has also developed a statewide catalog, called LAsernet. Over one million titles and four million holdings statements from over 100 public and academic libraries are included.[9] This catalog uses the Library Systems & Services Inc. LOANet CD-ROM based interlibrary loan system. The state of Mississippi is also involved with a similar system utilizing LOANet.[10]

A union catalog which is based on a network rather than a state is the Western Library Network's CD-ROM LaserCat. First introduced in 1987, the most current edition includes 2.56 million bibliographic records. WLN's members subscribing to this service include over 300 libraries in Washington, Idaho, Oregon, Montana, British Columbia, Arizona, and Alaska.[11]

Consortia covering smaller geographic areas or individual public library or public school systems have also been produced. In New York, The Nassau Library System, Suffolk Cooperative Library System, and Long Island Library Resources Council have developed a CD-ROM catalog.[12] Other examples include the 16 public and three academic libraries of the Waukesha County Federated Library System (WI), and the 30 public libraries in the Finger Lakes Library System (NY), which both use Le Pac for their CD-ROM products. One of the largest CD-ROM installations is the Los Angeles County Public Library system. Their installation includes 445 Le Pac public access catalogs distributed throughout the library system.[13]

These union catalogs have had varying effects, but in most cases they have increased overall interlibrary loan activity. These catalogs also have the potential to change dramatically the pattern of interlibrary loan transactions for libraries using these products. Smaller libraries may become much more involved with interlibrary loan, especially if their holdings have never before been available to other libraries. When a union catalog is provided for public access searching, patrons may become more interested in borrowing materials through interlibrary loan or in using the collections of a geographically close collection on-site. Libraries such as school libraries, which historically have been nonparticipants in interlibrary loan activities, may now become involved as they find the CD-ROM union catalog to be fitted to their resource sharing needs.

The provision of a statewide or regional catalog also tends to reinforce the traditional interlibrary loan concept of exhausting local resources before requesting items from libraries in another region or from out-of-state. Libraries using OCLC for interlibrary loan, for example, may find that requesting an item from a library across the country is just as convenient, and sometimes just as quick, as requesting from the library 30 miles down the road. In some respects, the OCLC ILL subsystem has caused an erosion of the concept of local resource sharing. CD-ROM catalogs may have revived this idea. Many CD-ROM products are used in conjunction with a local or statewide communications system which can also reinforce the local aspect of resource sharing.

Along with the Library Systems and Services interlibrary loan system previously mentioned, both Autographics and Brodart have developed interlibrary loan modules which can be used with their CD-ROM products. These systems can be used by consortia or networks to support their interlibrary loan transactions. Both systems allow for the downloading of data from the CD-ROM catalog to an interlibrary loan request form. Individual libraries are then linked together through a communications system so that requests can be sent electronically between the libraries.[14]

As the downloading components and communication systems used with the CD-ROM catalogs become more sophisticated, this type of interlibrary loan system will become an even more attractive option. Networks and consortia which have felt that more traditional online systems were financially out of their reach are finding CD-ROM based systems to be an attractive and viable option.

Bibliographic CD-ROM Databases

Most libraries find that online searching services increase interlibrary loan activity by making users aware of resources not owned by their own library. Some studies do seem to suggest that the impact of online searching on interlibrary loan is situation specific, with the types of databases searched, the nature of the searches, and the nature of the library collection being used by the searcher influencing the impact of the search on interlibrary loan services.[15] The impact of CD-ROM database searching seems to reinforce these beliefs, although the differences between online and CD-ROM searching may cause the impact to vary. One especially significant difference for academic libraries is that undergraduate students are major users of CD-ROM databases, but are typically not heavy users of online services. Undergraduate students are also lighter users of interlibrary loan services in general. While these characteristics may tend to minimize the impact on interlibrary loan services, the fact that these users are encountering more citations, as well as citations that they would not previously have had access to, probably causes an overall increase in interlibrary loan activity resulting from CD-ROM searching of bibliographic databases. In other libraries, such as many high school and smaller public libraries, online searching has never been available. In these cases, the provision of CD-ROM databases may dramatically increase the demand for interlibrary loan services.

Several libraries have, in fact, reported an increase in interlibrary loan activity which appears to be caused by CD-ROM database searching. The University of Vermont reported an increase in interlibrary loan activity with the introduction of end-user searching, primarily CD-ROM based searching. They found that total interlibrary loan requests increased 14% and interlibrary loan requests indicating verification by a computer search increased by 173%.[16] The University of North Carolina at Chapel Hill has also reported an increase in interlibrary loan requests attributed to their use of CD-ROM databases.[17] A study of the use of CD-ROM products in Canadian libraries found a corresponding increase in interlibrary loan activity.[18] Some libraries, however, have reported that the implementation of InfoTrak, used primarily by undergraduate students, did not increase interlibrary loan activity. This observation reinforces the concept that the patron and type of search being performed are important factors in predicting whether increased interlibrary loan and document delivery activity will occur.[19]

Another way in which CD-ROM databases may affect resource sharing is in the sharing of the databases themselves by libraries. Geographically close libraries may opt to either formally or informally coordinate their purchase of CD-ROM databases. Other libraries use telefacsimile or communications systems to transmit searches performed for other libraries in a consortium or system.

A $43,000 LSCA III grant provided the impetus for one such system. Coordinated by the DuPage Library System, this project called "Reference by GammaFax" included five libraries housing different CD-ROM databases. An additional five libraries were designated as receiving libraries. All ten libraries were networked with telefacsimile machines and GammaFax software, which made it possible to transmit search results directly from the microcomputer running the CD-ROM database to the library initiating a request by telefacsimile for a search of a CD-ROM database. The sharing of resources in this case not only meant the search results, but also the sharing of technological and database searching expertise. As a multi-type project including public, academic and high school, and hospital libraries, many of the participants had no previous direct experience with database searching.[20]

Full-Text CD-ROM Databases

Several full-text databases are now available in CD-ROM format. These databases pose some interesting questions regarding resource sharing activities, particularly in reference to copyright implications. How and whether the information included in these databases may be legally shared with others will have a definite impact on the resource sharing scene.

One of the most extensive full-text database projects is the international project ADONIS. This effort, sponsored by various agencies both public and private, has been in the planning stages since 1979, with a workable form not appearing until 1987. The ADONIS project includes the full-text of over 200 of the most heavily used biomedical journals. One of the concepts being tested by the publishers involved is whether copyright revenue can be obtained by supplying these journal articles on CD-ROM to document delivery sources. The document delivery suppliers then charge individual users for each article obtained via the CD-ROM text. The two document delivery suppliers involved in the test project in the U.S. are Information on Demand and University Microfilms International (UMI).[21] The results of this project will help determine whether full-text delivery of journals is an economically viable option. It may heavily influence whether other journal publishers will follow in distributing journals on CD-ROM.

UMI has introduced the Business Periodicals Ondisc system which provides the full-text on CD-ROM of 300 business and management journals indexed in the ABI/INFORM bibliographic database.[22]   Another example of full-text data is the Laserdisclosure system available from Disclosure.   This system provides access to Securities and Exchange documents, including 10-K's, 10-Q's, annual reports, and other filings.[23]   Moody's Manuals also produces a full-text database of business and financial information taken from their series of Manuals.[24]

A third example of a full-text database is the Cross-Cultural CD series being developed by SilverPlatter.   This series of databases is derived from texts included in the Human Relations Area Files (HRAF), which include information on societies and cultures worldwide.[25]   SilverPlatter also publishes the Peterson's College Database which includes over 3,000 detailed profiles of degree-granting colleges in the U.S. and Canada.   Searching by free text or by codes describing the institutions is possible.[26]

The Institute of Electrical and Electronics Engineers, Inc. (IEEE) and the Institution of Electrical Engineers (IEE) are also involved in a test CD-ROM full-text project.   In this project, they will be making available to 12 corporate, university, and government library test sites, the full text of their journals, magazines, conference proceedings, and standards.[27] A popular full-text product which has been purchased by many public and school libraries as well as academic libraries is *The New Grolier Electronic Encyclopedia*, which includes the full text of the *Academic American Encyclopedia*.[28]

As these products become more available on a wide range of subjects, and as new materials are produced which are only available in the CD-ROM format, libraries will need to deal with complicated access issues.   Just as some large microform sets are now owned only by a few research libraries, some CD-ROM products may only be available from a few libraries.   Other libraries may band together to purchase cooperatively CD-ROM full-text products, providing access to members of the consortium.   The potential for cooperative resource sharing projects for full-text databases seems quite good, especially as the technology for telefacsimile transmission and electronic transmission of large text files rapidly improves.   What may prove to be the stumbling block for resource sharing is the licensing and copyright implications for CD-ROM databases that have yet to be fully sorted out, both in a legal sense and in a marketing sense by the database producers and vendors.

U.S. copyright law does not provide any crystal clear guidance for traditional print materials, and provides even less for machine-readable databases.   Even the concept of "database" is not really defined.   At this point in time, libraries are understandably confused over the legal implications of downloading and other means of transferring database information to a wide variety of users with a variety of uses for the information. The most promising approach seems to be to negotiate with the vendor of the database a contract or licensing agreement which specifically spells out the rules, limits, and boundaries of a library's intended use of the product. [29]

Interlibrary Loan "Tools" Databases

CD-ROM databases are also being developed that can be used as interlibrary loan verification sources. As more CD-ROM products are developed, these types of tools will become increasingly significant, especially in the area of document delivery and communication networks. As these tools make the identification of bibliographic items easier, there will be increased pressure from users to quickly obtain the items found in these databases. These products are very well suited to the CD-ROM format, with the sophisticated searching software providing much greater access than their printed counterparts.

Two standard verification sources, *Books in Print* and *Ulrich's International Periodicals Directory* are available in CD-ROM format. The CD-ROM *Books in Print Plus* includes listings from *Books in Print, Subject Guide to Books in Print, Forthcoming Books in Print, Supplement to Books in Print, Children's Books in Print,* and the *Subject Guide to Children's Books in Print.* The CD-ROM *Ulrich's Plus* provides access to the information included in *Ulrich's International Periodicals Directory,* and *Irregular Serials and Annuals.*[30] A third source of this type is the CD-ROM version of *The Serials Directory: An International Reference Book* which includes information on over 114,000 series, irregular series, annuals, and ceased titles. Access is provided in twenty-three different ways along with the capability to use Boolean logic and truncations in searches.[31]

One of the most complex and massive projects being developed is the CD-ROM version of *The British Library General Catalogue of Printed Books to 1975.* It is being developed by Saztec Europe Ltd., and will be distributed by Chadwyck-Healey. This catalog will provide access to the over 8.5 million volumes of the British Library. The CD-ROM version will provide searching access that is impossible to achieve with the printed version. The advertising for this product may not be exaggerating when describing the impact of this product on researchers: "If indeed the library is the laboratory of the humanities and social science, then publication of *The British Library Catalogue on CD-ROM* puts into the hands of the scholar one of the most powerful research tools ever created. From now on scholars will be able to find information in the catalogue of one of the world's greatest libraries in a way that has never been possible before."[32]

Other similar products using the same search software include three national bibliographies. The *British National Bibliography* on CD-ROM includes all records from 1950 to the present. The German National Bibliography, *Deutsche Bibliographie* includes records from 1986 to the present. The third product, *Bibliographie Nationale Francaise Depuis 1975* is the cumulated version of the records of the Bibliotheque Nationale from 1975 to the present.[33] Chadwyck-Healey is also the publisher of *The Catalogue of United Kingdom Official Publications.* This CD-ROM product includes records for both HMSO and non-HMSO British publications. More than 160,000 records for publications published from 1980 to the present are included on this CD-ROM.[34]

U.S. Government Information

A wide variety of government information is being made available on CD-ROM. Since most government produced information is not copyrighted, publishers have often used government information and databases for their first forays into optical publishing. Government agencies have found that providing information in electronic format is more cost-effective than paper or microfiche products for many types of information. The massive amounts of data collected and disseminated by the government make CD-ROM technology an attractive alternative to online or magnetic tape distribution systems.

Agencies involved in CD-ROM projects range from the National Agricultural Library to the Postal Service. Some agencies, such as the Bureau of the Census, have already distributed products, whereas other agencies are still in the planning and prototype stage. How and if these products are distributed to the library community through depository libraries and sales programs is also very much in flux at this time.

Commercial vendors are also distributing products on CD-ROM. The ERIC, MEDLINE, and NTIS bibliographic databases were early commercial products. Production of individual products, such as the Central Intelligence Agency's *World Factbook* in CD-ROM by Quanta press is also beginning to appear.[35] Congressional Information Service (CIS) is also in the process of converting their massive statistical and congressional indexes to CD-ROM.[36]

Users of government data and information may soon find that CD-ROM is the only medium offered for certain types of information. Libraries may find an increasing pressure to obtain these CD-ROM governmental products as print and other format counterparts disappear. If CD-ROM format information is not distributed to depository libraries and that formal distribution and resource sharing mechanism is destroyed, then many libraries will find themselves scrambling to obtain information directly from agencies, buying the CD-ROM products themselves, or forming other resource sharing networks to obtain government data and information.

CD-ROM Cataloging Systems

A revolution in cataloging practices that is already having an impact on nationwide resource sharing has occurred among many libraries. In particular, smaller libraries have embraced the use of CD-ROM databases of MARC cataloging records, which they may use for retrospective or current acquisition cataloging. These records may be used only for local systems or for a statewide or regional database (often a CD-ROM product). The library's holdings, then, are often not available as part of a nationwide database.

Some of the libraries using these products never would have participated in a utility such as OCLC because of the costs involved, but many other libraries most likely would have or were using OCLC in the past before using CD-ROM technology. Coupled with the CD-ROM statewide and regional union catalog concept, this development may drastically change interlibrary loan from the nationwide network concept that has evolved back to the state-wide and regional concept that existed before the advent of OCLC. The danger with this is that the types of problems that often existed with more local interlibrary loan lending, such as a lack of speed in fulfilling requests, may occur again. In a resource sharing environment that has drastically changed, users no longer find a long waiting period for the fulfillment of interlibrary loan requests acceptable. Libraries moving back to the more local concept of resource sharing must actively monitor and adapt their interlibrary loan systems to compensate for the possible problems awaiting them.

Three major stand-alone products used for creating local machine-readable records include the Library Corporation's BiblioFile, Gaylord's SuperCAT, and General Research Corporation's (GRC) LaserQuest system. These systems do not require a link to an online system and may be used for both retrospective and current cataloging. OCLC offers the CAT CD450 product which requires membership in OCLC as well as the provision that those using it must update all records to the OCLC system. A CD-ROM product designed for retrospective conversion is the DisCon product available from Utlas. Utlas also offers its CD-CATSS for current cataloging. Western Library Network (WLN) produces LaserCat, which can be used in conjunction with its UltraCard system for the provision of cataloging records in addition to serving as a union catalog of WLN holdings.[37]

CD-ROM Local Catalogs

There are a number of products on the market which allow libraries to produce their own CD-ROM local catalogs, often after using one of the cataloging products described in the previous section. These catalogs have an impact on their immediate clientele by providing more access points and making materials held in the local collection more accessible. They may also increase local resource sharing, as a library system or group of local libraries may produce a catalog of their combined holdings. Some catalogs give the option of defining groups of locations to be searched. For example, a patron might search first their own branch library, then the library system as a whole, and finally a regional consortium of libraries. These systems used for local catalogs are also used for many of the statewide and regional union listings described in the first section of this chapter.

CD-ROM catalogs are produced by several major vendors. Brodart was one of the pioneers in this area with the development of their Le Pac catalog. Le Pac includes a variety of access points and two search modes. Another major vendor, Autographics, offers its CD-ROM catalog "Impact." As was mentioned earlier, both of these vendors provide an interlibrary loan module that interfaces with these catalogs. General Research Corporation (GRC) has its CD-ROM catalog, LaserGuide, on the market. The Library Corporation's Intelligent Catalog and MARCIVE's Marcive Pac are two other major catalogs available on CD-ROM.[38] CLSI produces its CD-CAT public access catalog, and WLN has developed its own CD-ROM public access catalog, LaserCat PAC.[39]

Collection Development

CD-ROM products and services carry a high price tag; money spent on CD-ROMs is not available for other purchases. This simple statement describes one of the major impacts of CD-ROM on collection development. In many libraries, the purchase of CD-ROM databases is at the expense of the purchase of book materials and serials. For other libraries, the conscious decision to emphasize access to materials over ownership of items has meant that there is an overall increased emphasis and dependence on resource sharing. These decisions, however, should be made in the context of overall collection development plans and follow a logical review and decision-making process. Where they are not, the impact on resource sharing may be quite negative over the long term.

A more direct impact on collection development activities which affect resource sharing, is the development of CD-ROM products which provide information to monitor and analyze collection development activities, and/or make specific collection development decisions. OCLC and AMIGOS are already developing one product specifically designed as a collection analysis tool: the "Collection Analysis CD." This product will provide the data to allow a library to analyze and compare their holdings of materials against other defined peer groups of institutions.[40] Other CD-ROM products may provide collection development information as a secondary by-product. As many of the CD-ROM catalogs increase in sophistication, collection management reports available from them are likely to increase both in number and usefulness.

Conclusion

CD-ROM technology has the potential to affect and change dramatically resource sharing at the local, national, and international levels. This impact will be felt by most libraries, including those which have not been involved with resource sharing activities in the past. The wide range of CD-ROM products and services involved have made it difficult for libraries and librarians to analyze and focus on the implications of this impact on resource sharing. If CD-ROM technology is to be adopted and used by libraries in any semblance of a planned and organized fashion, then this impact must be recognized and anticipated by all libraries from the smallest high school facility to the largest research institution. This chapter has identified and recognized that impact; the next step is to channel creatively CD-ROM technology to enhance our resource sharing activities.

Notes

1. Linda-Jean Smith, "Pennsylvania Libraries Hope for Success via 'ACCESS,'" *Special Libraries* 79 (Summer 1988): 215-220.
2. Doris M. Epler and Richard E. Cassel, "ACCESS PENNSYLVANIA: A CD-ROM Database Project," *Library Hi Tech News* 5 (Fall 1987): 81-88.
3. Karl Beiser, "Microcomputing," *Wilson Library Bulletin* 63 (February 1989): 72-73.
4. "Missouri Distributes Statewide Database," *Wilson Library Bulletin* 63 (January 1989): 11.
5. "Upddate on Brodart's LePac," *Information Retrieval and Library Automation* 25 (January 1989): 7.
6. "Libraries and Networks Sign with Brodart," *CD-ROM Librarian* 3 (April 1988): 7-8.
7. Information Systems Consultants Incorporated. *Resource Sharing in Iowa, Preliminary Report.* (Information Systems Consultants Incorporated, 1988) II-1-2.
8. "GRC's LaserGuide in Nevada State Library," *Information Retrieval and Library Automation* 24 (December 1988): 6-7.
9. "Louisiana's Public Libraries' Expanded LAsernet System," *Library Hi Tech News* 52 (September 1988): 8.
10. Publishers's brochure from Library Systems & Services Inc.
11. "Cross References in WLN's LaserCat," 7 *Information Intelligence Online Libraries and Microcomputers* (January 1989): 4.
12. "CD-ROM Union Catalog Forged by Three New York Systems," *Library Journal* 112 (May 15, 1987): 26.
13. *Communique*, (Winter 1989). Publisher's brochure from Brodart.
14. "Auto-Graphics Introduces IMPACT Inter-Library Loan Module," *Library Hi Tech News* 58 (March 1989): 15. "Brodart Automation Unveils Version 5.0 of LePac," *Library Hi Tech News* 49 (May 1988): 11.
15. Thomas J. Waldhart, "Patterns of Interlibrary Loan in the U.S.: A Review of Research," *Library and Information Science Research* 7 (1985): 217-218.
16. Nancy J. Eaton, Linda Brew McDonald, and Mara R. Saule, *CD-ROM and Other Optical Information Systems: Implementation Issues for Libraries.* (Phoenix: Oryx Press, 1989), 107.
17. "Implications of CD-ROM Reference," *Library Hotline* 6 (March 1989), 3.
18. Laura Neame, "View Fron Canada: A Report on CD-ROM Use in Canadian Libraries," *Laserdisk Professional* 1 (November 1988): 100-101.
19. Eaton, pp. 109, 118.
20. Diana Fitzwater and Bernard Fradkin, "CD-ROM + Fax=Shared Reference Resource," *American Libraries* 19 (May 1988): 385.
21. Barrie Stern and Robert Campbell, "International Document Delivery: The Adonnis Project," *Wilson Library Bulletin* 63 (February 1989): 36-41.
22. "UMI Introduces Full-Text Image Database," *Library Hi Tech News* 157 (February 1989): 12.
23. "Laserdisclosure," *Information Intelligence Online Newsletter* 10 (January 1989): 5.

24. "Moody's 5000 Plus," *Information Intelligence Online Newsletter* 10 (February 1989): 4.

25. "News & Forthcoming Databases," *Information Intelligence Online Newsletter* 10 (January 1989): 5.

26. Publisher's brochure from SilverPlatter.

27. "IEEE, IEE and UMI Join Forces to Conduct CD-ROM Experiment," *Information Retrieval and Library Automation* 24 (March 1989): 6.

28. Publisher's brochure from Grolier Electronic Publishing Inc.

29. Stephen A. Shaiman, Esq. and Howard B. Rein, "CD-ROM and Fair Use: A Lawyer Looks at the Copyright Law," *Laserdisk Professional* 2 (January 1989): 27-30.

30. Norman Desmarais, *The Librarian's CD-ROM Handbook.* (Westport, CT: Meckler, 1989), 79-80.

31. "Serials Directory on CD-ROM," *CD-ROM Librarian* 3 (July/August 1988): 8.

32. Publisher's brochure from Chadwyck-Healey.

33. *National Bibliographies on CD-ROM.* Publisher's brochure from Chadwyck-Healey.

34. *The Catalogue of United Kingdom Official Publications.* Publisher's brochure from Chadwyck-Healey.

35. "World Factbook CD-ROM," *Information Intelligence Online Libraries and Microcomputers*, 7 (May 1989): 11-12.

36. Publisher's brochure from Congressional Information Service.

37. Linda Bills and Linda Helgerson, "CD-ROM Catalog Production Products," *Library Hi Tech News* 7 (11989): 67-92.

38. Karl Beiser, "CD-ROM Catalogs: The State of the Art," *Wilson Library Bulletin,* 63 (November 1988): 25-34.

39. "CLSI Announces CD-CAT — A New Public Access Catalog," *Library Hi Tech News* 51 (July/August 1988): 8. "WLN Releases LaserCat PAC," *Library Hi Tech News*, 52 (September 1988): 12.

40. "Amigos and OCLC Announce Collection Analysis CD-ROM," *Information Intelligence Online Libraries and Microcomputers* 7 (April 1989): 8.

The ADONIS Project: The Brooklyn College Experience

Linda Meiseles
Deputy Associate Librarian for Technical Services
Brooklyn College, Brooklyn, NY

The rising costs of journals combined with the proliferation of titles are severely challenging serials librarians and collection development officers who are responsible for library materials budgets. The "serials crisis," as it is called in the profession, is the result of a combination of factors, including the publishing requirements for tenure and promotion along with publishers' desire for profits. Inflated prices are the result of the devaluation of the American dollar and the ever increasing subscription prices of scholarly material. This is especially true of the scientific, technical, and medical literature.[1]

The extent of this "crisis" is reflected in the profusion of journal articles on this topic, and has been a dominant theme of many seminars. At two such seminars sponsored by the Society for Scholarly Publishing, Joe A. Hewitt reports that it was agreed that the "high cost of scientific serials is distorting library spending, and doing so in a way that threatens all library dependent scholarly publishing. University presses and association publishers, well represented at the seminars, showed alarm at the threat to monographs in the humanities and social sciences and seemed committed to working with librarians to find solutions to the problem."[2]

Library materials budgets cannot continue to support the serials budget at the expense of the library collection; many libraries report as much as 50% to 80% on average are allotted to serials.[3] As the budget share for serials has increased, so too has the availability of new library materials and equipment on the market: CD-ROM products, computers, printers, and other electronic library products. Added to this is the diminished ability of libraries to purchase the more traditional materials: books, including rare books for special collections, and non-book materials, i.e. microforms, audio-visual materials, etc.

Clearly, this trend must reverse itself, resulting in a more rational allocation of funds. The September 1988 issue of the ARL SPEC KIT reports that many research libraries have instituted mass cancellation projects as a means of coping with this problem.[4] It should be remembered that cancellation of serials subscriptions does not necessarily imply deprivation of information.

Library managers must look for new ways to satisfy their users' needs while maintaining the integrity of their collections. Books not purchased this year may not get purchased at all, either because they go out of print, or are sacrificed for the current year's requests. Consequently there will be information needs not being met along with large gaps in the collection. It is time for libraries to start focusing on new ways to access information rather than on building collections. Instead of reacting to the "serials crisis," librarians should seek new approaches. Collection development strategies must be devised to provide alternative means of access, such as: making greater use of resource sharing, e.g., interlibrary loans, facsimile, photocopying, and other document delivery services.

In this paper, I will discuss document delivery services in general, and the ADONIS project, in particular, and will include a description of the Brooklyn College experience using the ADONIS material. For the purpose of this paper, document shall mean full-text retrieval of serial, or periodical articles.

Document Delivery Services

The concept of resource sharing is not new, but the emphasis on it has intensified. Academic librarians have long known that library material purchases had to be made selectively; most professionals also have relied upon outside sources to satisfy clients' needs. A search of the literature shows that there are many types of document delivery services. Historically, interlibrary loan has been the means of meeting these needs. The arrangements were formal, based on a regional cooperative agreement, or based on an informal agreement between individual libraries. These cooperative arrangements served libraries very well, but the turnaround time was poor, with unfilled requests leaving many frustrated and irate users. It was the time factor as well as the inconvenience that caused resistance from faculty when cancellations of titles were considered. They knew from past experience that interlibrary loan was not a viable alternative to having the journal on hand as part of the collection. In order for libraries to have control over their own budgets and not be dictated to by faculty insisting on proprietary ownership of journals, we must institute programs that can provide quick and efficient access to documents.

Electronic Document Delivery Services

Modern technology provides for a more efficient transfer of information, allowing for quicker access to journal and serial articles. There are two major library applications of electronic document delivery being used today. The first can be considered an enhanced interlibrary loan system. Via telefacsimile (fax), cooperating libraries with compatible equipment can transmit requests and receive articles instantaneously. Early attempts in the 1960s at using fax machines were not successful. Those libraries that experimented with it found that the copies were unclear; the transmission was either slow or faulty; and the equipment was unreliable. In addition, the demand for the service was so low that the participating libraries could not justify the cost and the staff time committed to the service.[5]

The 1980s have seen marked advances in facsimile with regard to speed of transmission, quality of reproduction, and lower costs. Fax technology is becoming very popular in libraries. Its potential is being demonstrated in numerous applications across the United States, including projects sponsored by the Fred Meyer Charitable Trust,[6] and those described by Mary Jackson in the May 1989 issue of the *Wilson Library Journal*,[7] on the performance, costs, and user acceptance of such systems. The preliminary reports from the testing libraries are encouraging, showing positive results. They also demonstrate that through cooperative agreements the profession is actively attempting to improve resource sharing by utilizing the new technology. Unlike most new systems introduced into libraries, facsimile can be integrated with the present interlibrary loan service without reallocation of staff.

Commercial Document Delivery Services

The other major library application of electronic document delivery is provided by the private sector, for commercial purposes. Currently, academic libraries are not major purchasers of full-text articles. Law school libraries and law firms, however, are active and long-term users of legal full-text systems such as Westlaw and Lexis. Other active users of commercial vendors include corporate libraries where the costs of the research and the delivered documents are passed on to clients.

Two document delivery vendors worth mentioning are the Institute for Scientific Information's The Genuine Article, and the UMI Article Clearing House. The Genuine Article provides actual pages or top quality photocopies to over millions of journal articles published over the last five years. The collection includes science, social science, and the arts and humanities materials; and can now be accessed over the OCLC Interlibrary Loan Subsystem. The UMI Article Clearing House also supplies document delivery to over 11,000 copyright-cleared articles including those from scholarly and technical journals, popular magazines, newspapers, and governmental documents. Many of the titles offered are indexed in major databases and indexes such as: ABI/INFORM, Abridged Index Medicus, Applied Science and Technology Index, etc. UMI is also available through the OCLC Interlibrary Loan Subsystem, plus ALANET and BRS. In addition, ARTIFAX takes advantage of the technology of telefacsimile, providing 24-hour processing combined with same-day or overnight transmission.

Some of the other major commercial online systems, which, in addition to providing bibliographic databases-indexes and abstracts, also support full-text article retrieval are: DIALOG, STN International (Chemical Abstracts Service Online), VU/TEXT, and Dow Jones News Retrieval. Additional databases appear almost on a monthly basis. This growth is evidenced by the presence of three directories that list online availability of periodicals: *Directory of Periodicals Online* (Vols. 1 & 2) published by the Federal Document Retrieval; *Books and Periodicals Online: A Guide to Publication Contents of Business and Legal Databases,* by Nuchine Nobari; and most recently, *Fulltext Sources Online: For Periodicals, Newspapers, Newletters and Newswires,* edited by Ruth Orenstein. These directories include listings of each periodical, newspaper, newsletter, and news-wire that provides full-text documents online.

One of the recognized disadvantages of the present services is that documents do not include graphics; it has been shown, however, that articles stored on CD-ROMs are nearly identical reproductions of the original document. Since CD-ROMs are not online, where there is a time constraint, more end users will be able to search and browse through the databases.

Information on Demand

Unlike commercial document delivery services previously discussed, Information on Demand (IOD) is not a specialized bibliographic database. As an information broker, IOD provides access to over 400 databases such as Dialog, BRS, Adrack, Nexis/Lexis, etc., on a fee-for-service basis. IOD performs research in all fields and locates and retrieves full-text of any publicly-available document, regardless of subject, date, or publication type, such as: journal articles, patents, conference reports, technical reports, etc.

The philosophy of Information on Demand is very much in agreement with that of the premise of shared resources. Accordingly, Cristine Maxwell, president of IOD, says: "Today there is more and more information available, and a person can get hold of less and less of it because the amount is growing so fast. Libraries today can no longer be libraries in the sense that they used to be, because they can never have everything anymore. They have to take on the new technology. If they don't, they will become museums of the past."[8]

An advantage of using Information on Demand is that as a member of the Copyright Clearance Center, they have a master list of all publishers and notify the Center when copyrighted material is used; clients, therefore, are assured of receiving proper lawful copies. Another advantage is that clients can order directly from Information on Demand using TELENET, thereby saving telecommunication charges. IOD has electronic mailbox capability, and claims that placing orders electronically hastens document delivery.[9]

ADONIS

Information on Demand and UMI are the United States document delivery centers that provide access to the ADONIS CD-ROM biomedical collection.

ADONIS is a trial document delivery service that supplies articles from over 200 biomedical journals published in 1987 and 1988 on CD-ROM. Discs are delivered approximately every week to major document centers in Europe, the United States, Mexico, Australia, and Japan, and are used to fulfill requests for individual articles received by centers in the course of their activities.[10]

Background

ADONIS was conceived in the late 1970s in response to publishers' concerns that the implementation of the "fair use" clause was resulting in widespread photocopying in document delivery centers and libraries. Although there was no direct proof of such activity, they believed that the increase in use of photocopying was resulting in a loss of copyright revenue, and a reduction in the number of subscriptions from libraries because copies were so readily available.[11]

To offset this potential loss of revenue, the consortium of publishers known as ADONIS began to look at the possiblility of providing document delivery centers with journals in machine-readable form, from which individual journal articles could be printed on demand at lower cost than photocopying from back runs of periodicals stored on shelves. The use of each article was to be measured automatically. Centers would be required to pay a subscription fee to the publishers plus a "use" or "copyright" fee. From the beginning it was thought that using newer technology based on optical storage might lead to cost savings.[12] It was hoped by this venture that the relationship between publishers and librarians would be improved by enlarging the scope of service to library users.[13]

In 1980, the British Library Document Supply Center (BLDSC), in collaboration with Elsevier Science Publishers, conducted a major use study to determine which articles were being requested from (BLDSC) and their number. A second survey was conducted in 1983 at the BLDSC (whose name had changed by now to the British Library Lending Division) to see if the pattern of use had changed with the advanced sophistication and increased use of online searching. To be as precise as possible, they conducted the second survey during the same two week period in May as the first study.[14]

It was determined by both studies that a small number of titles satisfied a relatively high proportion of demand, that about 50% of demand was for issues less than 3 1/2 years old, and that titles in the field of biomedicine accounted for over 60% of demand. Two subsequent document delivery surveys have since confirmed these results.[15]

The surveys also showed that for the project to succeed more publishers would need to be included; soon after Academic Press, Blackwell Scientific Publications, Pergamon Press, Springer Verlag, and John Wiley & Sons joined Elsevier Science Publishers and became part of the consortium.[16] The consortium called the project "ADONIS" in keeping with the custom of naming European documentation projects after Greek and Roman gods.[17]

The early efforts of ADONIS were not successful due to a combination of financial and technological factors; by 1985 the project was in a complete decline. Constance Orchard, of Information on Demand, says it is worth noting that, "because of the strong competition between non-commercial, subsidized, and commercial, non-subsidized document supply centers, the pricing of all documents was, and still is, well below real costs. The delivery of articles retrieved from the ADONIS discs is also subject to these same financial conderations. Consequently, by 1983, due to economic and technological causes the project went into complete decline."[18]

ADONIS was reborn in 1985 as a result of a combination of factors: rapidly developing CD-ROM technology, allowing for more information storage; the availability of less expensive printers; and the substantially lowered costs of retrieval work stations. In 1986, with the support of several major European libraries, and the Commission of European Communities, the ADONIS publishers agreed to resume the project. The intention was to trial test the project during years 1987 and 1988, and for the centers to use the discs until the end of June 1989.[19]

The Trial

The contents of over 200 biomedical journals, (including all editorial material, letters, book reviews, reports of conferences, abstracts of papers presented, as well as formal articles) published from January 1987 through June 1989 by consortium members and other publishers wishing to participate less fully in the trial, are indexed at Excerpta Medica in Amsterdam. Access is through title keyword, author, ADONIS number, but subjects are not indexed. A unique ADONIS number is assigned to each article, and the full-text of the material, along with its ASCII index, is sent to a facility operated by the Scanmedia Ltd. Bureau in the United Kingdom where the content of the articles is scanned. The scanning is performed in two modes. One is used for text scanning, and essentially reduces each area on a page to either black or white; the other is used to scan halftones and other graphics which require gradation. Although one method is faster than the other, the publishers decided to employ both methods because of the need for extremely detailed reproductions of the graphics which comprise about 20% of biomedical literature.[20] It is hoped that in the future, one page incorporating both text or graphics or halftones will be scanned by both modes producing high quality texts and graphics.[21]

Purpose and Objectives

The statistics generated will show the proportion of requests by type of user, (e.g., academic, governmental, industrial, or other) and country of origin, and also give insight into which journals are most heavily used, and how old the articles are. The statistics will also provide a basis for an analysis comparing the costs of using the ADONIS system and the conventional document supply service using photocopies.[22]

According to Barrie Stern, ADONIS project coordinator, and Robert Campbell, chairman of the ADONIS board and marketing director of Blackwell Scientific, another aim of the trial is to "learn about the impact of such a service on end users, which will contribute to knowledge about information packaging and (re)packaging. The trial explores aspects of the implementation of digital technology to effect savings that can be shared with publishers, thereby providing a solution to the conflict between publishers and document delivery services over the interpretation of copyright legislation. Also of interest will be the reception by the libraries of the ADONIS system and whether the system wll influence the way they work."[23]

ADONIS Workstation

The workstation requirements were developed by the British Library in cooperation with the Commission of the European Communities. The design basically consists of a Laser Data System with an IBM PC, an Hitachi CD ROM drive, and a Ricoh laser printer. Included in the retrieval workstation is the British library software to keep a log of articles copied (via the ADONIS identification number) providing the basis for the calculation of royalties.[24]

The time from receipt of the printed journal to delivery of discs at the centers should be about four weeks. This allows for one week each for indexing and scanning and ten days for disc production. It is important to both users and document suppliers that the discs be at the centers before current awareness services or other sources generate article requests to the centers.[25]

Brooklyn College Experience

There are twenty-three units within the City University of New York (CUNY) system, including senior colleges, community colleges, the Graduate Center, and the CUNY Law School. Brooklyn College, in Brooklyn, New York, is one of the CUNY senior colleges. The Brooklyn College Library provides integrated information support for the college's instructional, research, and administrative activities. Collections total 935,000 volumes, 3,800 current serial subscriptions, and 17,000 audiovisual units (chiefly sound recording and videotapes). The library adds approximately 10,000 new titles each year to its comprehensive humanities, social sciences collections, and participates in cooperative activities and arrangements with other libraries in the borough of Brooklyn, in the metropolitan area, in the State of New York, and nationally. Library resources and collections have been developed collaboratively by librarians and faculty. The library collection supports undergraduate and master's level study in the humanities, social sciences, and sciences.

In the fall of 1988, the City University of New York Central Administration for Library Automation Services purchased LINX for all the University libraries. LINX is an online remote access periodicals management system, developed by F.W. Faxon, and is available to a network of users through dedicated lines and dial-up access methods. The components of LINX used at Brooklyn College are: Datalinx, Faxon's operation files; Linx Courier, an electronic ordering, claiming and mail service; and INFOSERV, a collection development database.

INFOSERV offers a variety of databases, all with direct online orders, and electronic document delivery. INFOSERV's Biomedical Document Delivery Service (BDDS) allows users to order individual articles from the ADONIS file. The BDDS screen on INFOSERV provides a library with a complete list of the ADONIS serial titles (beginning with 1987), from which a user can order the desired citation directly through INFOSERV. To order an article through BDDS, one simply locates the serial title, then enters the citation on the order screen under that title. Faxon automatically transmits the order to Information on Demand, Inc. which will send the library a laser-printed copy of the article via first class mail on the same day. Express mail service is also available.

In the fall of 1988, the library began preparations for a serials cancellation project on the assumption that the 1989-1990 budget would be significantly lower than in previous years, and that the rate of inflation for serials subscriptions would outprice the current year's subscriptions. We started almost a year before the cancellations had to be made because we knew it was important that we plan for cuts of various magnitudes and to allow sufficient time for bibliographers to review titles and to consult with faculty in their assigned departments. The aim was to come up with lists by departments which would offer cuts of $25,000, $50,000, $75,000, and $100,000. We felt that even if these cuts did not have to made, the review of our subscriptions would be a worthwhile endeavor. It was never our intention to cancel any title that was part of the core collection.

Like many academic institutions, the major share of the library's serial's budget is spent on science and technical titles. Many of these are the more expensive ones with low usage, and, in all probability, candidates for cancellation. Because of this the serials librarians and the collection development officer hypothesized that purchasing journal articles from commercial document delivery services could be more cost effective than subscribing to less frequently used journals. The decision to choose ADONIS was based on several factors. Primarily, we hoped that by experimenting with a specialized subject database we could determine whether on demand full-text document delivery provided sufficient access to information needs without having a current subscription on-site; having access to ADONIS thru INFOSERV provided instantaneous ordering capability with promised quicker document delivery than the traditional interlibrary loan; and the low charge of $10.00 per article made it possible for the library to subsidize the project 100%.

In order for the library to learn from the project, certain limitations were set. The trial phase would run for the semester period, spring 1989. As it is a specialized database, access to the ADONIS collection would be offered to the faculty members in the Health Sciences, Biology, Psychology, Sociology, and Physical Education departments. No faculty member would be refused if they were not from the targeted departments. To test effectiveness of document delivery versus ownership, the ADONIS collection was limited to those journals not held by the Brooklyn College Library or Downstate, the CUNY Medical School.

At the start, we planned a major publicity campaign to ensure faculty awareness of the service. On November 14, 1988, we sent a letter to all concerned faculty detailing the ADONIS project, along with an invitation to a December 7, 1988 meeting to discuss their concerns, and answer any questions they might have relating to ADONIS. In addition, an article describing the ADONIS project was published in the December 1988, issue of *Password*, the College's Computing Center's newsletter.

The mechanics of the project were as follows:

1. Faculty requests for articles would be taken at the Reference Desk. Forms would be available there and in the Interlibrary Loan office, different in color to distinguish from other request forms.

2. The actual requests would be sent through INFOSERV by the serials staff, as DATALINX was already part of their daily routine. This meant that further staff training of the system was not needed.

3. Faculty would be given a list of journals in the collection indicating which are owned by Brooklyn College or Downstate (the regional medical library) to inform the requester that CUNY holds the journal.

4. The article would become the property of the requester.

5. The interlibrary loan officer and the serials librarians would monitor the project and gather statistics for evaluative purposes.

Results

On the face of it, the response to document delivery services was poor; of 120 potential participants, one professor requested five articles from the ADONIS file. In an effort to analyze the low demand, the 120 professors in the appropriate departments were sent a brief questionnaire; 9 returned responses.

1. The one professor who made use of the material claimed that the response time was disappointing, with turnaround time being two to three weeks. This was true, each order placed was held up by Information on Demand for one reason or another.

2. Two professors responded that they never heard of the project.

3. Two professors responded that they loved it, although they never used it.

4. The remaining respondents replied that the scope and range of the ADONIS collection did not fit their needs.

The low demand for articles from ADONIS makes it impossible to confirm the hypothesis that purchasing journal articles from commercial document delivery services could replace ownership of lesser used journals. Although we did not conduct a formal test, some conclusions can be drawn. It is possible the coverage and number of journals offered by ADONIS is too limited, with many of the titles already in our library. There is also the possibility that the nature or scope of research covered is not sufficiently relevant to Brooklyn College interest.

On the other hand, our participation in the project demonstrates to faculty members that Brooklyn College Library is committed to supporting their research information needs. If and when cancellations do occur, they should be assured that we are seeking new approaches to information access, and are actively investigating viable alternatives to proprietary ownership of journals.

References and Notes

1. Peter R. Young and Kathryn Hammell Carpenter, "Price Index for 1989: U.S. Periodicals," *Library Journal* 114, no. 7 (April 15, 1989): 43-49.
2. Joe A. Hewitt, "Altered States: Evolution or Revolution in Journal-Based Communications," *American Libraries* 20 no. 6 (June 1989): 487-500.
3. "Serials Control and Deselection Projects," Spec Kit, (Wash. D.C.: Association of Research Libraries, September 1988).
4. Ibid.
5. Mary Jackson, "Facsimile Transmission: The Next Generation of Document Delivery," *Wilson Library Bulletin*, 62 no. 9 (May 1988): 37-43.
6. Douglas K. Ferguson, "Electronic Information Delivery System: Reports on Five Projects Sponsored by the Fred Meyer Charitable Trust" *Library Hi Tech* 5 no. 2 (Summer 1987): 65-93.
7. Jackson, "Facsimile Transmission," 37-43.
8. Christine Maxwell, "The Business of Knowledge," *American Way* (March 15, 1987): 19-20.
9. Ibid., 20.
10. Barrie Stern and Robert Campbell, "The ADONIS Project," *Wilson Library Bulletin* (February 1989): 36.
11. Ibid., 36.
12. David Bradbury, "ADONIS–The View of the Users," *IFLA Journal* 14 no. 2 (1988): 132.
13. "Test Evaluates Feasibility of CD-ROM as Document Supply Medium," *Online Review* 12, no. 3 (1988): 139.
14. Bradbury, "ADONIS," 132.
15. Constance Orchard, "ADONIS and Electronically Stored Information: An Information Broker's Experience," Haworth Press, Inc. (1988): 85.
16. Stern and Campbell, "The ADONIS Project," 36.
17. Ibid., 36.
18. Orchard, "ADONIS and Electronically Stored Information," 86.
19. Ibid., 90.
20. Ibid., 87.
21. Ibid., 87.
22. Stern and Campbell, "The ADONIS Project," 39.
23. Ibid., 40.
24. Constance Orchard, "ADONIS and Electronically Stored Information," 88.
25. Stern and Campbell, "The ADONIS Project," 40.

Intellectual Property Rights and the 'Sacred Engine:' Scholarly Publishing in the Electronic Age

Adrian W. Alexander
Sales Manager, Academic Information Services
The Faxon Co., Inc.
and Julie S. Alexander
Assistant Director for Collection Development
University of Texas at Arlington

Thirteen years after the U.S. Congress, in its infinite wisdom, passed the 1976 Copyright Act, the debate over application of copyright in the electronic environment continues in earnest (some might say it has only just begun). It appears that Congress hoped to settle the copyright issue once and for all with that bill, which protects "original works of authorship fixed in any tangible medium of expression now known or later developed,"[1] but by 1980 it was already amending the act to handle the issue of computer software. Meanwhile, other amendments were being offered to address the equally unique problems of cable television, satellite reception, videotape, and other electronic media.[2]

Application of intellectual property rights to electronic information raises a number of interesting issues for libraries, especially as more and more information which previously was available only in paper or microtext formats becomes digitized. Downloading information from online databases continues to incite debate over the legality of such practices. Speaking at a Library of Congress Network Advisory Committee meeting in 1987, two representatives from the American Chemical Society expressed divergent views on the seriousness of that issue to the database producer.[3] With the increased use of microcomputers for downloading, authorship itself becomes an issue, as more and more "derivative" works are created by combining various elements of other works that are being downloaded. Another issue of concern to librarians in recent years has been that of copyright applications to bibliographic databases such as that stored at OCLC.[4]

A major resource-sharing issue of this decade for research libraries has been the spiraling cost of information published in serial form. Stories about serials consuming 70 to 80 percent of materials budgets in ARL libraries have become commonplace. Research by Hamaker and others suggests that a sizable portion of these serials expenditures go to a small group of commercial publishers which are focused on scientific, technical, and medical (STM) literature.[5] Journal prices continue to rise and, consequently, to have a greater impact on library budgets. At the same time, more of the STM journal literature has become available in electronic form, via such efforts as

Chemical Journals Online from ACS and the ADONIS CD-ROM venture from Information on Demand.

The question of whether the electronic journal will become the medium of choice for the publication and dissemination of scientific literature in the next century certainly remains to be answered, but strong voices in the market have already spoken on the subject. The new President-Elect of the American Library Association, Richard Dougherty, recently wrote, "it is highly improbable that the electronic journal will have a major impact for a number of years. Electronic publications will not become commonplace until the early part of the twenty-first century." But, says Dougherty, "Ultimately, we are talking about the eventual demise of the paperform journal."[6] Meanwhile, on the publisher side, a key executive for Elsevier has stated publicly that "CD ROM will have a direct impact on primary journal publishing." Michael Boswood went on to identify several possible ways in which this impact would be felt, including storing back volumes, reintroduction of individual/departmental prices for large scientific titles, replacement of print editions in some cases, and document delivery (i.e., ADONIS).[7]

From the standpoint of resource sharing, the possibility of large-scale migration over the next 10 to 15 years of scientific literature from print to electronic format has a number of implications, not the least of which is the question of copyright. There is also a related question of cost, if copyright indeed "turns information into property."[8] If, for example, the number of print subscriptions to a Pergamon journal available in the ADONIS database declines significantly as more libraries choose to order via ADONIS only the articles their clients request, how does the publisher (and, in this case, the holder of copyright) adjust the revenue stream? Does the library pay for the article ordered out of the materials budget, or pass on the cost directly to the user?

This chapter will explore these questions further by first examining two important investigations into the complexities of copyright in the electronic environment—the Congressional Office of Technology Assessment's landmark study, issued in 1986, and a subsequent discussion of that report, sponsored by the Library of Congress Network Advisory Committee in 1987. Finally, we will present some recent ideas regarding scholarly communication which could represent radical changes in the way in which we presently view copyright, access, and publishing.

The OTA Report

Much like the Library of Congress, the General Accounting Office, and the Congressional Budget Office, the Office of Technology Assessment (OTA) is a research arm of the U. S. Congress. It was created by passage of the Technology Assessment Act of 1972 as a result of heightened awareness by the Congress and the public at large of the growing impact, both positive and negative, of technology on society. More specifically, OTA was established to advise the Congress on the long-term impact of technology.[9]

As noted earlier, problems with application of the 1976 Copyright Act to electronic media were encountered almost immediately after its passage. By 1984, the Judiciary Committees of both houses of Congress realized that technology was outstripping the law, and asked OTA to conduct a study of the problem. The 310-page report resulting from the study was published in 1986.

The OTA study concluded that technology was complicating the intellectual property system and undermining the process by which intellectual property rights were granted and enforced. Furthermore, the study noted that this trend was likely to continue, since "today's technologies are the beginning, and not the end, of the information revolution."[10] The study also identified a number of specific problems created for the intellectual property system by technology. Several of these problems merit further discussion here.

Identifying Authorship

Protection under the Copyright Act is reserved for an "original work of authorship fixed in any tangible medium of expression, now known or later developed, from which they can be perceived, reproduced, or otherwise communicated, either directly, or with the aid of a machine or device."[11] The concept of "medium of expression" is important here because it is distinguished in intellectual property law from an idea, which cannot be protected by copyright. The case of *Baker v. Selden* (101 U.S. 841 [1880]) has long been regarded as a landmark in this important distinction between idea and expression, and it may be even more important today, in an age of digitized, easily shared and reproducible information. The case involved alleged infringement of a ledger book which contained a unique arrangement of columns and headings. The defendant's book contained a different system of arrangement, but achieved the same result of allowing the reader to review quickly the transactions for a given period of time. The Supreme Court agreed that the plaintiff's book might be copyrighted, but drew a "clear distinction" between the book itself and "the art that it is intended to illustrate." The court rejected the argument that the protection provided the author by copyright of the treatise extended to "the art or manufacture described therein."[12]

The ledger book which was the focal point of *Baker v. Selden* is what the OTA report describes as a "work of function," differing fundamentally from two other categories of expression: works of art and works of fact. These distinctions are important to the problem of authorship because: "The central problem of copyright law's continued accommodation to new technologies lies in the indiscriminate application of the doctrine of ideas and expression to three fundamentally different categories of works: works of art, works of fact, and works of function. Unless the law recognizes the inherent differences among these types of works, technology may make the boundaries of intellectual property ownership difficult or impossible to establish, and less relevant to the policy goals the law seeks to further."[13] Such a categorization of copyrightable works would provide a framework for the establishment of criteria for permissible copying and duration of protection which "more accurately reflect the perceived useful life of each of these types of works."[14]

The Report defines works of art as those "created for their own intrinsic value—whether that value is primarily aesthetic, entertaining, or educational in nature," and includes in this category such works as fiction, choreography, plays, music, film, and graphic works, while recognizing that firm boundaries cannot be fixed on any of the three categories. General characteristics of works of art are that they are more easily analyzed within the context of the idea/expression dichotomy (expression weighs heavily on the intrinsic value of the work) than the other categories, and that they "have always had a fixity and completeness to them." This latter characteristic makes the work of art much more amenable to basic elements of copyright law such as "the work, created by an author or authors," "belonging to him from the moment of creation," etc.[15]

Works of fact are those "whose value lies in the accurate representation of reality." This category too is amorphous and may overlap works of art in such areas as biography. Typically, maps, news programs, documentaries, scholarly (especially scientific) literature, statistical tables, and bibliographies fall into this category. Copyright protection is limited in works of fact to the way in which facts are expressed, not to the information itself. The problem for copyright law is that it is usually the underlying information that gives the work of fact its economic value, rather than the manner of expression. One of the major purposes of copyright law is to provide incentives for the production and dissemination of original works. In a free society, a critical public policy goal of copyright law should be to foster the sharing of information and ideas. So there is a conflict of principles with respect to works of fact, because copyright "does not necessarily protect the value of a work of fact." If the incentives are not sufficient to stimulate the creation and dissemination of some works of fact, then public access to information is at risk.[16]

Works of function are those that "use information to describe or implement a process, procedure, or algorithm." Examples given by OTA include recipes, instruction manuals, and, most importantly, a relatively new work, the computer program. Works of function seldom have intrinsic or aesthetic value, like works of art, and their worth is not dependent upon "what is," as with a work of fact, but rather, "what can be" if the procedure outlined in the work is followed. Copyright is restricted significantly for works of function because it does not protect the functional aspect of the work. Only the descriptive aspect of the work is protectable, which is a problem for computer programs, the descriptive part of which is the program code. "Because programs possess both a symbolic and functional nature, copyright may either protect too little if the copyrightable expression is limited to the literal program code, or too much if the copyrightable expression extends beyond the program code."[17]

From the standpoint of ownership, all three categories of copyrightable work are affected in the electronic environment. For works of art, interactive computing poses the biggest problem. Interactive fiction, for example, allows a writer to make choices about details of a story from a computer program, so the work is actually co-authored by human and machine. Interactive computer graphics enable one "artist" to use the work of another to produce new works. Images from a painting or a film, for example, can be digitized and stored in the machine, then reassembled with other images or in a different sequence. Music can be re-processed easily on a computer, resulting in an entirely new work. The problem of determining the line of demarcation between the programmer's expression and that of the user "stems from the fact that computers often mediate between the programmer and the user, and intermingle the creative efforts of both. Indeed, the program itself may contribute substantially to a creator's final artwork, and in ways that could be considered an autonomous or creative activity if done by a human being."[18]

For all three categories of works, computer networks could blur the lines by which copyright previously distinguished a work as "yours" or "mine." The ability in a network environment to create in a collaborative, online atmosphere "will demand rethinking several key aspects of copyright law." If, for example, a work is constantly embellished and revised by multiple contributors on a network, especially if each contributor finally ends up with a unique version of the original work, then questions of when copyright protection begins and ends become quite complex.[19] As one source frequently cited in the OTA report notes:

> ...the process of computer communication produces multitudinous versions of texts, which are partially authored by people and partly automatic. The receivers may be individuals, or they may be other machines that never print the words in visible form but use the information to produce something else again. So some of the text that is used exists electronically but it is never apparent; some is flashed briefly on the screen; and some is printed out in hard copy. What starts as one text varies and changes by degrees to a new one. Totally new concepts will have to be invented to compensate creative work in this environment.[20]

Oakley points out that current copyright law stipulates that the author is the initial holder of copyright, and that the Supreme Court has defined an "author" as "he to whom anything owes its origin, originator, or maker." But in the environment described above he notes that, "it may be extremely difficult to identify the author in any useful way."[21]

An electronic/copyright issue familiar to most librarians is that of databases. As noted earlier, copyright protection for works of fact extends only to the way in which the facts are expressed, not to the facts themselves, which usually give the database its economic value. OTA noted that this discrepancy is exaggerated by information technologies "because computers can easily manipulate the expression of a work of fact, and communications systems can quickly transfer the work."[22] In addition, OTA concluded that several unique characteristics of computer database technology (including storage media, searching ability, and distribution of information) could impair the usefulness of copyright protection for works of fact available online:

> ...expression may be easily and systematically changed by a person with access to the database and the ability to download and copy information from it with all evidence of copying erased. Once the information is modified, the user may no longer be liable for infringement, since the information, as such, is not protected. The downloading and the subsequent rearrangement of the information may be entirely legal, especially if the downloading onto disk is permitted under the contract. Since information that is rearranged and copied by hand may be legally appropriated, the same rearrangement might easily be done by the computer in real time as it is being received.[23]

The question of copyrightability of computer programs is equally complex, but not particularly germane to the issue of library resource sharing in the future. Briefly, Congress decided in 1980 that computer programs could be copyrighted as "literary works" under Section 102 of the 1976 legislation. Since that time, litigation over the issue has gone through two stages, first addressing the issue of whether software should be subject to copyright law or patent law, and then addressing the issue of what kind and how much protection should be afforded. OTA concluded that present copyright law "cannot be successfully applied to computer programs" because "one cannot arrive at a 'clear distinction' between idea and expression in a computer program by using traditional copyright analyses." More effective protection for software may lie within patent law, but OTA noted that presently there are limitations there as well.[24]

Identifying Infringements and Enforcing Rights

Chapter 4 of the OTA report deals with the issue of technology's impact on the enforcement of intellectual property rights. It begins by listing three major findings, which can be summarized as follows:
1. Technology is making it *cheaper* to copy, transfer, and manipulate information and intellectual property.
2. Technology is allowing the copy, transfer, and manipulation of information and intellectual property to occur *more quickly.*
3. Technology is making the copying, transfer, and manipulation of information and intellectual works *more private.*[25]

OTA first examined current trends in storage technologies, noting that it has become harder to enforce copyright as these technologies have dropped in cost while increasing in capacity. At the same time, they have also become more general in application; optical disks, for example, can handle many forms of information, including text, graphics, music, and video. Real problems with enforcement of copyright began with the advent of modern reprography in the middle of this century. As the technology became more widespread, it became too costly for owners of copyright to enforce their rights on a case by case basis. OTA noted that estimating the economic impact of unauthorized photocopying is difficult, but concluded that it had not had a serious impact on "general interest" publishing, while also citing a 1982 study by the Copyright Office which found no significant difference in this regard between scientific and technical publications and general interest periodicals.[26]

The first area where the impact of technology was felt on enforcement of copyright was that of audio and video taping. OTA cited studies showing that the technology was widespread in America by the early 1980s and that private copying was commonplace. Owners of copyright to these works, meanwhile, claimed that "commercial piracy" was widespread as well. OTA noted that, while considerable data proving economic loss had been compiled by proprietors, it was not definitive, nor did it answer the question of whether "a particular instance of copying actually displaced a sale of a copy."[27] In other words, if a viewer were unable for whatever reason to make a copy at home of a movie being shown on HBO (Home Box Office) would that mean necessarily that the viewer would go out and buy (or rent) a copy at the video store?

The computer, of course, made enforcement even more difficult. OTA identified three major problems posed by computer storage technology:

1. Copying digital information is much less costly and much faster than either photocopying or tape dubbing.
2. The very nature of digital information creates the possibility of an infinite number of perfect copies, so "original" quality does not necessitate possession of the original itself. That means that content is no longer tied to medium; it can be "unbundled" at the user's discretion.
3. As a matter of normal operation, a computer makes many copies of parts of works; some of those copies may only exist for a nanosecond. But other copies may be held in the machine indefinitely, or may be copied to tape or disk for backup.

While recognizing that computer users presently receive "a relatively small amount of copyrighted material in digital, computer-readable form—computer programs and a small but rapidly growing amount of material made available through online databases," OTA rightly pointed out that this circumstance is changing just as rapidly as any other area of computer technology, and some of the others also pose problems for copyright enforcement. These include optical scanning devices, laser printers, and that most formidable of storage devices, the digital disk, which will become even more fearsome when it is finally erasable. The conclusion reached by OTA in its analysis of storage technologies was that they "are making the old definitions of 'rights,' 'infringements,' and 'fair use' ambiguous and largely obsolete." Furthermore, said OTA, traditional enforcement via civil suit "may no longer be effective in protecting the creative and economic interests of copyright owners."[28]

Concurrently, trends in communication technology have affected copyright enforcement since the advent, in the 1920s, of electronic broadcasting, which allowed for the dispersal of a "performance" beyond the walls of a concert hall or theatre. Television, in particular, presented enforcement problems for owners of copyright, who joined with broadcasters in the development of a system of commercial support (sponsors) for broadcasts and established contracts with organizations that would monitor use of copyrighted work and pay royalties. OTA noted that cable television is especially troublesome for copyright holders because it is susceptible to "theft of service," or the deliberate, unauthorized connection to a cable service. Additionally, cable companies must deal with high transaction costs in handling royalty payments to the many owners of copyright represented by their diverse programming.[29]

More important to libraries, however, are some other communications technologies, including facsimile transmission and data communications. Unfortunately, OTA devoted only three paragraphs to facsimile technology, but did describe it as one with "potentially significant implications for copyright enforcement." OTA identified cost as the major reason why telefacsimile was not a more important technology.[30] It should be remembered, however, that this report was issued in 1986, and that costs indeed have declined, while usage among libraries has proliferated.

Within the realm of data communications ("computer to computer transfer of digital information"), OTA includes databases, computer bulletin boards, local area networks, and the developing Integrated Services Digital Network (ISDN), and rightly recognizes that "as more and more copyrighted material is available in computer-mediated form, people will be able to transfer it widely and quickly without the knowledge or consent of copyright holders."[31] The report notes that data communications is expanding in scope, scale, and speed. In other words, more people are moving more digital information along communications lines that allow the data to travel faster than ever before. The real key here for copyright enforcement, however, is the relatively high degree of secrecy with which such massive amounts of digital transmission can be achieved. OTA's conclusion:

> ...unless significant changes are made in the operation of public telecommunications networks, the increasing volume of data communications will make it essentially impossible for proprietors to trace the subsequent movements of their works once they are captured by users' computer and data communications systems. This raises the issue of whether proprietors should, and in practical terms can, control the transfer of their works after users first receive them.[32]

Current trends in processing technology are also troublesome for copyright holders, especially since they put technology directly in the hands of the end-user of information, at home and in the office. OTA's greatest concern in this area is the increased ability of the end-user to prepare "derivatives" of copyrighted material, by selectively modifying and re-assembling protected works in such a way that they become "new, or apparently new works."[33] In its discussion of text derivation, OTA describes the increasing use of integrated PC software (word-processing, database management, communications) packages which enable the user to download copyrighted works from online databases, and then manipulate the information on the PC until its original source is obscured. OTA expects such database derivation to become more prevalent and enforcement to become, therefore, much more difficult, and perhaps impossible. Newer technologies, such as automatic indexing, abstracting, and document preparation systems that combine the latest in optical storage, high-speed communications, and intelligent text processing could be disastrous for holders of copyright.[34]

OTA identified three basic strategies that copyright proprietors are using to protect themselves in these increasingly difficult circumstances: technological protection, public relations and lobbying. The first involves a variety of methods, depending upon the medium, and includes security measures such as signal encryption or scrambling, monitoring information flow, and proprietary channels for distribution. In assessing the pros and cons of technological protection, OTA noted that a vicious circle of increasingly sophisticated methods of protection, followed by copying, would likely result. More importantly, from the standpoint of public policy, better technological protection could compromise the public welfare goals related to dissemination of and access to information.

In the public relations arena, the information industry has pursued three basic strategies, according to OTA. First, they have tried to make the public more aware of the fact that copying is illegal and can be prosecuted. Second, they have tried to establish a link between end-users and the "fair compensation" of creators, publishers, and distributors of intellectual property (we all have a stake in this). Finally, they have attempted to educate the public about copyright, appealing to Americans' general inclination to abide by the law. OTA concluded that these strategies had met with varying success and that the public would respect copyright law only if it was perceived as fair. In fact, a public opinion survey commissioned by OTA found that:

1. Most people did not know much about intellectual property rights or feel that they were affected by them;
2. The vast majority of those surveyed found some forms of unauthorized copying (probably videotaping movies on TV) acceptable;
3. Most people felt it was not right to infringe copyright if done for profit or in a business setting;
4. Most people saw the issue as a marketplace problem that should be solved by the information industry.

A similar survey of small business executives found that this group generally was more sympathetic than the general public to the position of the information industry, but agreed with the public that copying for personal use was acceptable. They also agreed with the public that nongovernmental solutions were best, but likewise felt there was little demand for solutions at present. OTA's conclusion from both of these surveys was that public relations strategies were more likely to be effective if they focused on the relationship between the copyright holder and the end-user than on the rights of the former.[35]

The Intellectual Property Bargain

Chapter 7 of the OTA report addresses the effects of new information technologies on what it describes as an "intellectual property bargain" between proprietors and users of copyrighted information; a *quid pro quo* which was based on the sale of information goods by the copy. OTA found that the present copyright law "offers little guidance to courts in resolving conflicts over who shall benefit from new uses afforded by technology," and suggested therefore that "because electronically disseminated works are not sold in copies, but accessed through communications media, Congress may need to rethink the intellectual property bargain to ensure adequate access to information goods."[36]

According to OTA, it was the intention of the framers of the Constitution (especially Madison) that "copyright benefit the public by encouraging learning through the dissemination of works," and that the Supreme Court has "consistently interpreted the intellectual property bargain to be 'primarily' for the benefit of the public." But Madison and others also worried that governmentally granted exclusive rights like copyright and patents could be monopolistic and subsequently detrimental to the public good, so early American intellectual property law was much more limited, with respect to authors' rights, than present legislation. For example, once a work had been printed and sold, anyone could "display it, read from it publicly, or even write other books based on it, without infringing the author's copyright."[37]

Since the first copyright act in 1790, the intellectual property bargain has been transformed by both the expansion of copyrightable subject matter (dramatic performances, 1856; musical compositions, 1897; mechanical recording of musical compositions, 1909) and, more importantly, the expansion of authors' rights. At the same time, the courts began to broaden their interpretation of "copying" from mere mechanical duplication to similarities in "expression." "It was Congress however," says OTA, "that, unwittingly and perhaps accidentally, granted written works the most far reaching rights in the act of 1909," by adding the right to *copy* to those already granted—printing, reprinting, publishing, and vending. According to OTA, this was a critical juncture in intellectual property law, "for the ambiguity of the word 'copy' subsequently endowed proprietors with rights, not only against commercial piracy, but also against noncommercial personal and private use," and just in time for later emerging technologies such as the photocopier and the tape recorder to make private copying practical.[38]

The courts subsequently interpreted the right to copy literally, transforming copyright from "the right to control the use of copyright for commercial profit (vis `a vis competing publishers) to the right to control the copyrighted work itself (vis `a vis the user of the work)." OTA believes that this distinction is a critical one, because it suggests that, in the former case, copyright is a form of *regulation* "designed to ensure that only an author will be allowed to sell his work to the public," and that "end-users of the work are free to copy, store, manipulate, and share copies that they have purchased." But if the copyrighted work itself is what is controlled, "then it is a form of *property*; a bundle of rights that follows each and every copy of a book, record, or computer program," and includes "rights to profit from the uses to which the work is put." The question of regulation vs. property has never been answered completely by Congress or the courts, but OTA believes that it must be resolved if we are to determine who will benefit (copyright holders or end-users) from new information technologies.[39]

In forging a new intellectual property bargain which would accommodate emerging information technologies, OTA points out that Congress must first recognize the fact that the activities of printing, publishing, and reproducing are now in the hands of the end-user as well as the proprietor, thanks to technology. Subsequently, the question of private use of copyrighted works ("whether the copyright proprietor is to be remunerated for end-user activities"), which is ambiguous under present copyright law, must be addressed. Furthermore, recommends OTA, such a policy should be based on a number of criteria, including "whether it causes *harm* to copyright proprietors, whether it would be economically *efficient* to extend rights, whether *political support* for an extension of rights exists, and whether *access* to information can be ensured."[40] OTA also concluded that the judicially developed doctrine of "fair use," which was codified by Congress in the 1976 Copyright Act but not defined, is of "limited value in addressing the private use issue to which the new technologies give rise."[41]

The Conference on Intellectual Property Rights

In April of 1987, the Network Advisory Committee of the Library of Congress sponsored a conference on intellectual property rights which used the OTA report as its major focus. The first speaker was D. Linda Garcia, the OTA project director, who began by answering (at least from a personal perspective) the earlier question of regulation vs. property. Garcia declared that the granting of intellectual property rights "give[s] intellectual works the status of property" and "allow[s] intellectual works to be treated as commodities." The most vexing problems created for intellectual property rights by digital technologies, said Garcia, include the identification of "authorship" and "works," both of which may be intangible and reprocessible in digital form. Derivative use makes it more difficult to determine who should be rewarded for what contributions, prompting Garcia to question whether "an incentive system which favors the original creator is still appropriate." Her conclusion is that the rapid and fundamental changes which are occurring in information technology "will antiquate many of the policy mechanisms now in force" and that the problems for the intellectual property system are long term ones which may only be resolved by "significant changes in the system itself."[42]

The next speaker, in fact, titled his presentation "The End of Copyright." Robert Kost, also an OTA staffer (and an attorney), focused on the basic problem of a copyright system based on "Static Media" which revolved around the printer/publisher but must now come to terms with a "user-centered universe" created by computers and telecommunications. He agrees with Garcia that "copyright turns information into property," but considers information "a very reluctant form of property," which unlike tangible property, can be possessed by more than one person at the same time. In an age of "Static Media," it was easier to make intellectual property behave like tangible property by printing it on paper and selling the paper. The printing press, claimed Kost, made copyright both necessary and possible.[43]

When the present century brought with it "Dynamic Media" such as the photocopier and the tape recorder, the printing press became less of a copyright regulation mechanism because it could not control the sale and distribution of copies. Kost maintains that the 1976 legislation, which "sought to control the use of the work itself," was 50 years too late in its response to dynamic media. Furthermore, its distinction between the work and the copy "is a recognition of the fact that information is reverting to its elemental, non-property, form." That process has only been accelerated in the present age of "Digital Media," he believes, noting for example that "electronic distribution is not distribution at all—at least in the legal sense—since one can distribute only copies of a work, and copies are material objects under the law." For computer processible works of fact especially, Kost believes, "copyright is a slender reed upon which to hang protection," because it technically protects not the underlying information in works of fact, but the arrangement, organization, design, and selection, all of which are activities which modern computers perform very well indeed. Ultimately, says Kost, the real question is whether we should continue to find "patchwork solutions for the sake of preserving copyright," or whether we should simply look for better ways to take full advantage of everything that information technology has to offer.[44]

Two representatives from the American Chemical Society, John Hearty and Barbara Polansky, presented differing opinions on the importance of copyright to their company's family of full-text databases, Chemical Journals Online. Hearty works in marketing, and thus felt that a database vendor's first concern "is to sell information." Copyright violations were his fourth concern, with customer support and product development second and third, respectively. Hearty identified three types of copyright violations which ACS encounters:

1. downloading by an individual who then resells the information elec-

tronically or in hard copy (a major violation);
2. downloading by an individual who then uses the information deriva-
   tively by merging it with other downloaded information to create a
   new, value-added product (Hearty believes that little can be done about
   this);
3. downloading by an individual who then shares the information with
   others at no cost (Hearty classifies this as a "minor" violation).

Finally, in reiterating his belief that a database owner's primary concern is to
make money, Hearty acknowledged that owners are also concerned that availability of the electronic database does not adversely affect subscriptions to
the print form of a journal. "After all," he says, "publishers make their money, by and large, from the original printed form. They do not make it, at least
at this time, from the electronic distribution of their information."[45]

Barbara Polansky, responsible for copyright issues related to the printed publications of ACS, noted in her presentation that publishers such as ACS
are concerned about copyright violations via downloading, which is why they
insist on granting rights to download by contractual means. This concern also
means that they are not afraid to sue a copyright violator, which they have
done. Polansky also described the concerns which she had when ACS first
granted downloading rights, which basically were that users would not be content to limit their downloading to the terms of the contract. In an online, full-
text environment, she does not believe that copyright alone will be enough to
both protect the rights of users and meet the needs of users. This "delicate balance...will be upset every time a newer and faster technology is created. And
with the advancement of technology, the use, reuse, and repackaging of information becomes even easier, faster, and cheaper." Her conclusion was that contracts for downloading provide clear guidelines for use and that the terms of
contracts be communicated to everyone in the user organization who might be
downloading. The key, says Polansky, is for database owners, vendors, and users to make their needs and concerns known to one another.[46]

Copyright and the Electronic Journal

As noted in the beginning of this chapter, the continually rising cost of serial-
ly published scholarly information, particularly in the sciences, has been an
important resource-sharing issue of the 1980s. In a very real sense, copyright
is at the heart of this issue, for the rights for most published scholarly information are ceded by the author to the publisher, who then sells the information back to the author and his peers in a journal which may be becoming pro-
hibitively expensive. This is a price which most scholars and their institutions
are still willing to meet in order to fuel the sacred engine of promotion and
tenure, but it is a price which most of their libraries are finding increasingly
difficult to pay.

The present system of scholarly communication is very much a
product of the "Static Media" age described by Kost, revolving around the

publisher, who holds the rights, as well as most of the economic benefits. As OTA pointed out, "Profits flow for the most part to the investors, not to those who found the data, organized the presentation, or created the efficient expression."[47] The author benefits economically only in the sense that he or she increases his or her chances of promotion and tenure by publishing; the author's institution benefits, presumably, by retention of the author. But without the publisher, who edits, prints, publishes, and distributes the information, the author, until recently, had no effective means of disseminating his or her research.

The "Digital Media" age, however, could change that scenario. As OTA observed:

> Working on an electronic network, for example, the author of a book can now edit, print, publish, and distribute his works; tasks that were traditionally within the purview of the publisher. Under these circumstances, the author may be less inclined to assign his rights to the publisher.[48]

Specifically regarding information published in scientific journals, OTA also observed that information now distributed electronically differed from journal literature primarily in that the former was more likely to be a work in progress, but concluded that: "Eventually, scientific research may actually be published on such networks instead of paper. This practice would have far-reaching consequences for scholarship."[49]

Richard Dougherty believes that academic libraries could not only benefit from a scholarly communications system based on new information technologies, but play an important role as well. In his judgment, "the skyrocketing costs of maintaining the new STM (scientific, technical, medical) publishing infrastructure, ... and the new information technologies available to support a new generation of STM communications media will inevitably lead to a reassessment of the current system."[50] Dougherty believes that the long-term solution to the problem lies with the university becoming a major force in scholarly publishing, fundamentally changing the way "higher education produces, distributes and uses the information products of university research." He advocates a marriage of "the technological capabilities of computing centers with the expertise of university presses as publishers and libraries as retailers and distributors of STM information," in which libraries would manage resource-sharing networks and distribute electronic journals and articles on demand.[51]

Dougherty acknowledges that the initial costs of such a system of scholarly communication would be high, but believes that the long-term benefits would be even greater. Among those benefits would be the likelihood that:

> Universities would be able to regain control of copyrights in the name of their faculty. If easy and inexpensive access to information through networks is a desired goal of universities, ownership

of copyrights by universities could prove to be a particularly significant benefit in the long run.[52]

James Thompson, chair of ACRL's Discussion Group on Journal Costs in Academic and Research Libraries, concurs with the idea that the university must become more involved in publishing its research, pointing out that "scholarly information originates here in the academy; there's no reason why it shouldn't become a financial asset for education rather than a liability."[53] Scholarly information, says Thompson, "is produced with our resources, and the copyright, until reassigned, belongs to us."[54]

Dougherty too believes that scholarly information could become a university asset instead of an economic liability, maintaining that "university-initiated publishing and distribution ventures would in time generate millions of dollars in revenues," and noting that university libraries currently are spending hundreds of millions of dollars on journal subscriptions.[55]

Approaching the same idea from another angle, Richard R. Rowe, President and CEO of the Faxon Company, addressed a meeting in February 1989 of the Professional and Scholarly Publishers Division of the Association of American Publishers. Speaking on the economics of scholarly communication, Rowe noted that escalating costs and declining public subsidies for higher education will force universities to intensify their efforts to "seek new ways to fund their enterprises. One obvious way to do this is to capitalize upon the intellectual products of the university's faculty. That process is well under way in the sciences, and we can expect it to expand considerably in the years ahead."[56]

Rowe also raised the possibility of a disturbing consequence of this trend toward viewing "faculty products" as sources of revenue. Rowe warned that scholars and researchers may become increasingly responsive to "immediate financial demands," and that scholarship will subsequently "shift away from long-term, disinterested inquiry toward those matters that can return a fairly quick dollar to the institutions that pay for the development and support of scholars and researchers." The result, he believes, will be an increasing privatization of scientific discoveries for the purpose of competitive advantage, a development which would place in serious jeopardy Madison's vision that copyright benefits the public by encouraging learning through the dissemination of works.[57]

In describing his new electronic system of scholarly communication, Dougherty does not foresee a role for library cooperation and resource-sharing in the traditional sense, but does seem to suggest that libraries would maintain the databases and resource-sharing networks, distributing the information to users.[58] He also sees an opportunity for libraries to assume a leadership role in this effort, noting that researchers are too narrowly focused on promotion and tenure. It would seem that one area in which librarians could provide their institutions with a great deal of expertise is in educating administrators and researchers alike on the copyright issues related to electronic information. It is an education which they will sorely need if Dougherty's assertion is correct that "easy and inexpensive access to information through networks is a desired goal of universities,"[59] because such a goal is in direct conflict with the goals of commercial publishers such as Robert Maxwell, who is "determined that Maxwell Communications Corporation will be one of what I expect will be only ten surviving global publishing companies."[60] As long as commercial publishers can acquire and hold copyright to much of America's scholarly information, it will be Maxwell's, rather than Dougherty's, dream that will be realized, and libraries that will foot the bill.

Notes

1. 17 U.S.C. Sec. 102(a).
2. David Peyton, "A New View of Copyright," *Journal of Policy Analysis and Management* 6 (1): 92.
3. John A. Hearty and Barbara F. Polansky, "ACS Chemical Journals Online: Is It Being Downloaded, Do We Care?," In *Intellectual Property Rights in an Electronic Age*, ed. S. G. Harriman, Proceedings of the Library of Congress Network Advisory Committee Meeting (Washington, D. C., April 22-24, 1987), Network Planning Paper No. 16, 45.
4. For an excellent analysis of this question, see Marilyn Gell Mason, "Copyright in Context: The OCLC Database," *Library Journal* 113 (12): 31-35.
5. Charles Hamaker, "Library Serials Budgets: Publishers and the Twenty Percent Effect," *Library Acquisitions: Practice & Theory* 12 (2): 212-214.
6. Richard M. Dougherty, "Turning the Serials Crisis to Our Advantage: An Opportunity for Leadership," *Library Administration and Management* 3 (2): 61.
7. Michael Boswood, "The Future of Serials, 1976-2000: A Publisher's Perspective," *Serials Librarian* 11 (3,4): 15.
8. Robert J. Kost, "The End of Copyright." In *Intellectual Property Rights in an Electronic Age*, ed. S. G. Harriman, Proceedings of the Library of Congress Network Advisory Committee Meeting (Washington, D. C., April 22-24, 1987), Network Planning Paper No. 16, 20.
9. D. Linda Garcia, "The OTA Report on Intellectual Property Rights," in *Intellectual Property Rights in an Electronic Age*, 10.
10. U. S. Congress, Office of Technology Assessment, *Intellectual Property Rights in an Age of Electronics and Information* (Washington, D. C.; Government Printing Office, 1986), 3 (hereafter cited as OTA Report).
11. 17 U.S.C. Sec. 102(a).
12. OTA Report, 62.
13. OTA Report, 65.
14. Robert L. Oakley, "Intellectual Property Issues and Information Networks: A Background Paper," (Discussion Paper prepared for the Library of Congress Network Advisory Committee), 10.
15. Ibid., 66.
16. Ibid., 73.
17. Ibid., 78.
18. Ibid., 70.
19. Ibid., 68-69.
20. Ithiel de sola Pool, *Technologies of Freedom* (Cambridge, Mass.: Belknap Press, 1983), 215.

21. Oakley, 12.
22. OTA Report, 73.
23. Ibid., 75.
24. Ibid., 79-85.
25. Ibid., 97.
26. Ibid., 99-100.
27. Ibid., 101.
28. Ibid., 102-103.
29. Ibid., 105.
30. Ibid., 107.
31. Ibid., 107-108.
32. Ibid., 109.
33. Ibid., 112.
34. Ibid., 112.
35. Ibid., 121-123.
36. Ibid., 187.
37. Ibid., 189-190.
38. Ibid., 190-192.
39. Ibid., 192-193.
40. Ibid., 193.
41. Ibid., 197.
42. Garcia, 9-18.
43. Kost, 19-21.
44. Ibid., 24-25.
45. Hearty and Polansky, 46-48.
46. Ibid., 50-56.
47. OTA Report, 152.
48. OTA Report, 5.
49. Ibid., 152.
50. Dougherty, 61.
51. Ibid., 62.
52. Ibid.
53. James C. Thompson, "Journal Costs: Perception and Reality in the Dialogue," guest editorial, *College & Research Libraries* 49 (6): 482.
54. James C. Thompson, "Confronting the Serials Cost Problem," *Serials Review*, 15(1): 46.
55. Dougherty, 62.
56. Richard R. Rowe, "The Economics of Scholarly Communication." Paper presented at the annual meeting of the Association of American Publishers, Professional & Scholarly Publishers Division, Boston, February 1989.
57. Ibid.
58. Dougherty, 62.
59. Ibid.
60. William Kay, "A Global Vision," *Global Business* 1 (1): 41.

An Accountability Model for Authors in the Electronic Age

Bonnie Juergens and Gloriana St. Clair

Some years ago, a clever commercial for XEROX copiers showed a monk being asked by his superior to produce copies of a thick manuscript in a short time. The viewer's assumption is that scribes in the scriptorium will make the copies. In medieval times, each copy of a manuscript could have—and, due to human error as well as deliberate intervention, did have—different content. However, since XEROX solves the problem in the commercial, each of the manuscript copies is identical.

In a communications exercise used to teach management, four or five persons will sometimes sit in a room with identical looking sheets of paper trying to solve the problem described on the papers for thirty or forty minutes without discovering that each page contains different pieces of information.

These two examples remind us of the modern reader's assumption that pieces of printed material are the same. The uniformity of currently published materials is taken for granted in our paper-based society. Yet, as we enter an age of electronic publication, we enter a time when individual copies of a "published" document could easily be different. One of the clear advantages of electronic publication will be the ability to change content during the publication process and/or after publication has occurred. But who will change documents? What records will be kept of document changes? And what impact will this have on bibliography? These questions can be addressed with an accountability model.

The elements of this accountability model are:

1. Content changing
2. Citations changing with content, and the necessity for audit trails
3. Scrambling systems
4. Publisher selection for protection
5. Copyright continuation.

Bonnie Juergens is Executive Director of AMIGOS Bibliographic Council, Inc., a non-profit resource-sharing network providing services to over 300 member libraries throughout the Southwest. Gloriana St. Clair is Assistant Dean for Access Services at Pennsylvania State University.

Content Changing

Control of the content in today's electronic publishing process is, without intervention, dependent upon individuals in much the same fashion that it was in the scriptorium. Since content can readily be changed, it will become the task of the electronic publisher to ensure that such changes take place only in accordance with the rules.

For purposes of this discussion, the authors will focus primarily on the publication of scholarly and scientific journals. We are not including the commercial publication of fiction and non-fiction books, although the principles being proposed can apply to general publishing. Also, in grappling with the issues surrounding the replacement of paper journals with electronic journals, it is useful to consider the distinctions between a "database" and a "text." The authors are restricting this discussion to the electronic publication of "text." Briscoe describes the differences quite succinctly in his statement that

> ...text may be defined as the original written or printed words and form of a literary work. Elaborate and quite scientific methods of scholarship have been developed to establish the text of tens of thousands of culturally important works. A text is usually fixed and stable, notwithstanding known variants and editions. It has a distinct beginning and end and is read linearly. A database, on the other hand, is mutable, expandable, revisable.[1]

The assumption here is that electronic publishing produces a database rather than a text with "a distinct beginning and end." But electronic publishing can and will produce both. For the publication of scientific and scholarly texts, the pertinent constraints of traditional "publishing" are possible if we use the electronic medium to develop, disseminate, modify, and also *finalize* the content. Rather than allowing the medium to control the standards, let us use the medium as a tool to support the standards. And, further, let us expand the capabilities of the medium to impose order on the electronic publishing process. The distinctions, based on purpose instead of medium, between electronic publications and databases will ultimately define the controls that are applied.

A major part of the bibliographer's concern for control is the ability to cite properly, correctly, and finally. The scholar's bibliographic concern is with the *finality* that is inherent in the citation. In electronic publishing as currently practiced, the writer is perceived to have the ability to change the content once it has been made available to readers, i.e., published. Just as the copyist or scribe could—and did—change the contents of documents with each round of copying, the electronic writer—or, in fact, reader—could—and, it is conceded, will—change the content of documents after they are published.

Citations Changing With Content: The Audit Trail

The analogy of the scribe to today's electronic writer is an apt one. It suggests the solution to the bibliographic and moral problems associated with returning the power of convenient change to the writer, or for that matter, to anyone involved in the publication process. Just as bibliographers adapted to the limitations of the scribe's technology by noting textual differences, bibliographers can and must adapt to the limitations of electronic technology. To forbid change would be as foolhardy as to allow unlimited change. T. S. Eliot's phrase "visions and revisions with the taking of a toast and tea" may take on new meaning as versions proliferate.

The bibliographic solution is that of clear, convenient, consistent identification. Each variation in the content of an electronic publication must be carefully documented. A consistent and meaningful identification scheme must be employed as part of bibliographic control. A simple scheme comes to mind:

0.1-nnn	for "internal" or draft documents
1.0-1.nn	for "in publication" occurrences of the document (today's preprints)
2.01-n.nnn	for subsequent changed versions (today's editions).

The publisher will be responsible for defining the "final" version—in today's terms, the edition—of an electronically-produced document. Subsequent changes will literally define a later edition. Examples: 1.0 through 1.05 may constitute progressive versions of an article-in-publication. Readers and bibliographers will need a signal indicating that the document is no longer "in production," but has been finalized. The number of successive iterations will vary from document to document, so a predesignated final number—say, "1.10" or "1.99"—does not appear to be sufficient. A standard finalizing notation must be adopted—such as "F" for "Final version." Thus, the publisher's notation "1.06F" would tell a very important tale: the document in hand is the sixth and final version of the first edition of the work. The critical role of the publisher must be, at this point, to "lock in" the contents of the document and disallow further changing in its electronic form. Subsequent changes will initiate the second edition, and will be tracked as "2.0 – 2.nn" up to the publisher-defined completion of the second edition, which in this case might be identified as "2.16F."

Prior to the publisher's involvement, the internal "draft" versions of a document can be numbered 0.1-nnn; these would be outside the control and thus the protection of the publication industry. They would share the basic production mechanism of electronic word processing and even electronic dissemination, but not yet be under the protection of a publisher's network.

It is also reasonable to expect that a date will be incorporated into the status-of-publication statement, and that inclusion of this coded information will become a routine part of both verbal and visually-displayed references to "published" documents. More importantly, documents that do not contain such identifiable information will be suspect. Serious researchers, scholars, and commentators will not accept or use information that is not thus qualified.

Scrambling Systems

As described above, a structure that allows an audit trail to accompany legitimate publications must be devised if the dual purposes of sharing information and accruing credit are to be met in the academic electronic publishing environment. The authors' point is not that our scheme need be adopted, but that *some* scheme must be standardized and adopted quickly so that control can begin to reign over chaos at an early stage in the adoption of this ubiquitous technology.

But the audit trail will not be effective unless "someone" makes decisions throughout the publishing process: when does a document change from an internal or private draft to a publication? When does a work in progress become a finalized edition? A second edition? Who can make "authorized" changes to a document in process? The publisher is the one who currently makes these decisions. The task of the electronic publisher will be to ensure that changes in content take place only in accordance with the rules. And the publisher will ensure that no tampering takes place by relying on the same technology that gives rise to the problem. Sophisticated programs may be written to protect the data via scrambling just as security-conscious data systems have done for years.

Along with devices to protect the integrity of the documents and to make accountable individuals who change data once the document is in distribution, publishers will have to devise systems that prevent direct electronic theft of data through downloading. This is particularly complex because there will be many instances in which downloading is an acceptable and, in fact, desirable practice. There will also be instances in which downloading constitutes theft. In the print-publishing environment, the dependence of copyright upon peer pressure and financial cost-of-diminishing-returns tells us that copyright in the electronic environment must be protected by strong means that do not rely upon direct policing of citizens.

Thus, publishers must develop systems that account for downloading activities of users. Perhaps electronic controls similar to those developed by the recording industry will be applied to electronic publishing: programs which can distinguish between users with copying authorization and those without such authorization, and thus prohibit or interfere with unauthorized copying. Such systems must allow only authorized users to download, will credit or debit their accounts, and will provide realistic audit trailing that will be legally justifiable. Similar accounting will apply to uploading activities, an inevitable part of electronic publishing. The challenge for electronic publishers will be to prevent unauthorized data modification as well as unauthorized copying.

Publisher Selection for Protective Abilities

Electronic publishers will develop protective audit trails and automatic checks in order to attract quality writers to the medium. Just as scholars currently limit their submissions to the prestigious publications in their fields, and reputable researchers do not trust information from non-authoritative sources, so will the electronic scholarly writers of the future qualify the range of publication sources they are willing to use.

High-quality electronic publishers will be those whose systems protect content while they are providing a full bibliographic audit trail. The "paperback" publishers of the electronic medium will be those of lesser quality. In their publications, editing mistakes will be more frequently overlooked and security precautions will be less stringently applied.

The tabloid equivalents of the electronic publishing world will be those systems that do not protect the data, the writer, or in fact, even the publisher. Serious scholars, researchers, and literary writers who make their living by selling original works of fiction will not trust their work to publishers of lesser quality.

Whatever technology-based controls are developed by publishers to support the audit trail, the primary rule for creating the intellectual content of publications will be similar to today's rules: proper credit must be given for another's work. In the academic community, peer pressure and scholarly regard will continue to be primary enforcers of this rule, as they are in the paper environment.

Copyright Continuation

In the preceding discussion, historical antecedents to the print-publishing environment were examined. The accountability model itself was based on concepts related to citation of medieval manuscripts. Similarly, history provides some insights into related issues on copyright. In earliest times, the creator wrote out beautiful thoughts. Classical and medieval copyists made these thoughts available to others. After the introduction of the printing press, the task of the copyist was taken over by the printer. Most recently, the roles of the copyist/printer have been taken by the publisher. Can that continue to be true in the era of electronic publishing?

Ithiel de Sola Pool believed not:

> The recognition of a copyright and the practice of paying royalties emerged with the printing press. With the arrival of electronic reproduction these practices become unworkable. Electronic publishing is analogous not so much to the print shop of the eighteenth century as to word-of-mouth communication, to which copyright was never applied.[2]

However, the word-of-mouth analogy is not completely adequate, because individuals participating in scholarly publishing desire two distinct results: communication and recognition. Understanding the importance of communication between and among researchers, one can recognize that the paper-based communications medium must logically give way to the electronic medium that allows scholars and researchers to communicate quickly, directly, and inter-actively. This shift from paper to electronic information-sharing has been taking place for as long as equipment (originally terminals; more recently networked personal computers) has been available to researchers. As Lewis describes it:

> ...the scholarly journal was created because scientists could no longer keep up with each other's work through word of mouth and correspondence. The weight of the system, based on the printed scholarly journal, has become more than existing structures can bear...Publishing delays are such that no self-respecting scholar depends on journal publication as a primary means of staying current. Preprints and working papers have become a way of life, and formal journal publication is more for posterity and tenure committees than communicating with colleagues.[3]

Indeed, a second element associated with scholarly communication is that of the credit accruing to the publication of scholarly works. In an earlier society in which only the wealthy could afford the luxury of both time and the education required for scientific inquiry, the free exchange of ideas could take place via letters and—as de Sola Pool says—by "word of mouth." In today's scholarly research community, legitimate contributors depend upon the reward system (promotion and tenure) as straightforwardly as professional writers and publishing firms depend upon the earnings that accrue from copyright protection.

Just as there have been changes in mechanisms for sharing intellectual ideas, there have been changes in perceptions of what constitutes originality. Today's perceptions of originality are part of why we have copyright. When William Shakespeare was busy borrowing heavily from North's translation of Plutarch's *Lives of the Noble Greeks and Romans* to produce the play *Antony and Cleopatra*, originality was not considered important. In fact, not to derive materials from classical and Biblical sources would have been gauche.

A dual system for defining what constitutes originality exists. In the purely artistic endeavors, such as art, music, poetry, and drama, the final work of art is ladled from a soup pot filled with earlier works of art, music, literature, history, and everyday occurrences. Thus, the evidence of borrowing from others' materials is diffuse, delayed, and covert.

In the scholarly world, the components of a finished work are the same as above. Bits and pieces of others' works are recycled to fit the necessities of the current work. These works by common consent and by conventional acceptance may be borrowed from one another as long as the proper credit is given. Direct financial remuneration for these borrowings is not expected or required. Our conventions require that the person borrowing give credit to the creators for their exact wording and for any facts or opinions not also available in a second source. Thus evidence of conventional use of non-original materials in scholarly work is direct, immediate, and overt.

In electronic publishing of scholarly works, downloading facilitates borrowing exact wordings from others because microcomputers easily transfer contents from one document to another. Online databases now provide powerful new means for retrieving materials on quite specific topics. The technology facilitates plagiarism. Little-known items in local databases could be retrieved, copied, and submitted as work for degrees in other localities. While this kind of scholarly heist occurred from time to time in the past, subject database access and electronic publication make new recombination on little-known topics much easier.

A well-known example from the print-publishing environment is Alex Haley's purported appropriation of passages from an earlier and somewhat obscure African novel. Haley gained notoriety, publicity, and profit. Financial success mitigates censure. However, successful and continuing abuse of plagiarism would be disastrous to a society basing its practices on willing compliance to established custom. It will be important for publishers to counter the current electronic publishing environment in which downloading makes very easy the kind of borrowing Haley purportedly did in *Roots*.

Financial reimbursement for written words is managed through copyright. Or, as Robert J. Kost reminds us, "copyright turns information into property."[4] Since information is in fact not quantifiable, controllable property, it had to be turned into property in order to be used as a profitable commodity. This is an important concept in copyright, as described by Kost:

> Scarcity and exclusivity, which do not come naturally to information, are nevertheless fundamental to the notion of property, and at the very heart of a market economy...And this is where copyright comes in. Because the Framers of the constitution, and before them, the House of Lords, decided that having lots of books and maps and charts around was a good idea, and because the free market was so adept at providing other types of goods demanded by society, some mechanism had to be found to remedy the market failure of information. Copyright was a truly ingenious solution; it made information plentiful by making it scarce, and available to all by making it exclusive. This was possible because information was always and everywhere to be found embedded in tangible goods—copies—which went proxy for information in the marketplace...What we had going was a product compromise: information could be sold like goods as long as it acted like them.[5]

Thus for many years, society has been successfully treating information like property. The publisher as the primary facilitator in the creator-consumer relationship has been able to make the copyright system work. Because the publisher understood the cost-of-diminishing-returns, small aberrations were not worth pursuing.

But major aberrations in the system cannot be tolerated. Such a violation of book copyright occurred when Ace Books pirated the text of *The Lord of the Rings* in 1965. Ace Books reproduced the hardback edition to satisfy a paperback market demand in the United States. Tolkien made revisions to the text to create a new edition, and American publisher Houghton Mifflin collaborated with Ballantine books to create a legitimate paperback edition. In a letter to one of his sons, Tolkien says:

> My campaign in U.S.A. has gone well. Ace Books are in quite a spot, and many institutions have banned all their products. They are selling their pirate edition quite well, but it is being discovered to be very badly and erroneously printed, and I am getting such an advt. from the rumpus that I expect my "authorized" paper-back will in fact sell more copies than it would, if there had

been no trouble or competition.[6]

In 1966, Tolkien signed an "amicable agreement" with Ace Books which paid a royalty of four percent and agreed not to reprint.[7] Pressure from fan clubs and the Science Fiction Writers of America to use the authorized edition helped reduce sales of the pirated version. However, the availability of the legitimate Ballantine edition, which cost twenty cents more because of the royalties paid, was the key to controlling the violation of copyright.[8]

More recent copyright decisions have renewed discussions about the practicality of copyright. The Library of Congress Network Advisory Committee hosted a 1987 discussion of the critical issues related to copyright and electronic publishing, and the proceedings constitute a seminal work that should be perused by any librarian interested in this important topic. In his presentation to NAC participants, Ralph Oman, Register of Copyrights, reminded us of a recent court decision against copyright enforcement:

> In the celebrated *Betamax* case the U.S. Supreme Court held that home taping of copyrighted television broadcasts for time-shifting purposes amounted to "fair use," notwithstanding that entire works were copied and that the cumulative effect was to erode a large potential market. The majority opinion says that "...it is not our job to apply laws that have not yet been written." What the Court failed to note was that the law *had* been written. It simply chose to ignore it.[9]

Do radio and television offer an alternative "copyright" model for electronic publishing? Ed Brownrigg and Clifford Lynch propose that they do, and offer a persuasive argument in their 1985 *ITAL* discussion of electronic publishing:

> Perhaps the management of copyright over display should be patterned after the management of certain performance rights rather than after the management of reproduction rights to printed material. ...Without [the performance professions'] central licensing agencies, each radio station would require copyright clearance experts and would undergo programming delays while contacting the owners for each performance. ...Authors and publishers could submit their copyrighted material to the catalog of a clearing agency, which would collect royalties on their behalf according to [an agreed-upon] scheme.[10]

Economics remains the consistent bottom line on the problem of copying and copyright. In the print-publishing environment, economies of scale, more than copyright enforcement, mitigate against excessive photocopying and even hand copying. In most instances, it remains less expensive to buy a copy of a book rather than to photocopy one, and certainly than to type or hand copy one. It is clear, however, that in the electronic age, the economics of copying will change. Copying from diskette to diskette and performing downloading operations are less laborious than photocopying or scribal hand copying. This ease of pirating must give publishers an economic incentive to establish technological safeguards to protect their legal copyright status. And if the current concept of copyright is replaced because it is not feasible in the electronic publishing environment, its replacement must still deal directly and successfully with the underlying scholarly as well as commercial motivations for publishing.

Today, many people are struggling to identify, comprehend, and cope with the issues relating to copyright in an electronic environment. The concept of copyright was basically self-policing in a print-publishing environment; that is not true in an electronic environment. But the primary elements described above as an accountability model for authors in the electronic age can, if applied, serve scholarly and scientific writers no matter how the copyright issues are resolved. Perhaps electronic scrambling devices to protect the author's work from unauthorized emendation will not be required, although it is difficult to see how the protection associated with selecting a high-quality and professionally prestigious publisher will apply without such technological safeguards. But the concept of a publisher-instituted numbering system for each successive text to maintain bibliographic control and to establish an audit trail speaks for itself. Electronic authors can and will change the content of their works after publication. Let us use our technological capabilities to support, rather than frustrate, this superior capability.

Notes

1. Peter Briscoe, "Electronic Publishing—Its Darker Side," *Technicalities* 1 (8): 14-15 (July 1981).
2. Ithiel de Sola Pool, *Technologies of Freedom*, (Cambridge, Mass.: Belknap, 1983).
3. David W. Lewis, "Inventing the Electronic University," *College & Research Libraries* 49: 291-304 (July 1988).
4. Robert J. Kost, "The End of Copyright," in *Intellectual Property Rights in an Electronic Age: Proceedings of the Library of Congress Network Advisory Committee Meeting, April 22-24, 1987* (Washington, D.C.: Network Development and MARC Standards Office, Library of Congress, 1987), p. 20.
5. Ibid., pp. 20-21.

6. Tolkien, J. R. R. *The Letters of J. R. R. Tolkien*, ed. Humphrey Carpenter. Boston: Houghton Mifflin, 1981. p. 364.
7. Ibid., p. 367.
8. Carpenter, Humphrey, *Tolkien, a Biography*, (Boston, Mass.: Houghton Mifflin, 1977), pp. 225-229.
9. Ralph Oman, "The Copyright Law: Can It Wrap Itself Around the New Technologies?," in *Intellectual Property Rights in an Electronic Age, Proceedings of the Library of Congress Network Advisory Committee Meeting, April 22-24, 1987*, (Washington, D.C.: Network Development and MARC Standards Office, Library of Congress, 1987), p. 29.
10. Edwin B. Brownrigg and Clifford A. Lynch, "Electrons, Electronic Publishing, and Electronic Display," *Information Technology and Libraries*, pp. 201-207 (September 1985), p. 206.

Resource Sharing: A Selective Bibliography of Recent Publications

Gloriana St. Clair, Karyle S. Butcher, and Shirley R. Scott

Resource sharing is one of the prides of librarianship. In "A Century of Cooperative Programs Among Academic Libraries,"[1] David Weber observes a correlation between cooperative programs and prevailing national policy and economic conditions. This correlation seems to explain common attitudes towards resource sharing among European, Commonwealth, and United States libraries.

The first century of United States history, from 1770 to 1870, witnessed the founding, and destruction by fire, of many collections in emerging academic libraries. By 1876, the year in which the American Library Association was founded, many great libraries had been firmly established. In 1898, a move towards cooperative lending was begun by the University of California which announced a willingness to lend to libraries who would in turn loan to them. The tools to enable this reciprocal lending were also being developed about this time. The first, cooperative cataloging, had a committee for standardization of cataloging rules and one to continue the production of Poole's *Index to Periodical Literature*. The American Library Association began to publish analytic cards as a shared indexing/cataloging program. Copy was prepared by five libraries and became the nucleus of H. W. Wilson's 1919 *International Index of Periodicals*.[2] Weber believes the increase in publishing in the 1850s and Civil War economics ended production of library catalogs in book form.

In the early 1900s, the Library of Congress became a lending library for other libraries. ALA first published an interlibrary loan code in 1916. Union catalogs as a tool of cooperation and resource sharing also arose. The *National Union Catalog* was established in 1900, and the Library of Congress began selling printed catalog cards and card galley proofs. The California State Library created the first regional union catalog of periodicals in 1901. Major universities joined in publishing printed cards and analytics for serials,

Gloriana St. Clair was formerly the Assistant Director for Technical Automation and Administrative Services, and is now the Assistant Dean for Access Services at Pennsylvania State University. Karyle S. Butcher is Assistant Director for Research and Reference Services, and Shirley R. Scott is the Head of Research Services for the William Jasper Kerr Library, Oregon State University, Corvallis, Oregon.

and the Library of Congress established its Cooperative Cataloging Division in 1932. Cooperative collection development or joint acquisitions programs also began early with a 1913-14 South American buying trip on behalf of Northwestern University, Harvard University, Brown University, the John Crerar Library, and the American Antiquarian Society.[3]

Federal relief monies stimulated new union card catalogs, and a number of cooperative arrangements developed. Reciprocal borrowing privileges were established in Atlanta; and the Oregon State Board of Higher Education, in an effort to enforce cooperation in that state, appointed one director of libraries for the entire state system. The decades of the 40s, 50s, 60s, and 70s produced a number of impressive examples of cooperation. However, as Weber also records, some notable failures in resource sharing occurred.[4]

Today, cooperative agreements are commonplace. The most prevalent programs include: reciprocal borrowing privileges, expanded interlibrary loan service, union catalogs, photocopying services, reference, delivery services, mutual purchase notification, special communications, publication programs, catalog production and support, joint purchases, and assigned subject specialization of acquisitions. While cooperative agreements are philosophically supported by many libraries, Weber has found that local libraries assign cooperative activities low priority and little or no budget.[5] Factors contributing to the success or failure of cooperative efforts are:

- distance among participants
- inadequacy of book resources
- positive responsibilities and direct benefits
- agreements allowing for expansion and adjustment
- acceptance of reasonable duplication
- substantial contributions to cooperation on a research level from only a few libraries.[6]

Major contributions to resource sharing have derived from the establishment of the Center for Research Libraries (1949) Ohio College Library Center (1967); [now OCLC, Inc.]; and Research Libraries Group (1974). Although the literature does not provide a comprehensive cost-effectiveness study of cooperation, institutions have recognized that filling that last one percent of service is disproportionately expensive. Weber predicts accurately that new technologies will greatly enhance cooperative programs but that the central problems will continue to be political ones.[7]

This selective bibliography focuses on articles about resource sharing in the decade of the 1980s. Since neither Library Literature nor ERIC employs "resource sharing" as a subject heading, a variety of less inclusive headings were surveyed. Generally, the leadership in resource sharing seems to be among academic libraries in the United States and Canada; materials presented here reflect that dominance. Many, many more articles appear in the literature than are discussed here. The intention has been to delineate areas of success and failure in resource sharing and to present representative publications in each area.

General Resource Sharing

Listed here are representative articles on resource sharing in general. A few additional articles appear in a final section on the future of resource sharing.

Battin, Patricia. "Research Libraries in the Network Environment: The Case for Cooperation." *EDUCOM Bulletin* 15, no. 2 (Summer 1980): 26-31. *Journal of Academic Librarianship* 6, no. 2 (May 1980): 68-73.

Patricia Battin sets the tone for discussions of resource sharing in the 1980s with this article on the practical needs for a new commitment by research libraries. Economics necessitate a change; if trends continue, a research library will require 27% of the University's budget to survive at its current 3% level. Battin labels the new cooperation needed a "sharing of dependencies." She believes that research libraries must shift their emphasis to the provision of information rather than the storing of materials. Changes demanding this re-evaluation include:
- the inability of individual institutions to continue to acquire and house comprehensive collections;
- the changing role of the Library of Congress;
- the staggering preservation problem;
- the changing needs of clientele.

Battin reminds librarians that their business is information and communication, not the maintenance of an entity called "the Library." She calls for the re-invention of the research library in the network environment.

Dougherty, Richard M. "Research Libraries in an International Setting: Requirements for Expanded Resource Sharing." *College and Research Libraries* 46, no. 5 (September 1985): 383-89.

Mounting costs of lending and borrowing and physical deterioration of the collection are primary concerns of research libraries. In this context, Dougherty compares U.S. practices with those observed in the European community. He posits a discontinuity between the technological age of bibliographical access and the "horse-and-buggy era of document delivery." A discussion of collection use cites the Bradford-Zipf law and the "Pittsburgh Studies." Dougherty concludes that long-term goals for both European and U.S. libraries need to include shared-collection development, more bibliographic access, and effective document delivery.

Pond, Kurt, and Dwight F. Burlingame. "Library Cooperation: A Serials Model Based on Philosophical Principles." *College and Research Libraries* 45, no. 4 (July 1984): 299-305.

Pond and Burlingame describe the factors in a successful serials project: willingness of staff to cooperate, close physical proximity, van service to transport serials, a common OCLC system, involvement of campus faculty, and interinstitutional evaluation of serials. They believe that cooperation is a rational response to user needs and to increasing serials costs.

Rothstein, Samuel. "The Extended Library and the Dedicated Library: a Sceptical Outsider Looks at Union Catalogues and Bibliographic Networks." *Cataloging & Classification Quarterly* 2, no. 1-2 (1982): 103-20.

Rothstein posits two background principles—a profit factor in which libraries must share from the benefits of cooperation and an equity factor in which libraries must share efforts more or less equally. He discusses the costs of interlibrary loan; the tendency to leave the work to the larger institutions (British Library Lending Division, Library of Congress, and the National Library of Canada). He believes that union catalogs play a distinctly secondary role, and he recalls that book availability should be a library's first priority. He concludes that libraries should play down their emphasis on interdependence, and press for direct service and dedicated libraries.

Stevens, Norman D. "Library Networks and Resource Sharing in the United States: An Historical and Philosophical Overview." *Journal of the American Society for Information Science* 31, no. 6 (November 1980): 405-12.

Stevens traces the history of network development, of MARC format, and of evolution of interlibrary loans. He believes cooperative programs have had little significant impact on the acquisitions practices of American libraries. Although many strong resource sharing programs exist at the local and state levels, the total national structure is not yet established. Stevens' final caveat is that networks have an enormous amount of work yet to do in effectively integrating badly needed resource sharing programs.

Wilcox, Alice E. "Library Cooperative Relationships in Connection with Emerging Service Patterns." *Library Trends* 28, no. 2 (Fall 1979): 329-35.

In a brief history of library cooperation, Wilcox notes a post-World War II change in the development of county systems, the establishment of reciprocal borrowing cards, and the publication of area collection guides. She notes that most change was attitudinal. The past fifteen years have brought networks, systems, and consortia. Public libraries have gravitated toward busy areas as a sign of their commitment to service rather than to archival activities. Wilcox concludes with a plea for a re-examination of acquisitions policies and a more effective utilization of personnel.

Cooperative Collection Development

A 1985 conference, "Coordinating Cooperative Collection Development: A National Perspective," was sponsored by Eastern Illinois University and the Illinois Board of Higher Education. The proceedings from the conference provide the most comprehensive view of cooperative collection development in the 1980s. The proceedings were published in *Resource Sharing and Information Networks* (2, no. 3-4) and by Haworth Press. Several related articles are also cited here.

Coordinating Cooperative Collection Development: A National Perspective, edited by Wilson Luquire. New York: Haworth Press, 1986.

In "A National Scheme for Collaborative Development: The RLG-NCIP Effort," Paul Mosher attacks the myth of the self-sufficient collection. The numbers show that no library can afford to adhere to Polonius' advice to be neither a borrower nor a lender. Mosher further contends that the results of overlap studies argue strongly for interdependency. Citing Battin, De Gennaro, and others, Mosher argues that we must go beyond cooperation to collaboration. Collaborative efforts require librarians to be active rather than static, professional rather than clerical, change agents rather than reagents. Mosher outlines the development of the Research Libraries Group Conspectus, noting the vision of research collections as extensions and David Stam's injunction to "Think nationally, act locally." He also touts Ross Atkinson's concept of complementary synergy in collection development. Mosher delineates the uses of the RLG Conspectus to negotiate about collection strengths, to distribute collection responsibilities, and to examine interlibrary borrowing strategies. He examines the North American Collections Inventory Project, which builds on the techniques of the RLG Conspectus. Benefits of these two projects are enumerated.

Accompanying Mosher's treatise are a number of articles about local collection projects. In "The North American Collections Inventory Project (NCIP): 1984 Phase II Results in Indiana," David Farrell discusses the common framework and its applications to the Indiana project, defines coordinated cooperative collection development, describes four local contributing programs, and notes the progress of the Indiana project. In "A System Level Coordinated Cooperative Collection Development Model for Illinois," Karen Krueger explains how state library support provided a data collection methodology for Illinois. The model developed incorporated client-centered assessments of collections for non-research collections and had implications in making local as well as cooperative collection development decisions. In "Cooperative Collection Development Among Research Libraries: The Colorado Experience," Joel Rutstein and Johannah Sherrer describe a formal structure for cooperative purchases; a special emphasis is given to the development of uniform policy statements. In "Cooperative Acquisitions within a System: The University of California Shared Purchase Program," Marion L.

Buzzard describes the nine-year history of a program to prevent unnecessary duplication among nine campuses of the University of California and Stanford University. Methods for funding, successes of the program, and difficulties with methodology and access are presented. Joan Neumann discusses how a coordinated program grew from a well-established regional multi-type library resource sharing system. Coordination, bibliographic access, and delivery are discussed in "The New York State Experience with Coordinated Collection Development: Funding the Stimulus."

Cooperation between Duke University and University of North Carolina at Chapel Hill, with participation by North Carolina State University and the University of Virginia on a limited basis, is summarized by Joe A. Hewitt in "Cooperative Collection Development Programs of the Triangle Research Libraries Network." Hewitt not only describes the programs, but also makes general observations about the operation of cooperative collection development programs.

In "HILC at Thirty-Four: A View from Within," Billie Rae Boxzone evaluates the Hampshire Inter-Library Center's repository for little-used serials, a program which became the umbrella for other cooperative programs. Dennis Stephens in "A Stitch in Time: The Alaska Cooperative Collection Development Project," outlines a resource-poor state's utilization of the resources of academic, public, special and school libraries to put together a resource sharing program. The program concentrates on training librarians for collection development policy formulation, on liaison among officers, and on the formation of an Alaska Conspectus to map collection building strengths and serve as a basis for coordinated collection building. Finally, Anne Haley and Douglas K. Ferguson describe the Pacific Northwest Conspectus, funded by the Fred Meyer Charitable Trust's Library and Information Resources for the Northwest project. Regional assessment, training, database development, collection survey, and cooperative acquisitions plans have been the results. The value of the whole volume is increased by the presence of reactions to the papers and panel discussions.

"Cooperative Library Resource Sharing among Universities Supporting Graduate Study in Alabama." Montgomery, AL: Alabama Commission on Higher Education, Council of Libraries, 1982. (ED 224 497)

This document details the progress of a group of regional libraries to provide a plan for cooperative resource sharing. The poverty of resources in the area led the authors (Highfill, Lowry, Gapen, French, Spence, Stephens, and Heath) to address a variety of needs: collection development, staff adequacy, space requirements, bibliographic and physical accessibility to services, and computerization/networking. The report calls for the establishment of an Alabama Academic Libraries Network, lays down a number of strictures about financial support for collections, institutes a collection analysis program, calls for interlibrary loan and delivery system agreements, institutes a union list of serials, and established a graduate borrower's card to facilitate resource sharing. The conclusion warns that inadequate funding will leave area librarians understaffed, poorly housed, bibliographically inadequate, and isolated from the mainstream of academic library computing. The Alabama experience appears in other articles, too, especially in *Issues in Cooperative Collection Development* (Papers presented at the SOLINET Resource Sharing Networks Support Program, 11 March 1988, edited by June L. Engle and Sue O. Medina).

Linda McNair Cohen in "Resource Sharing and Coordinated Collection Development in the Network of Alabama Academic Libraries" also describes the creation of the Network of Alabama Academic Libraries (NAAL) in *Collection Management* (10, no. 3-4 [1988]: 149-62).

"Report on the Conoco Project in German Literature and Geology." Stanford, CA: Research Libraries Group, 24 June 1986.

Based on a study of Germanists and geology bibliographers, collection managers report that they would be willing, subject to certain conditions, to change up to half of the selecting decisions they make under a well-established consortial collection development plan. The Conoco Study also reveals that coverage in foreign languages is poor, causing major gaps, while duplication in serials makes science collections more homogeneous than humanities collections. A three-day turnaround time was acceptable for more than 70 per cent of materials. Selectors distinguish between collection for research and potential future use, and collecting for instructional support; in the latter they are less willing to share.

In a critique in the *Journal of Library Administration*, Sheila Dowd addresses the results of the study. She says, "It is very doubtful that 40 to 50 per cent of our acquisitions could be dropped without incurring quite prohibitive borrowing costs, profound user dissatisfaction, and severe damage to collections as integrated, orderly research sources."[8]

Boucher, Virginia, and others. "Resource Sharing at the University Libraries, University of Colorado, Boulder. A Report of the Resource Sharing Task Force." Boulder CO: University of Colorado, 1982. (ED 226 743)

As a result of a Collection Assessment Project, the Task Force on Resource Sharing was organized to recommend directions for the future. Especially noteworthy in this report is the establishment of Colorado Alliance of Research Libraries (CARL). The task force concludes:

- The practice of resource sharing has risen dramatically.
- University of Colorado will continue its commitment to that practice.
- Library users will benefit by improved resource sharing services.
- Document delivery remains a concern.
- CARL and OCLC remain preeminent programs for support and use.
- Long range planning and other activities should be developed.

- National activities should be monitored to assess the potential for participation.

Branin, Joseph J. "Issues in Cooperative Collection Development: The Promise and Frustration of Resource Sharing." In *Issues in Cooperative Collection Development*, edited by June L. Engle and Sue O. Medina. Atlanta, GA: Southeastern Library Network, Inc., 1986.

The strength of Branin's article is its focus on the obstacles to cooperative collection development and correlative strategies to overcome them. Obstacles are:
1. A desire for everything here and now
2. Changing priorities for collection development
3. Control of collection policies and priorities
4. Staff and faculty attitudes
5. Document delivery time
6. Lack of education for users about need for cooperation
7. Needed support services
8. Required administrative structure and support
9. Political environment
10. Reluctance to yield autonomy
11. Lack of common language for analysis and description.

Strategies used against these obstacles include education of users, improved document delivery, structuring of agreements, common language, and good administration.

Branin, Joseph J., David Farrell, and Mariann Tiblin. "The National Shelflist Count Project: Its History, Limitations, and Usefulness." *Library Resources and Technical Services* 29, no. 4 (October/December 1985): 333-42.

Branin, Farrell, and Tiblin describe the origin and workings of the national shelflist count project with its 490 subject areas defined by Library of Congress classification ranges. Concerns about the usefulness of the national shelflist count include its reflection of cataloged holdings only, its approximation of holdings, its variations through number of cards per title, its inclusion/exclusion of branches according to local practice, its representation by titles rather than volumes, and its difficulties with handling additional classification schemes. Branin, et al., provide an excellent comparison of the relative subject detail between the RLG conspectus and the national shelflist count. The authors recommend continuing the count, undertaking it once every two years, assigning the responsibility for reports, providing technical assistance for the conversion of holdings in other classification schemes, encouraging other libraries to participate, seeking consensus for changes in procedures, and implementing a discussion group for Chief Collection Development officers.

Farrell, David. "The NCIP Option for Coordinated Collection Management." *Library Resources and Technical Services* 30, no. 1 (January/March 1986): 47-56.

This "Best of Conference" paper discusses the implementation of NCIP in Indiana. After describing the implementation process, Farrell examines the benefits of coordinating research collection management for Indiana: the completion of seven conspectus division cooperatives and their entry into the Conspectus Online; the introduction of new ideas and methodologies for collection planning and assessment to collection development librarians; increased knowledge of national collection management issues and activities; establishment of regular contacts among the collection development officers and the subject specialists; preparation for cooperative decision-making and for local uses of the data in collection budget management; and preparation for drafting a LC class-based, conspectus-based, standard terminology collection development policy. Farrell concludes that coordination and cooperation are difficult to achieve. He believes cooperative collection development will pay increasingly larger dividends.

Henige, David. "Epistemological Dead End and Ergonomic Disaster? The North American Collections Inventory Project." *The Journal of Academic Librarianship* 13, no. 4 (September 1987): 209-13.

Henige argues that the NCIP project and its conspectus are too imprecise to be instructive, too untestable to invoke belief, and too laborious ever to repay the effort. He notes its value for resource sharing is limited since the interlibrary loan is usually a request for a specific item rather than a request for knowledge about depth of collections. Henige asserts that conspectus do not yield single datum and are, therefore, of little use in the interlibrary loan process. He describes the conspectus as being "little more than an extravagantly designed and assiduously propagated bushel full of best guesses." Henige does believe, however, that the conspectus can and will enhance resource sharing by increasing the reliability and efficiency of a knowledge base which underlies cooperative activity.

Hewitt, Joe A., and John S. Shipman. "Cooperative Collection Development among Research Libraries in the Age of Networking: Report of a Survey of ARL Libraries." *Advances in Library Automation and Networking* 1 (1987): 189-232.

A resurgence of interest in cooperative collection development arose from the economics of research libraries and from the availability of new technologies. Hewitt and Shipman surveyed the membership of the Association of Research Libraries to assess the impact of these changes on their practice of cooperative collection development. They found that two-thirds of the membership were involved in such programs, in which relationships with other institutions were more important than specific program activities. An observed schism between levels of aspiration and accomplishment should not diminish the significance of the cooperation. The "idea" necessarily precedes concrete goals, and ultimately, cooperative collection development will realize its greater potential.

Mosher, Paul, and Marcia Pankake. "Guide to Coordinated and Cooperative Collection Development." *Library Resources & Technical Services* 27, no. 4 (October/December 1983): 417-31.

Mosher and Pankake prepared this draft guide to help librarians who are responsible for planning or establishing coordinated and cooperative collection development programs within libraries. The plan suggests contexts, goals, methods, organizations, effects and processes needed to achieve cooperation. In addition, Mosher and Pankake provide an outline of approaches to cooperative collection development: Farmington Plan Approach, National Program for Acquisitions and Cataloging System, Library of Congress, Center for Research Libraries Approach, A Mosaic Overlap of Collection Development Policies, The Status Quo Approach, and the Combined Self-interest Plan. They also list suggestions for planning cooperative collection development systems.

Peel, Bruce, and William J. Kurmey. "Cooperation among Ontario University Libraries." Toronto: Council of Ontario Universities, 1983. (ED 233 744)

The purpose of the Council of Ontario Universities is to extend university library cooperation in the province. Cooperative acquisitions and resource sharing projects are among the stated goals. Objectives and guidelines are similar to those of other libraries involved in such projects with the usual pleas for a common set of protocols. The consortium admits limited success in the area of collection rationalization; timely sharing of information about purchases over $2,000 and local needs limited potential effectiveness. However, some notable purchases are detailed. Establishing the idea of a provincial resource has been successful.

Sohn, Jeanne. "Cooperative Collection Development: A Brief Overview." *Collection Management* 8, no. 2 (Summer 1986): 1-9.

Sohn discusses the history of cooperative collection development and examines projects conceived, implemented, and discontinued in the past forty years. Her primary focus is on current regional projects and the ARL sponsored North American Collections Inventory Projects. Sohn touches briefly on the barriers to interlibrary cooperation and notes ARL's attempts to avoid such barriers. She projects that truly meaningful cooperative collection development consortia may be formed through the agency of individual libraries which decide to become resource libraries in their regions. Although cooperation is difficult, leadership in collection development can foster it.

Gateways and Networks

The technological methods available for resource sharing are running far ahead of the political solutions for active programs. Here are gathered representative articles treating the emergence of gateway technologies, networks, and their impact on resource sharing.

Avram, Henriette D. "Toward a Nationwide Library Network." *Journal of Library Administration* 8, no. 3-4 (Fall-Winter 1987): 95-116.

Avram notes several problems in the expansion of networking: lack of international cataloging standards, lack of international subject control, language barriers, and non-roman alphabets. She also addresses the issue of database copyright and suggests that the Networking Advisory Committee may play some role in resolution. After a discussion of the Linked Systems Project, she concludes that the lack of an effective vehicle for national planning and coordination constitutes a serious problem for which the 1988/91 White House Conference may provide some solution.

Avram, Henriette D., and Beacher Wiggins. "The Role of the Linked Systems Project in Cooperation and Resource Sharing among Libraries." *Journal of Academic Librarianship* 13, no. 2 (May 1987): 100-A-D.

Avram and Wiggins describe the development of the MARC format as a key technology for resource sharing and outline the development of bibliographic utilities. The challenge to the Linked Systems Project will be to link without modification to individual systems, to include new participants without a negative impact on older ones, and to allow users to continue with familiar system-inquiry language. Standard Network Interconnection and Open System Interconnection are described. The authors conclude with a recognition of the importance of standards, and an affirmation of that importance in achieving a high level of cooperation.

Avram, Henriette D. "The Linked Systems Project: Its Implications for Resource Sharing." In *New Information Technologies and Libraries*, edited by H. Liebaers, W. J. Haas, and W. E. Biervliet, 244-60. Dordrecht: Reidel, 1985.

After describing the Linked Systems Project, Avram focuses on its implications for resource sharing: the exchange of cataloging data, the ability to upload and download records, the exchange of library items themselves through LSP links, and the sharing through computer-to-computer links of full texts of monographs. Underneath all this will be a strong basis in national and international standards. (Several other articles treat Linked System Project, Standard Network Interconnection, Open Systems Interconnection; they have not been included here. Clearly, technical developments have implications for resource sharing but do not fall within the scope of this literature review.)

Burton, Hilary D., Gladys A. Cotter, and Richard W. Hartt. "Resource Sharing through Integration of an Intelligent Gateway and Library Support Software." *Special Libraries* 77, no. 1 (Winter 1986): 28-35.

The purpose of this project is to improve resource utilization by facilitating information sharing in a group of unique technical libraries. Major objectives included the identification of commercially available software/ hardware, development of information transfer and format conversion mechanisms, and creation of a gateway system to provide access. The result was a single terminal providing a full spectrum of bibliographic, administrative, and computational resources.

De Gennaro, Richard. "Library Automation and Networking Perspectives on Three Decades." *Library Journal* 108, no. 7 (1 April 1983): 629-35.

De Gennaro touts the 1970s as cooperation's golden age, which has been tempered by the economic realities of the 1980s. The hard lesson learned in the 70s is that cooperation is "a difficult, time-consuming, and expensive way to do something and the results are frequently disappointing." The decade's successes were often tied to LSCA funding, which is now diminishing; additional curtailment of public funding has required reappraisal of many cooperative ventures. Kilgour's phrase that "the National Library was the nation's libraries" finds a corollary in the totality of computer systems and online catalogs of the nation's libraries and networks. The multiplicity developing in these resources reflects the major trends shaping the information society.

De Gennaro, Richard. "Libraries and Networks in Transition: Problems and Prospects for the 1980's." *Library Journal* 106, no. 10 (15 May 1981): 1045-49.

While most of this article deals with automation and networking, De Gennaro does make some incisive statements about cataloging in a network environment. He hypothesizes that catalogers have become so much more careful about their work that the attendant stage fright results in "fear of inputting." He believes that small and medium-sized libraries have been better served by networking than large ones: "but local original cataloging in large libraries, like the state under communism, is not withering away." De Gennaro believes that librarians should stop apologizing for the high cost of libraries because information is a valuable and expensive resource. He concludes that the formation of the Resource Libraries Group is the most promising development in U.S. librarianship.

Gherman, Paul M. "Vision and Reality: the Research Libraries and Networking." *Journal of Library Administration* 8, no. 3-4 (Fall-Winter 1987): 51-57.

Gherman believes that research libraries will diverge from other library types as they spend the remainder of the decade concentrating on development of local systems, delivery of library services and information products on Local Area Networks. Their participation in multitype networks will be reluctant and they will not be strong supporters of the egalitarian ambitions of the NAC statement. He believes regional networks will be foregone in an attempt to establish regional direct relationships with OCLC. He expects research libraries to become gateways to end-users, key consumers of new information products, within their own academic communities.

Kilgour, Frederick G. "Problems Related to Interlinking Online Interactive Library Networks." *Electronic Library* 1, no. 1 (January 1983): 49-57.

Kilgour outlines the two major benefits of interlinking: an increase in library resources available to users and significant reductions in per-unit library costs. Problems in the interlinking of international systems include: political climate, professional attitudes, incompatibility of organizations, differences in management and staff, threats to financial stability, telecommunications and computerization problems, and concerns of library origins. Kilgour concludes while combinations of lesser elements could set up a barrier, the most likely unresolvables would be disparate competence of personnel, lack of audited balance sheets, extensive incompatibility of descriptive cataloging rules, and unilateral prohibition of transborder data flow. The *Collected Papers of Frederick G. Kilgour* provide much more information on this topic and others related to resource sharing. [9]

Schuman, Patricia Glass. "Library Networks: A Means, Not an End." *Library Journal* 112, no. 2 (1 February 1987): 33-37.

Schuman examines three myths [misconceptions] about library networks: First, networks save money. Schuman finds no evidence of savings, even though much work can now be accomplished by paraprofessional copy catalogers. She revisits De Gennaro's concerns about catalogers immobilized from "fear of inputting." Schuman believes that networks can help libraries and librarians to become more cost effective. Second, networks blur the lines between technical and public services, breaking down traditional organization services. While some libraries have gotten away from traditions, most have not, although communications inside the library have increased in importance. Third, networks will break down the barriers between libraries. While Schuman doesn't believe it has happened yet, she does see the concept of ownership changing. She says what we have done best so far is to convince the user to wait. In conclusion, she believes that networks can be used to automate or to inform; smart people can be combined with smart machines for innovation and change.

Trochim, Mary Kane. "Academic Library Resource Sharing through Bibliographic Utility Program Participation." Washington, D. C.: Office of Educational Research and Improvement (EDD00020), and Office of Libraries and Learning Technologies (EDD00036), 1982. (ED 227 853) Executive Summary (ED 227 854)

In this ERIC document, Trochim summarizes the impact of the growth of bibliographic utilities and academic library networking on the interlibrary loan practices of six academic libraries. Interlibrary loan practice has been affected through bibliographic utility membership: quantity of material increased, regional and local use remained high, reporting procedures proved obsolescent, new demands were made of ILL staff, patron expectations varied by location, as did record keeping and availability of background information. Issues for the future include the integration of a number of bibliographic utilities into one database, the lack of standardization about reporting resource sharing information, and the paucity of research on interlibrary loan program and bibliographic utilities as they relate to resource sharing.

Established Resource Sharing Programs

Although these three resource sharing programs have been included in discussions under other headings, a few representative articles are cited here. Commentators on the future of resource sharing cherish these successes.

Research Libraries Group

Gwinn, Nancy E., and Paul H. Mosher. "Coordinating Collection Development: The RLG Conspectus." *College and Research Libraries* 44 (March 1983): 128-40.

The RLG Conspectus, an overview arranged by subject, of existing collection strengths and future collection intentions, serves as a location device for ascertaining national resources and primary collecting responsibilities. Gwinn and Mosher trace its antecedents to ALA committee work, an RLG collection committee, and GNOMES + 2 (collection development officers for several large libraries). Gwinn and Mosher recognize the conspectus as being equivalent to the development of the National Union Catalog in its impact on librarianship. Stronger research collections with less redundancy and unnecessary expenditure will not be easy to accomplish because interdependence must be laid upon a foundation of trust. They believe the conspectus represents an insurance policy against future uncertain times, a new vehicle for improved service, and an opportunity to improve bibliographic access and rapid delivery.

McDonald, David R., and Robert Hurowitz. "Research Libraries—Automation and Cooperation." *Perspectives in Computing* 2, no. 4 (December 1982): 4-11.

McDonald and Hurowitz define and describe the Research Libraries Information Network as a means by which RLG member libraries can work together to provide resources for teaching and research through the cooperative sharing of bibliographic data and through improved access to collections. The authors also underline the importance of RLIN for cooperative collection development. Reduction of clerical labor, greater resource sharing, improved information retrieval, and access to a union database for reference service are the advantages outlined.

Center for Research Libraries

At the ALA annual conference in New Orleans, several librarians presented views of the value of the Center for Research Libraries in a program entitled "The Center for Research Libraries: What's There and How to Get It." The texts were printed in *Library Acquisitions: Practice and Theory*.

Naru, Linda A. "Transforming Concept into Practice: How Collection Development, Interlibrary Loan, and Reference Staff Utilize the Center for Research Libraries." *Library Acquisitions: Practice and Theory* 12 (1988): 397-99.

Naru's brief article outlines the holdings of the center, describes the membership, and discusses its collection development policies. Naru then introduces five papers which constituted a 1988 ALA program panel entitled "The Center for Research Libraries: What's There and How to Get It".

Boisse, Joseph A. "CRL Membership: The Library Director's Perspective." *Library Acquisitions: Practice and Theory* 12 (1988): 399-402.

Boisse, a member of the Board, testifies to the benefits of CRL membership: the opportunity to practice cooperative collection development through cooperative acquisitions and the dedicated and responsive access to a large but specialized collection. The center has a research-oriented collection of 3.5-4 million volumes and 1.1 million microforms. The center's Purchase Proposal Program allows member libraries to avoid unnecessary duplication; items are selected for cooperative acquisition by a democratic vote of the membership thus expanding local access to resources. Boisse contends membership in the center allows directors to ask for additional resources to combat inflation while giving assurances that resource sharing attempts are being made.

Dowd, Sheila. "Major Collection Components and Policies of the CRL." *Library Acquisitions: Practice and Theory* 12 (1988): 403-5.

Dowd defines the CRL as a library's library whose single purpose is to extend the collections of its members and to enhance their service. Dowd describes the general miscellaneous collection and enumerates the following special collections: foreign dissertations, foreign and domestic newspapers, archival materials in microform, foreign scientific and technical publications, children's books, foreign bank reports, textbooks, and college catalogs. The center also has a well-defined program for major purchases.

Boucher, Virginia. "Bibliographic Access to the Center for Research Libraries' Collections." *Library Acquisitions: Practice and Theory* 12 (1988): 407-10.

Boucher describes a number of aids available to librarians seeking information about the uncataloged holdings of the center. Published bibliographies, guides, checklists, and collection descriptions are discussed. Cataloged materials at the center are available through the major bibliographic utilities, the *National Union Catalog*, and equivalent serial lists.

Loring, Christopher B. "Maximizing Use of the Center for Research Libraries through Interlibrary Loan: CRL as the Lender of First Resort and Other Strategies." *Library Acquisitions: Practice and Theory* 12 (1988): 411-14.

Loring outlines five areas of activity in order to foster maximum use of the center for interlibrary loan operations. First, local library administrators must commit to the center, second the library must foster a special attitude towards CRL; these need to translate into a concrete interlibrary loan policy for the center's collections. Third, interlibrary loan staff must be trained about the center, and finally, ILL procedures must include CRL wherever appropriate. With these strategies, local libraries can maximize their investment in the Center for Research Libraries.

Mateer, Carolyn. "The Role of Public Service Librarians in Promoting Use of CRL's Collections." *Library Acquisitions: Practice and Theory* 12 (1988): 415-18.

Mateer notes that CRL's rapid delivery service and its policy of allowing researchers to retain materials until they are needed by another user allows the center to function as an extension of the local library. She identifies reference librarians as the primary catalysts in the process of merging the center's collection with local holdings. In addition to discussing the use of specific tools as finding mechanisms, she also relates several instances of researchers whose needs have been met through use of the center's materials.

Illinois' Library Computer System

Sloan, Bernard G. "Resource Sharing among Academic Libraries: The LCS Experience." *Journal of Academic Librarianship* 12, no. 1 (March 1986): 26-29.

The State of Illinois' Library Computer System (LCS) provides circulation of over a million items a year with holdings of over fifteen million volumes. This amount of traffic makes it the largest circulation system in the world. Sloan outlines four factors contributing to the success of this large enterprise: an established spirit of cooperation among libraries, a high level of administrative support, a cost effective resource sharing system, and an effective document delivery system.

Several other articles deal admirably with the LCS experience, but they have not been included here.

Copyright

The 1976 Copyright Law continues to plague interlibrary loan librarians as they go about the business of trying to bring information and users together. The primary difficulty with the law is the use of language which in many cases is so vague it defies any standard definition. This is particularly true with the phrase "aggregate quantities" as used in the section of the law related to interlibrary loans. The law states that libraries may engage in interlibrary arrangements "that do not have, as their purpose or effect, that the library or archives receiving such copies ... for distribution does so in such aggregate quantities as to substitute for a subscription to or purchase of such work."

Not feeling comfortable with such language, the National Commission on New Technological Uses of Copyrighted Works (CONTU) developed guidelines which were quickly adopted by Congress. It is the CONTU guidelines which established the so called "rule of five," meaning that up to and including five requests for articles published within five years prior to the date of the request and filled within the year are within the "aggregate" number allowable. Most of the articles cited in this work indicate that while the CONTU guidelines have resulted in excessive record keeping, they have not been a barrier to access to information.

"Copyright Observations of the International Federation of Library Associations." *International Journal of Legal Information* 10, no. 5 (October 1982): 239-41.

These observations, from the International Federation of Library Associations, reflect IFLA's attempt to put copyright issues into an international perspective. Major points covered in the article concern questions of fair use, decisions on adding additional subscriptions, and passage of new fees to the user. In looking at use patterns for most libraries, it is clear that while the volume of photocopying of articles is high, few journals are copied so extensively as to violate the rule of five. The discussion ends with a brief look at the future of document delivery. For the short term, it is sufficient for most libraries to proceed as they are now. Future considerations will focus on the use of full text for high-demand journals, and ultimately, to direct access by users to materials on optical disc and in machine-readable format.

Anderson, Patricia E. "Librarians' Rights and Responsibilities under the Copyright Law." *Catholic Library World* 55, no. 7 (February 1984): 305-8.

This is a lucid overview of the effects of the 1976 Copyright Law on libraries. Anderson spends some time talking about the CONTU guidelines, noting they were an attempt to bring focus to the rather vague provisions of the law. While there is nothing new in her discussions, they are clear, concise, and she appends a useful annotated bibliography to her article.

Berger, Patricia W. "Complying with Copyright in Scientific Libraries. The National Bureau of Standards Experience." *Journal of Chemical Information and Computer Sciences* 22, no. 2 (May 1982): 74-78.

In this article on the effect of the 1974 copyright law on the library at the National Bureau of Standards, Berger notes the NBS seldom exceeds the "limit of five" rule. However, "keeping records necessary to assure compliance has resulted in considerable cost. . ." to the NBS. The inability to exchange materials freely is also impeding the dissemination of scientific information. Journal costs are increasingly forcing librarians to rely more on ILL for information sharing. Publishers must understand that libraries are turning to photocopying as a means to obtain information, not as a means to avoid journal purchases.

Butler, Meredeth A. "Copyright and Academic Library Copying." *College & Research Libraries News* 43, no. 4 (April 1982): 123-25.

In this discussion of the relationship between libraries and the New Copyright Law, Butler looks at the survey conducted by ACRL in 1978 to determine how the law had been affecting academic libraries. In terms of interlibrary loans, Butler discovered 43 libraries, of the 100 surveyed, indicated they were unable to fill photocopy requests because of the "limit of five" rule. Users with unmet needs were urged to travel to nearby libraries owning the journal or to seek alternative sources. Butler also notes 56 libraries were purchasing additional journals in order to be in copyright compliance.

Byrd, Gary D. "Copyright Compliance in Health Sciences Libraries: a Status Report Two Years after the Implementation of PL 94-553." *Bulletin of the Medical Library Association* 69, no. 2 (April 1981): 224-30.

A survey was sent to 373 health science libraries to discover how they were complying with the copyright law of 1976 and how they felt about it. Overall response was 57% with 157 usable returns. Most libraries indicated they were familiar with the law and most speculated it would adversely affect the flow of information. Of the respondees, only twelve were registered with the Copyright Clearance Center and fewer than that made regular use of the CCC services. The author concludes that after two years of experience with the copyright law most health science librarians find the law an annoyance, but not a real threat to interlibrary loan activity.

Crews, Kenneth D. "University Copyright Policies in ARL Libraries." SPEC Kit 138. Washington, D. C.: Association of Research Libraries, Office of Management Studies, 1987. (ED 289 526)

As with most ARL SPEC Kits, its usefulness is in the broad range of policies provided. While some libraries address the issue of copyright and ILL less thoroughly than others, in all this is a good source for anyone who is just starting the data-gathering phase. Particularly helpful are sample letters requesting copyright permission and the selected reading list.

Hood, Howard A. "A Survey and Critique of Photocopying Provisions of the New American Copyright Act." *International Journal of Law Libraries* 6, no. 2 (July 1978): 159-69.

At the time of this article, Hood was a reference librarian from Vanderbilt University. It is his view that the Copyright Act, as enacted by Congress, is vague to the point of being misleading in the way that it addresses the concerns of interlibrary loan. Because of this, various library organizations, including the American Library Association, have worked out their own "informal, unofficial interpretations of the law, called guidelines." Hood contends that these guidelines, though not a part of the Copyright Act, are treated as gospel and adhered to rigidly. Hood's objections to this acceptance are grounded in his belief that the guidelines act as private legislation and an abdication of governmental responsibility. Hood argues that the guidelines are more restrictive than the law and, in this case, entail libraries voluntarily relinquishing privileges granted to them by Congress. Finally, he believes that the narrow, detailed guidelines will require large amounts of record keeping. Hood concludes that the Copyright Act, far from being a model for other countries, "exemplifies in many ways the errors they should seek to avoid."

Hopkins, Richard. "Copyright: Complexities and Concerns." *Canadian Library Journal* 44, no. 5 (October 1987): 273-78.

Hopkins is representing the Canadian Library Association's Copyright Committee. He provides a historical overview of copyright in Canada focusing on the issue of "fair dealing" ("fair use"). While fair dealing has been a part of earlier Canadian copyright laws, there is a movement among Canadian authors to remove this from a proposed new law. Authors want to be paid for each page of their work which is photocopied and recommend this cost be passed on to the user of the information. Librarians object. Authors counter that if libraries do not want to pass on charges, they could buy additional copies of and/or subscriptions to often requested items. Hopkins looks at these various arguments and recommends an alternative which he hopes will provide financial reward for authors, but not heavily penalize libraries or their users.

McDonald, Dennis D., and Colleen G. Bush. "Libraries, Publishers and Photocopying: Final Report of Surveys." Rockville, MD: King Research, Inc., 1982. (BBB05336) Washington, D.C.: Library of Congress, Copyright Office. (ED 226 732)

In 1981, King Research, Inc. conducted six surveys to determine how libraries were coping with the 1976 copyright law. The section on interlibrary loan showed the majority of ILL requests were for photocopying. While the libraries surveyed refused to copy 1.9 per cent of the requests, the CONTU "five-copy guideline" was cited as a reason in only a minority of the cases. In 1981, 6.5 million serial ILL requests were filled with photocopies—an increase of nine percent over 1976. Of the libraries sampled which supplied data in both the 1976 photocopying study and the King survey, 33% of the public and 42% of the academic libraries reported actual decreases in annual outgoing ILL requests. The authors conclude that growth or decline in ILL activities is related to a variety of factors including the possible restrictions of the copyright law.

Merriam, Elizabeth B., David R. Salazar, and Mary E. Struckmeyer. "Coping with Copyright." Madison, WI: Wisconsin Department of Public Instruction, 1978. (ED 172 829)

This article is a good overview of the copyright law aimed at clarifying those areas which particularly affect librarians. Especially useful is the discussion of the CONTU guidelines in defining "aggregate quantities." The authors remind librarians that borrowing should not be a substitute for journal subscriptions; that CONTU guidelines are just that—guidelines, not absolute requirements; and that the duty of record keeping lies with the requesting library. A section of questions and answers on subjects such as copyright clearance, fair use, and copyright clearance centers is informative and helpful.

Miller, Jerome K. *Applying the New Copyright Law: a Guide for Educators and Librarians.* Chicago: American Library Association, 1979.

This publication by the American Library Association is useful for its straightforward explanation of copyright and photocopying for interlibrary loans. It takes the "opaque legal language" of the CONTU guidelines and translates them into "common language," providing a helpful and easy to understand source for ILL and other librarians.

Oboler, Eli M. "Watch the Shells, Watch the Pea: Paying for Copyright Rights to Articles." *Serials Librarian* 4, no. 1 (Fall 1979): 65-67.

This is a critical look at the services provided by the Copyright Clearance Center. While not totally denying the CCC's uses, Oboler cautions librarians to examine its pricing structure. There are cases in which a library would be better off, financially, to subscribe to a journal rather than to pay the permission-to-copy fee to the center.

Sharma, Ravindra N. "Copyright-U.S.A.: the Librarian's View." *Libri* 31, no. 1 (March 1981): 57-68.

> In discussing the history of copyright in the United States, Sharma devotes a portion of the article to copyright and interlibrary loans. Three points emerge from this discussion. First, while libraries are limited in borrowing photocopies of articles because of the "limit of five" rule, there is no provision for apprehending violators. Second, record keeping because of the "limit of five" rule has increased the ILL workload, especially in libraries with active ILL departments. Third, the combination of increasing journal prices and "limit of five" rule is effectively eroding resource sharing.

Steuben, John. "Interlibrary Loan of Photocopies of Articles under the New Copyright Law." *Special Libraries* 70, no. 5-6 (May-June 1979): 227-32.

> The National Commission on New Technological Uses of Copyright Works (CONTU) has been instrumental in helping to define what "aggregate quantities" means as used in Subsection 108 of the copyright law. Using these guidelines, the National Oceanic and Atmospheric Library examines its own use of photocopying through ILL. This article presents the results of that study. Most requests involved five or fewer articles from periodicals per year. The library found six is the break-even point in terms of requesting a journal; after that it is more economical to subscribe than to pay for copyright clearance. However, because of journal cuts and heavier use of online bibliographies, journal requests for NOAA are increasing. Steuben predicts in the future NOAA will have more difficulty in complying with the CONTU guidelines.

Tallman, Johanna E. "One Year's Experience with CONTU Guidelines for Interlibrary Loan Photocopies." *Journal of Academic Librarianship* 5, no. 2 (May 1979): 71-74.

> In this discussion of the experiences of the Millikan Library at California Institute of Technology, librarians tracked their use of photocopying for ILL over a nine-year period. They discovered in 90% of the cases, they had no difficulty in following the CONTU guidelines on copyright. In the cases where the "limit of five" might be exceeded, the library called upon alternative sources. These include subscribing to the needed journal, writing to the publisher for copyright permission, writing to the author for permission, purchasing a second-hand copy, ordering from OATS (Original Article Tear Service), and paying royalties to a copyright clearing house.

Thatcher, Sanford G. "On Fair Use and Library Photocopying." *Scholarly*

Publishing 9, no. 4 (July 1978): 313-34.

This article is written from the perspective of the publisher of scholarly materials and is an attempt to help "all scholarly publishers to become familiar at least in a general way with the problems and challenges posed by fair use and library photocopying." After a general discussion of the history of copyright and interlibrary loan practices in the United States, Thatcher looks at the current situation. To him, it is a "no win" predicament. Publishers are in need of protecting their investments in the information they publish and libraries are interested in facilitating the flow of information at no cost, or as inexpensively as possible. Thatcher believes the Copyright Clearance Center offers some help, but the fundamental problem is that the Copyright Law itself is too loosely written. Only if aid "comes from outside the publisher-library system—from private foundation support, from government subsidization of users, or directly from the government itself—can the system survive for long into the future."

Tseng, Henry P. "The Ethical Aspects of Photocopying as They Pertain to the Library, the User, and the Owner of Copyright." *Law Library Journal* 72, no. 1 (Winter 1979): 86-90.

This interesting article explores the copyright law from an ethical point of view. Are librarians and teachers who do multiple photocopies acting unprofessionally? Is the publishers' adherence to strict guidelines unethical? Having asked these questions, Tseng discusses the intent of the copyright law and moves into a fuller look at the concept of fair use. Weighing the classroom and scholar's need for information against the author's potential financial loss poses an ethical dilemma. Finally, Tseng discusses the Copyright Clearance Center which claims to be a not-for-profit institution but assigns, in some cases, such high per-page royalties that it effectively limits access to some publications. Tseng concludes by offering a proposed royalty schedule for the CCC and a proposed code of professional conduct for librarians, teachers and publishers.

Weil, Ben H., and Barbara F. Polansky. "Copyright, Serials, and the Impacts of Technology." *Serials Review* 12, no. 2-3 (Summer-Fall 1986): 25-32.

In discussing copyright concerns as they relate to interlibrary loans, Weil and Polansky first examine current practices of libraries and how well they are following the CONTU guidelines. They then discuss the establishment of the Copyright Clearance Center and examine how well it is helping libraries meet the requirements of the CONTU guidelines. The remainder of the article focuses on the increase of technology as it impacts on electronic publishing and raises the question of what type of provisions will a future copyright law need to insure that authors, publishers, and libraries are all served well.

Interlibrary Loan

The following are representative of the ILL literature, including statewide networks or systems, the effect of automation on ILL, ILL in academic libraries, various ILL practices and research.

Statewide ILL Networks

"Plan for Restructuring Interlibrary Loan in Michigan." Lansing, MI: Bureau of Library Services, Michigan State Department of Education, 1980. (ED 231 358)

An Interlibrary Loan Task Force was established to work with Michigan State Library Services staff to examine the problems of the state's ILL structure and to develop policies to enable it to function more effectively and efficiently. In addition, the task force was asked to make long-term recommendations about the evolution of the ILL system into a regional multi-type network involving school, public, academic and special libraries, with support from the state's five major research libraries (Detroit Public Library, Michigan State University, Michigan State Library, University of Michigan, and Wayne State University). The report includes a listing of task force members; description of a regions-of-cooperation concept and criteria for statewide ILL; guidelines for development of regional ILL services; profile for a multi-type region of cooperation; guidelines for ILL relationships; directions for establishing a state-level Board of Review for resolving conflicts; criteria for 1980 LSCA Title III grants; protocol for using State Library ILL services; and a map of the 15 multi-type regions of cooperation.

"Wisconsin Interlibrary Loan Guidelines," 3rd ed. Bulletin No. 6212. Madison, WI: Wisconsin State Department of Public Instruction, 1985. (ED 266 792)

The Wisconsin Council on Library and Network Development recommended a revision of ILL guidelines to reflect changed patterns of ILL and to clarify concepts. This edition describes the responsibilities of lending and borrowing libraries; definitions, principles and goals of statewide ILL; purposes and development of area ILL plans; and ILL patterns for public, school, academic, vocational-technical school, and special libraries. Changes in the "Guidelines" include the following: area plan development is still voluntary, but public library systems have been assigned the responsibility of coordinating the plan development process; definitions have been clarified and expanded; ILL patterns have been clarified and expanded; patterns for reference requests are included if they differ from ILL patterns; vocational-technical school libraries were added; section on special libraries was expanded; and a section was added for libraries not located in system areas.

"Wisconsin Interlibrary Loan Telecommunications Committee and Implementation Progress." Final Report. Madison, WI: Wisconsin State Department of Public Instruction, 1985. (ED 264 893)

The Wisconsin Interlibrary Loan Telecommunications Committee reviewed and assessed major ILL issues and problems in Wisconsin for a two-year period. Specifically, the committee's charge was to study and make recommendations on the best use by Wisconsin libraries of telecommunications equipment for transmission of ILL and reference requests. The state's goal was to ensure compatibility of resource sharing equipment among libraries around the state, improve efficiency, keep costs as low as possible, and enable state-level ILL providers to respond efficiently to requests for service. Included in this report is a list of committee members and results of their meetings throughout 1983 and 1984. The committee reviewed and discussed background on major ILL planning efforts and resource sharing tools in Wisconsin; reviewed and discussed ILL telecommunications methods and studies in Wisconsin and other states; defined key ILL telecommunications issues and problems; defined basic statewide ILL telecommunications needs; defined and analyzed optional ways of meeting ILL telecommunication needs; and developed short- and long-term recommendations for ILL telecommunications in the state. The last section reports progress toward implementation of its recommendations during the following fiscal year. An appendix lists formatting options for ILL requests.

Flanders, Bruce. "Interlibrary Loan in Kansas: a Low Cost Alternative to OCLC." *Wilson Library Bulletin* 61, no. 7 (March 1987): 31-34.

The author describes problems encountered with the in-house development of a statewide ILL and electronic mail telecommunications network in Kansas, and makes recommendations about avoiding the pitfalls encountered there. He suggests making automation decisions with broad-based input, soliciting expert advice on hardware and software considerations, purchasing conservative-design hardware, projecting realistic completion deadlines, and software review by a knowledgeable expert.

Matthews, Joseph R. "Resource Sharing in Montana: a Study of Interlibrary Loan and Alternatives for a Montana Union Catalog." Grass Valley, CA: Matthews (Joseph R.) and Associates, 1980. (ED 198 821)

This report by Matthews and Associates, prepared for the Resource Sharing Task Force of the Montana State Library, is the result of a study of ILL and automated networking in the state. Alternatives studied included: installation of WLN at each of the six federation headquarters libraries, the State Library, and the six units of the university system; installation of WLN in a few selected locations—the State Library, three university-system libraries, and two federation headquarters libraries; the "poor person's" union catalog—microfilming existing card catalogs in selected libraries; linking circulation systems; and merging of four existing COM catalogs.

Recommendations include several actions to create and maintain a Montana union catalog (MONCAT) for more efficient resource sharing and ILL within the state. Specific recommendations include: merging of existing COM, machine-readable bibliographic records and OCLC tapes into a single microform catalog; acceptance of only MARC records for new acquisitions; installation of WLN at five additional sites; initiation of a selective retrospective conversion project; implementation of a temporary "round robin" communication of ILL requests; designation of funding to support the Union List of Montana Serials; development of MONCAT to allow a smooth transition to an online catalog; and upgrading equipment to improve ILL communications and reduce costs. The study also recommends state legislative support for university ILL activities and re-allocation of federal Library Services and Construction Act funds.

Shoffner, Ralph M., et al. "Interlibrary Loan in New York State. Recommended Redesign. Results of a Study: Redesign of Interlibrary Loan in New York State." Beaverton, OR: Ringgold Management Systems, Inc., 1986. (ED 274 351)

This study by Ringgold Management Systems for the New York State Library was conducted for the purpose of redesigning ILL in the state of New York. The scope of the study included the following: to provide an overview of ILL structure and patterns in the state; to collect and analyze statistical data on ILL in the state and evaluate the performance of local and regional networks; to review and analyze the impact of national ILL networks such as OCLC, RLIN and RML within the state, and identify and analyze major trends in other states; to identify major problems with the present ILL system in New York State; to review ILL technology used and recommend changes; to review document delivery procedures and suggest improvements; to identify and evaluate major alternatives in ILL redesign; to analyze fiscal responsibility in local, regional, and state level programs; to review and define the statewide ILL role of the State Library, research libraries, regional systems and local libraries; to address the implementation of an ILL code for the state; to recommend performance standards and evaluation criteria for ILL; and to develop ongoing data collection models and monitoring of ILL performance at local, regional and state levels.

The study based its findings on site visits, field meetings, statistics, and a survey of public, academic, school, special, and other libraries throughout the state. Included are major findings and recommendations for a "mixed system" redesign of ILL, and appendices with summaries of interviews and meetings, statistical data, trends, and examples of survey forms used.

OCLC/Automation

Bills, Linda G. "Interlibrary Loan Before and After OCLC." Illinois Valley

Library System OCLC Experimental Project, Report No. 7. Springfield, IL: Illinois State Library, 1984. (ED 252 244)

One of eight reports describing the experimental project of the Illinois Valley Library System (IVLS) to test the costs and benefits of OCLC use in the system, this document examines ILL activities before and after the OCLC ILL subsystem was used in the 33 project libraries. Comparisons are made of protocol, time, costs, and staffing. In addition, effects of the project on resource sharing patterns and ILL staff attitudes toward online ILL are examined. Helpful appendices include statistical information on project libraries and a map of the IVLS; IVLS ILL protocols; request forms and flow chart of IVLS ILL department procedures; a transaction study form; worklog study forms; and instructions for OCLC and non-OCLC ILL activity.

Kelsey, Ann L., and John M. Cohn. "The Impact of Automation on Interlibrary Loan: One College Library's Experience." *Journal of Academic Librarianship* 13, no. 3 (July 1987): 163-66.

The author argues that the significant growth of ILL activity at the library of the County College of Morris derives from computerization in the library. Using a software package named FILLS (Fast Interlibrary Loans and Statistics), the library was able to retrieve data on return time, average cost, and total number of requests to analyze this growth pattern. Several automation ventures have contributed to ILL growth in the library: joining a network, thus making its holdings information available online; rapid turnaround time using the OCLC ILL Subsystem, encouraging patron satisfaction and creating more requests; and online searching's generating more citations, which increases the number of ILL requests. To deal with the growth in ILL, the library responded by redistributing staff and striving to provide efficient service to its clientele.

Kilgour, Frederick G. "Description of a Computerized, Online Interlibrary Loan System." Paper presented at the Conference of the International Federation of Library Associations and Institutions. Forty-fifth, Copenhagen, Denmark, 27 August-1 September 1979.

The OCLC Interlibrary Loan Subsystem was the first system of its kind: a computerized, online system designed to increase the efficiency and speed of interlibrary lending and borrowing. Testing of the subsystem began in January 1979 and it became available system-wide in April 1979. This paper describes the way the system functions and reports on its first two months of operation. The subsystem supports: 1) bibliographic verification of interlibrary loan requests and holdings information using OCLC catalog records; 2) online transmission of interlibrary loan requests and responses; 3) automatic forwarding of requests to potential lenders; 4) multiple online access points to interlibrary loan records; and 5) automatic updating of interlibrary loan record status.

Kilgour, Frederick G. "Interlibrary Loans On-line." *Library Journal* 104, no. 4 (15 February 1979): 460-63.

   A survey of 37 Ohio academic libraries using OCLC was conducted prior to the advent of the OCLC ILL Subsystem. These libraries were queried about the number of books loaned three years prior to the library's participation in OCLC (1971) and the following six years. The results indicated a sharp increase in ILL lending beginning with the third year of participation for most libraries, except for those with the largest number of loans, where the increase was small. Increases were significantly greater (75%) than those projected in *A Study of the Characteristics, Costs and Magnitude of Interlibrary Loans in Academic Libraries* (Westport, CT: Greenwood Publishing Co., 1972). Kilgour concludes that the entry of holdings of academic libraries in an online union catalog such as OCLC significantly accelerates interlibrary lending by those libraries.

Academic Libraries

Howland, Joan S. "Interlibrary Loan In ARL Libraries." SPEC Kit 127. Washington, D. C.: Association of Research Libraries, Office of Management Studies, 1986.

   Based on the results of a spring 1986 survey of 32 members of the Association of Research Libraries (ARL), who were selected on the basis of their ILL activities and programs, this SPEC Kit details online ILL services and cooperative borrowing/consortium activities of the 22 responding libraries. All of the respondents conduct at least part of their ILL activities electronically, and all are involved in one or more cooperative borrowing arrangements. Nine of the responding libraries have individual arrangements with local libraries; six participate in regional consortia; 15 participate in statewide agreements; 13 participate in statewide networks; 22 participate in RLIN (Research Libraries Information Network) or OCLC (Online Computer Library Center); three are involved in subscription-based activities; and 15 participate in other types of cooperative borrowing arrangements. Included in this document are a list of responding libraries, ILL trends in ARL libraries, annual reports of five libraries, ILL statistics of three libraries, organization charts for ILL, policies and fee schedules, ILL codes, descriptions of cooperative programs and services, and documents related to telefacsimile projects of three ARL libraries.

Linsley, Laurie S. "Academic Libraries in an Interlibrary Loan Network." *College & Research Libraries* 43, no. 4 (July 1982): 292-99.

   A survey of participants in the Florida Library Information Network (FLIN) was conducted to analyze ILL patterns and problems in the network and make recommendations for improvement. Libraries were questioned about book collection size, ILL staffing, volume of ILL, OCLC utilization, verification tools, and FLIN performance. Results of the survey indicated the greatest level of borrowing was by academic and public libraries, and the majority of materials requested were borrowed from the academic libraries. Most of the lending systemwide was by academic and public libraries, and together these libraries borrowed 66 percent of all items and loaned 88 percent of all items. Academic and public libraries also accounted for more than half of all OCLC ILL subsystem use. Indeed, though academic libraries represented only 12 percent of respondents to the survey, it was found that they play a vital role in Florida's ILL network.

Paustian, P. Robert. "Collection Size and Interlibrary Loan in Large Academic Libraries." *Library Research* 3, no.4 (Winter, 1981): 393-403.

The common assumption has been total collection size significantly influences the ILL lending and borrowing activity of libraries. This study contends collection size alone is not necessarily an adequate measure of fulfilling a patron's research needs, and tests the hypothesis that the amount and type of ILL activity is correlated with the size of large university library collections. The results of the study did not strongly support this theory. The largest private university libraries examined in the study, Harvard and Yale, did not do, proportionately, as much lending as some of the largest public university libraries, such as Minnesota and Illinois. The largest public university libraries are thus handling the largest portion of the academic ILL workload. Possible reasons for this include total staff size, geographical constraints, delivery time, perceived likelihood of the lending library's ability to provide ILL documents, and membership in networks and consortia.

Waldhart, Thomas J. "The Growth of Interlibrary Loans among ARL University Libraries." *Journal of Academic Librarianship* 10, no. 4 (September 1984): 204-8.

The reduced availability of local resources in ARL libraries; the liberalization by the American Library Association of the interlibrary loan code; the development of online interlibrary loan systems; the increased awareness by users of materials not owned by their libraries; and the state and federal support for the development of library networks would all seem to encourage the increased use of interlibrary loan as a means of meeting library users' needs. At the same time, the introduction of interlibrary loan fees by many of the net lending libraries, the new copyright legislation, and online document ordering systems would be expected to have a negative effect on the growth of interlibrary loan activities. In order to determine the growth and impact of interlibrary loan in ARL university libraries, this paper analyzes ARL interlibrary loan statistics over a period from 1974-75 through 1982-83.

The author concludes that a significant change occurred during this period in the relationship between large university libraries and smaller libraries which have in the past relied on them for interlibrary loan purposes. The introduction of the OCLC interlibrary loan system in 1979 made available the holdings of more libraries for interlibrary loan. A large increase in borrowing activity by ARL libraries in 1982-83 indicates they are attempting to meet some of the needs of their local patrons through interlibrary loan. Because of the costs associated with borrowing transactions, the author concludes that ARL libraries will be forced to reconsider their traditional stance with regard to fees for this service.

ILL Practice

Ballard, Thomas H. "Public Library Resource Sharing in the United States." *Interlending & Document Supply* 14, no. 2 (April 1986): 35-39.

Ballard explores the prevailing U.S. library service paradigm which states public libraries should, along with academic, special and other libraries, make the resources of the nation, region or state available to all citizens, regardless of the patron's geographic location or ability to pay. In order to evaluate this model and resource sharing in the U.S., a library must also consider costs, usage, and alternatives and then examine the possible ways to provide the service.

Users have rejected bibliographical access to books as a substitute for physical access, and creating many large book collections seems to be the best approach for providing the access patrons demand. Reciprocal borrowing is the only important resource sharing strategy that makes sense for public libraries today. American libraries purchase elaborate systems to provide potential access to what their patrons may want, while the British Library Document Supply Centre provides access to millions of books, incurring expense only if there is actual use of the collections.

Budd, John. "Interlibrary Loan Service: a Study of Turnaround Time." *RQ* 26, no. 1 (Fall 1986): 75-80.

Turnaround time for ILL transactions using the OCLC subsystem was studied using data collected from requests made to the ILL Department of the Southeastern Louisiana University Library and filled between January 1 and December 31, 1985. Total turnaround time was defined as the time elapsed from the date the request was made by the patron to the date it was received. The average turnaround time in this study was almost two weeks (13.76 days for a periodical article and 11.29 days for book requests), which shows little change in turnaround times found in other studies, since the subsystem was introduced in 1979. Budd suggests that libraries view ILL as an auxiliary service, and recommends further research on staffing, ILL economics, and alternative means of transmission such as telefacsimile and commercial document delivery.

Cline, Gloria S. "The High Price of Interlibrary Loan Service." *RQ* 27, no. 1 (Fall 1987): 80-86.

Cline documents the large increase in ILL fees from 1975 to 1984 by certain large private and public university libraries; overall prices were considerably higher in private academic libraries than they were in public academic libraries. The higher prices charged by these private libraries have reduced their overall lending by 38%.

Conversely, large, public university libraries were lending more than twice as many items as private libraries did in 1974-75, but by 1983-84 were lending 4.5 times as many. Related ILL problems discussed include confusing terminology, inconsistent application of fees, poor invoicing practices, and a trend toward increased restrictions regarding to whom a library will lend materials. Suggestions for resolving these problems include a national ILL coupon system to alleviate library accounting costs, implementation of structured user fees, and standardization supported by the ILL Committee of ALA's Reference and Adult Services Division.

Everett, David. "Verification in Interlibrary Loan: a Key to Success?" *Library Journal* 112, no. 18 (1 November 1987): 37-40.

ILL standards require that the library requesting photocopies of periodical articles verify both the bibliographic citation and the location of the needed journal. By sampling photocopy requests submitted to Colgate University Library for one month, the author determined current verification practices and their effect on the library's ability to fill requests. Each incoming request was examined for the stated source of citation verification and for holdings verification. The study showed that more than half of the requests (60%) provided no citation verification, and these were filled 68 percent of the time. Requests with primary verification (using a standard index, abstract or bibliography) were filled 90 percent of the time. Holdings verification, particularly the use of union lists when available, greatly increases the fill rate of ILL requests and has greater effect on the success of ILL transactions than citation verification.

Thompson, Dorothea M. "The Correct Use of Library Databases Can Improve Interlibrary Loan Efficiency." *Journal of Academic Librarianship* 6, no. 2 (May 1980): 83-86.

This study of ILL requests received at the Hunt Library of Carnegie-Mellon University demonstrates that proper use of location information in the OCLC and NUC databases can reduce costs and increase efficiency of the ILL process. Requests to the Hunt Library which were verified on OCLC had a high fill rate (90%), while improperly verified requests had a decreasing success rate of 72 percent in 1975 to 58 percent in 1978. ILL costs and unsubstantiated requests for loans would decrease markedly if location verification were adhered to as a standard.

ILL Research

Waldhart, Thomas J. "I. Patterns of Interlibrary Loan in the U.S.: a Review of Research," *Library and Information Science Research* 7, no. 3, (July-September 1985): 209-29.

In this first of a two-part review of ILL research in the U.S., Waldhart places primary emphasis on research published since 1970. Included here are patterns of ILL, specifically total volume, growth rate, the nature of exchange relationships between libraries, the characteristics of ILL requests, users and uses of ILL, and financing. Based on four studies, an estimate of total ILL activity is made for public, academic and other libraries, with the volume falling between 12 million and 24 million requests per year. While there is no comprehensive statistical data available for growth measurement, one analysis of the limited data indicates that from 1974-75 through 1980-81, the total ILL activities of academic libraries grew 43.9%, with an average annual growth rate of 7.4%.

Another study found that growth rate for academic libraries was 2.4% for ARL libraries. Factors influencing growth rate have been studied, including online searching, the emergence of online union catalogs, the implementation of the OCLC ILL Subsystem, and the 1976 Copyright Law. The nature of exchange relationships is a complex one involving the interaction of academic, public and special libraries, and several studies have attempted to analyze this relationship. Research has shown that most requests from public libraries are for books, while academic libraries borrow books and serials, with an emphasis on serials. Special libraries rely heavily on academic libraries for their primarily serial requests. Subject content and language of materials borrowed are other characteristics of requests that have been researched. Users and uses of ILL materials studied include employees of special libraries needing materials for job-related purposes and faculty in academic institutions requesting materials for teaching, study, and research. Little direct research has been done on financing ILL services, but some studies indicate that ILL is funded by state subsidies, charges by lending libraries for loans to businesses, photocopy charges, and subsidization of ILL by the lending library.

Waldhart, Thomas J. "Performance Evaluation of Interlibrary Loan in the United States: a Review of Research." *Library and Information Science Research* 7, no. 4 (October-December, 1985): 313-31.

In his second article reviewing research on ILL in the U.S., Waldhart covers research into the five criteria used for evaluating ILL performance: satisfaction rate (fill rate), speed of supply (turnaround time), cost (efficiency), user satisfaction, and user inconvenience. Also included are methods of document delivery and mode of communication, which contribute to ILL performance as well. Fill rate examines the relationship between the total number of requests and requests successfully transacted. This rate depends on several factors, including the complexity of the requests, availability of location information, accuracy of the requests, and persistence of the borrowing institution. Most success rate studies are concerned with borrowing activities, which are commonly found to be 80% to 90%. Cost studies examine the amount of resources utilized in ILL transactions. Cost is especially vulnerable to differing interpretations, and central to this type of study is the determination of which costs are relevant. Level of staff, supplies, postage, insurance, communications, photocopy, delivery services, and salaries and wages, are factors considered in cost studies, while the extent of the effect of technology on ILL has not yet been investigated.

Response time examines the amount of time elapsed between receipt of requests and their completion, though there is considerable variation in how this time is measured. Total response time is dependent on a number of components, including borrowing library processing time before sending out the request, request transit time, lending library processing time, material transit time, and borrowing library processing time on receipt of materials. Existing research indicates that OCLC's ILL system contributes to reduced response time because it saves time in bibliographic verification, location verification, request preparation, communicating requests and information to other libraries.

User satisfaction determines the level of users' satisfaction with the different aspects of ILL service, frequently turnaround time, while user dissatisfaction examines the amount of user inconvenience caused by ILL delays. Improvements in document delivery can result in significant reduction of turnaround time, and libraries are keenly interested in investigating alternative delivery services such as United Parcel Service, Express Mail, courier services, and telefacsimile transmission. Despite these alternatives, most libraries continue to rely heavily on the U.S. Postal Service for delivery of ILL requests, because U. S. mail continues to be the least expensive method. Initial communication of requests may be accomplished in several ways, including mail, TWX, telephone, electronic mail, telefacsimile, shared online circulation systems and online ILL systems, which have all been compared for efficiency and cost.

The Future of Resource Sharing

Many authors speculate on the future of resource sharing for libraries facing rising costs and new technologies. Here are a few of their visions.

Atkinson, Hugh C. "Atkinson on Networks." *American Libraries*, 18, no. 6 (June 1987): 432-9. "The Importance of People Networking." *Resource Sharing and Information Networks*, 4, no. 1 (1987): 83-90.

Commenting on the importance of networks to resource sharing, Atkinson notes that results really count, not equities. He believes that our commitment towards library materials themselves affects our attitudes about networks. Free or relatively free access to information and an awareness of patron's expanding needs for a growing universe of information meet with a knowledge of how little we have in any given library. Resource sharing must be an essential and integral part of every library's program. Atkinson urges libraries to act on interlibrary activity and multitype systems. Although no absolute guarantees of success exist, attempts, with their attendant risks, must be made to provide better library service through resource sharing.

Battin, Patricia. "The Electronic Library: A Vision for the Future." *EDUCOM Bulletin* 19, no. 2 (Summer 1984): 12-17, 34.

Battin discusses not technology but the concept of the scholar using electronic work station. She defines a need for three types of access: printed format, machine-readable databases, and mediated access to the electronic and print access. Costs will be incremental, not substitutional. She believes the fragmentation of access is inimical to the academic purposes of the institution and traditional procedures for allocation of costs have undergone radical transformation. She thinks merging libraries and computer centers can provide an information infrastructure to stimulate the continuing autonomous use of information sources. Battin suggests amending the traditional cliche´ that the library is the heart of the university. She believes a new metaphor is more appropriately based upon the structure of DNA. The process will be a helix; the scholarly information center will provide a basic set of services and technical capabilities while users interact and experiment with new technical solutions. The character and quality of a scholarly information center will become a genetic code for the institution.

"Costs and New Technologies: Libraries, Network, Utilities." Program presented at American Library Association 108th Annual Conference, 24-29 June 1989, Dallas, TX.

Paul Mosher discusses a primary impetus for resource sharing: the inability of a single library to meet all the information needs of its clientele. He predicts interlibrary loan will continue to grow. Mosher believes librarians have been effective against the specter of library journal costs and libraries will not be forced to ground by greedy journal publishers. He decries the peculiar logic of withdrawing from network cataloging to reduce local costs. He believes our network resource sharing devices should be made more apparent to users so libraries will receive greater support from external constituents.

"Costs and New Technologies: Libraries, Network, Utilities." Program presented at American Library Association 108th Annual Conference, 24-29 June 1989, Dallas, TX.

Bonnie Juergens discusses the value of the 1-3% of local library budgets that are spent for network services. Moves to enhance the biliographic record with table of contents information should maximize use of local collections. In this decade, librarians have a rejuvenated commitment to resource sharing which is translating into action under a new level of leadership. Cooperative agendas for the future must include continued and expanded interlibrary loan, a focus on electronic document delivery, more and more formalization of resource sharing, balancing between net borrowers and net lenders, supplying data for interlibrary loan within the local system, and increasing awareness of ownership versus access as an issue in librarianship. Juergens stresses that networks can enhance service by making resource sharing more effective and efficient.

Downes, Robin. "Resource Sharing and New Information Technology—An Idea Whose Time Has Come." *Journal of Library Administration* 10, no. 1 (1989): 115-25.

Within the context of crises deriving from increasing materials costs and steady-state budgets, Downes challenges the idea that every device has been exploited. He believes that collection-centered cooperative networks and collection development can offer further opportunites for resource sharing. He cites the successes of the Triangle Research Libraries Network and the Illinois LCS model. He notes that smaller libraries make contributions to the effectiveness of the whole and that overlap studies rarely exceed 50%. Downes believes cooperative collection development offers only a short-term defense against current journal price increases. While technology and network composition offer some succor, the traditional system of scholarly communication is out of control. Electronic publishing, desktop publishing, and the introduction of new regional publishers may offer some relief, but a partnership between librarians and publishers, both middle agents in information dissemination, could be as productive as the 25 year history of the application of computers to bibliographic systems has been. The entire issue of the *Journal of Library Administration*, "The Impact of Rising Costs of Serials and Monographs on Library Services and Programs," has relevance for resource sharing.

Martin, Susan K. *Library Networks, 1986-87: Libraries in Partnership.* White Plains, NY: Knowledge Industry Publications, 1986.

In her chapter "Library Cooperation: Two Definitions," Martin discusses traditional cooperative activities—interlibrary loan, reciprocal borrowing, shared storage, and union catalogs—and a second level of cooperation involving automated library networks—bibliographic utilities, shared local development, and reference networks. She also devotes chapters to the history and evolution of automated library networking, OCLC, RLG, regional networks, and nationwide programs. Martin believes networks are tools which will help libraries to reach "a level of sophistication and breadth heretofore unimaginable."

Notes

1. David C. Weber, "A Century of Cooperative Programs Among Academic Libraries," *College & Research Libraries* 37 (May 1976): 205-21.
2. Weber, 185-86.
3. Weber, 187-88.
4. Weber, 188-92.
5. Weber, 192-93.
6. Robert B. Downs, "American Library Cooperation in Review," *College & Research Libraries* 6 (September 1945): 407-15.
7. Weber, 194-99.
8. Sheila T. Dowd, "Fee, Fie, Foe, Fum: Will the Serials Giants Eat Us," *Journal of Library Administration* 10, no. 1 (1989): 29.
9. *Collected Papers of Frederick G. Kilgour*, compiled by Patricia A. Becher, and Ann T. Dodson; edited by Lois L. Yoakam. Dublin, OH: Online Computer Library Center, 1984. 2v.